GLOBAL DIVAS

Perverse

Modernities

A series edited by

Judith Halberstam

and Lisa Lowe

A JOHN HOPE FRANKLIN CENTER BOOK

MARTIN F. MANALANSAN IV

Filipino
Gay Men in the
Diaspora

GLOBAL DIVAS

DUKE
UNIVERSITY
PRESS

DURHAM
AND LONDON
2003

The distribution of this book is supported
by a generous grant from the Gill Foundation

Printed in the United States of America on acid-free paper ∞
Designed by Rebecca Giménez   Typeset in Sabon and Futura
by Keystone Typesetting Inc.   Library of Congress Cataloging-
in-Publication Data appear on the last printed page of this book.

Contents

Preface, vii

Introduction: Points of Departure, 1

1 The Borders between *Bakla* and *Gay*, 21

2 Speaking in Transit: Queer Language and Translated Lives, 45

3 "Out There": The Topography of Race and Desire in the
Global City, 62

4 The Biyuti and Drama of Everyday Life, 89

5 "To Play with the World": The Pageantry of Identities, 126

6 Tita Aida: Intimate Geographies of Suffering, 152

Conclusion: Locating the Diasporic Deviant/Diva, 184

Notes, 193

An Elusive Glossary, 199

Works Cited, 205

Index, 219

Resty, a Filipino gay man in his thirties and one of the people I interviewed for this book, once asked me, "What is the title of the book you are writing?"[1]

"*Global Divas*," I answered.

"Global divas?" Looking puzzled for a minute, Resty then smiled and exclaimed, "Ah! Global *'di va?*" [Global, isn't it?]

Resty realized another meaning of the book's title by utilizing *swardspeak*, which is a particular argot deployed by Filipino gay men. He performed a linguistic play on the word *diva* by using neither mainstream English nor Tagalog. Had he used standard Tagalog, the sentence would have been "Global, 'di ba?" But by substituting a "v" instead of a "b," he playfully transformed the word *diva* into a conspiratorial and rhetorical question in a style that encoded the speaker as gay.

This short encounter between Resty and me speaks to the important ways in which this book confronts and queries globalization and diaspora via vernacular and queer terms through the lives and words of Filipino gay men living in New York City. By doing so, this book presents a critical view of globalized modern gay identity. While numerous scholars and activists have heralded the coming of age of global gay identities, it has increasingly become apparent that even the gayest global spaces such as New York City are rife with cultural fissures and divides between various queer communities.

Throughout the book, I use the term *gay* both provisionally and strategically. My usage points both to the various ways in which the histories and lives of Filipino men are enmeshed with the cultural politics of gay identity and to the fact that other identity categories such as transgender are not typical in their arsenal of categories.[2] In this book, the term *queer* marks the moments when *gay* is insufficient or inappropriate and highlights these Filipinos' cultural and social *dis-ease* and displacement from mainstream gay practices.

Global Divas is an ethnographic study of Filipino gay men in New York City. Of course, this study does not purport to give a complete picture, nor does it pretend to represent all Filipino gay experiences at all times and spaces. As in any ethnographic project, the views and ideas are always partial and highly specific. Based on fieldwork and interviews conducted between 1990 and 1995,[3] this work focuses on the life narratives of fifty Filipino gay men who create a sense of self and belonging, or citizenship, amid the exigencies of immigration and in the face of emerging notions of global gay identity and cultural practices. These life narratives are diverse, but taken together they show how these informants are agentive narrators and social actors.[4] The life-narrative interviews were semistructured and were conducted mostly in Taglish.[5] The interviews included questions about life experiences such as growing up and immigration. In addition, I solicited informants' views about racial, ethnic, and class issues, identity categories, and the AIDS pandemic.[6] Although I placed ads to recruit potential informants in a gay-Asian organization newsletter, most of the life-narrative interviews came about through word of mouth and social networks. The fifty main informants lived in the greater New York area with a majority residing in Manhattan, Queens, Brooklyn, and Jersey City, New Jersey. Their ages ranged from twenty-two to more than sixty years (two mature informants were intentionally vague about their ages) with a median age of thirty-one.[7]

This work draws on participant observation in various private and public sites such as homes, bars, hospitals, and Filipino restaurants, as well as public social gatherings (both gay and straight) such as the Gay Pride Parade and the Philippine Independence Day Parades. From 1990 until 1999, I also conducted short informal interviews with more than a hundred Filipino gay men in New York, San Francisco, Atlanta, Washington, D.C., and Philadelphia; among these men were Filipino gay men who were tourists visiting from the Philippines. Family members and non-Filipino partners or boyfriends of these men were also interviewed. In addition to interviews and observations, I critically draw from various cultural forms such as novels and theatrical performances.

I demonstrate how these men negotiate between Filipino and American sexual and gender traditions, more specifically between *bakla* and gay ideologies. *Bakla* is the Tagalog term that encompasses homosexuality, hermaphroditism, cross-dressing, and effeminacy. One of the bakla's singular attributes is a sense of self entrenched in the process of transformation. Works by anthropologists Fenella Cannell (1999) and Mark Johnson (1997) suggest that Filipino queers are concerned with the processes of transformation and shifting of selves that are not moored to any fixed category. Both authors were concerned with the idea of beauty as a process where selves are made and remade in such public events as the beauty pageant. Both agree that beauty is about appropriating American symbols of glamour, creating hybrid cultures, and gaining a level of intimacy with the powerful yet distant America.

Throughout the book, I focus on two idioms, *biyuti* and *drama,* that permeate swardspeak discourse and which, more than anything, reflect the self-conscious construction of the bakla not as a static monolithic category but as a basis of multiple performances. My use of *biyuti* rather than the English word *beauty* faithfully captures the ways in which Filipino gay men manipulate its pronunciation and meanings. While biyuti's provenance is clearly from the English word, its precise meaning can shift depending on its context and the person of whom it is used. In this context, it means both physical feminine beauty and countenance. In many conversations, informants would refer to their person or present state of mind using the term *biyuti*. For example, if the informant wanted to show how something or someone has ruined his day or dampened his disposition, he could say, *nasira ang biyuti ko* or *naukray ang biyuti ko*. Both literally mean "my biyuti was ruined," although the latter statement utilizes the word *ukray,* which can, depending on the context, mean to ruin, to destroy, to kill, or to vilify something or someone.

The idiom of "drama" is based on the idea of the bakla as a system of generative practices that at one time or other reconfigures various environments and inflects gender, class, race, and ethnicity through dramaturgical or theatrical idioms. For example, "Ano ang drama mo [what is your drama]?" can be a question about personal problems, sexuality, schemes/plans, or mundane tasks. Therefore, the category of bakla is less about identity than about shifting positions and conditions that are part of its mercurial and dynamic quality.

I suggest that Filipino gay men's experiences and discourses do not construct a consistent monolithic self. Instead, we find a configuration of possible scripts of self/selves that shift according to the situation. Furthermore, I suggest that these men's sense of selves are inflected and reconfigured by race, class, gender, sexual orientation, and immigration status. As immigrants, these Filipino men straddle competing cultural traditions, memories, and material conditions. Their claims toward membership or citizenship in gay and mainstream communities and the meanings that they create as part of this struggle are the results of dynamic maneuverings and strategic manipulation of their social, cultural, economic, and racial positions. Therefore, I would argue that Filipino gay men do not readily assimilate into modern gay personhood and instead actively recuperate the bakla as a way to assert a particular kind of modernity.

Gay identity, as I deploy the term throughout the book, is negotiated, translated, reproduced, and performed by the Filipino men living in the global city of New York and away from the Philippine homeland. Therefore, the book grounds diasporic, transnational, and global dimensions of gay and other queer identities and locates them within the frame of quotidian struggles. Departing from popular and scholarly works that read immigrant and diasporic queer lives in abstract and textual terms, this ethnography sifts through the gritty, contradictory, and mundane deeds and utterances of Filipino immigrant gay men, enabling me to position queer diaspora and globalization "from below."[8] Filipino immigrant gay men are not passively assimilating into a mature or self-realized state of gay modernity, but rather are contesting the boundaries of gay identity and rearticulating its modern contours. In other words, Filipino gay men in the diaspora are charting hybrid and complex paths that deviate from a teleological and developmental route to gay modernity. Gay identity functions not as a consumable product alone but as a pivot in the mobilization of multi-stranded relationships and struggles forged by queers living away from the homeland and confronting the tribulations of a globalizing world.

By beginning this work with an example of ironic and linguistic play, I challenge facile views of globalization, transnationalism, and diaspora by interrogating the premises of everyday local existence and the ways Filipino gay men struggle and maneuver in order to survive and even to flourish. I suggest that these Filipino gay men are neither heroes of a triumphant story of queer liberation nor are they dupes or victims of perpetual displacement, cultural forlornness, or oppression. Rather, these Filipinos are queer subjects constituted through struggles that oscillate between exuberance and pathos and between survival and loss.

This work is a product of numerous travails and travels. At the same time, its creation is the result of staying put, or being marooned, in one place — for one reason or another. I have shaped and reshaped its contours after numerous rides on New York City trains and many years of stepping back from the chaos of living away from the Philippines. After more than a decade of inhabiting what my late *ninong* (godfather) called, with all the strength of cliché, the "land of milk and honey," it is time to take stock. The exigencies of my life are inscribed in this work despite its lack of a confessional or overtly reflexive tone as some readers have pointed out to me. I believe this book resonates with the tensions of diasporic life. Such tensions evoke particular images, smells, sounds, and peoples dancing on the rim of a life spanning two cultures and thousands of miles.

In the classic anthropological manner, I start my acknowledgments by charting my rather unusual kinship web. I want first to recognize my intellectual lineage, my foremothers and forefathers whose works not only influenced my own but made its very existence possible because of what they went through to pursue a research topic that was both socially stigmatized and professionally scorned in the 1970s and 1980s. These people include Evie Blackwood, Gil Herdt, Liz Kennedy, Bill Leap, Ellen Lewin, Steve Murray, Esther Newton, Kath Weston, and Walter Williams. Lesbian and Gay Studies was just an emerging field when I started my research in 1989, and I felt very much alone. The Society of Lesbian and Gay Anthropologists (SOLGA) became my second university and another home whose many members became surrogate mentors.

In Asian American, Asian, and ethnic studies, I am grateful for the encouragement and intellectual guidance of Kim Alidio, Nerissa Balce-Cortes, Victor Bascara, Kandice Chuh, Evelyn Hu Dehart, Mercedes Dujunco, David Eng, Yen Espiritu, Dorothy Fujita-Rony, Jessica Hagedorn, Alice Hom, Allan Isaac, Peter Kwong, Russell Leong, George Lipsitz, David Lloyd, Andrea Louie, Linda Maram, Gary Okihiro, Vince Rafael, Karen Shimakawa, Steve Sumida, Jack Tchen, Sunny Vergara, and Linda Trinh Võ. I would like to make special mention of Chandan Reddy, whose stunning intellect coupled with a humble yet ebullient personality has helped me sort through philosophical muddles and political quandaries.

I also want to thank my colleagues in the fields of anthropology, area, queer, and sexuality studies such as Henry Abelove, Tani Barlow, Alan Berube, Tom Boellstorff, George Chauncey, Rosemarie Chierici, Lawrence Cohen, Ann Cvetkovich, John D'Emilio, Jill Dolan, Amy Donovan, Lisa Duggan, Deborah Elliston, Carolyn Dinshaw, Licia Fiol-Matta, Rod Ferguson, Rudy Gaudio, Rosemary George, David Halperin, Wolfram Hartmann, Neville Hoad, Miranda Joseph, Caren Kaplan, Eithne Luibheid, Arnaldo Cruz Malave, Purnima Mankekar, Jose Muñoz, Benjamin Pang, Geeta Patel, Beth Povinelli, Frank Proschan, Louisa Schein, Alisa Solomon, John Wiggins, and Alan Yang.

The AIDS pandemic was the context in which this work was conceived and realized. While my own exploration of the cultural meanings of sexuality and gender were first hatched in the relatively strain-free environs of Manila in the early 1980s, little did I know that I would be exploring the topic in the war-ravaged battlegrounds of the pandemic. During my research, I worked at Gay Men's Health Crisis, Inc. (GMHC) and at the Asian Pacific Islander Coalition against HIV/ AIDS (APICHA) in Manhattan. Both jobs were rewarding experiences. Anthropological fieldwork has always been seen as a particularly hazardous and exotic bildungsroman. Living in New York, conducting fieldwork, and surviving the AIDS epidemic have added a special dimension to my professional and personal life.

Craig Harris, Ben McDaniel, and Dario Marano were my late colleagues at GMHC. They, among others, taught me about the realities of the epidemic and the wider implications of my work. Dario, who came to America from Italy in his teens, was especially instructive in the drama of being an immigrant gay man. I wrote the chapter on AIDS with the joy and pain of the memories of working alongside these dear colleagues. My former GMHC and APICHA co-workers included Joey Almoradie, Kevin W. Bratholt, Leo Cairo, John Chin, Dawn Cunningham, Lance Dronkers, Ron Frederick, Ruben Garcia, Michael Paquette, Jack Guza, Ernesto Hinojos, the late Ramon Hodel, Jennifer Kaplan, Karyn Kaplan, Li Ma, John Manzon-Santos, Robin Miller, Ana Morais, Jane Po, Ludy Resurreccion, Therese Rodriguez, Vince Sales, Javid Syed, Bert Wang, and David Whittier, who taught me the values and pitfalls of activism and service in the pandemic.

At the University of Illinois, Urbana-Champaign, numerous colleagues were generous in providing me with an intellectual community that enabled me to step back from years of living in New York City and write the book. I especially thank Ed Bruner, Julie Chang, C. L. Cole, Clark Cunningham, Tim Dean, Elena Delgado, Augusto Espiritu, Jed Esty, Brenda Farnell, Paul Garber, Alma Gottlieb, Masumi Iriye, Eva Lynn Jagoe, Moon-Kie Jung, Suvir Kaul, Janet Dixon Keller, Bill Kelleher, Esther Kim, Sharon Lee, Steve Leigh, Chris Lehman, Ania Loomba, Alejandro Lugo, Janet Lyon, Anita Mannur, Bill Maxwell, David O'Brien, Andy Orta, Yoon Pak, Simona Sawhney, Larry Schehr, Helaine Silverman, Olga Soffer, Siobhan Somerville, Adam Sutcliffe, Arlene Torres, Billy Vaughn, Richard Wheeler, Julia Walker, Norman Whitten, and George Yu. Shanshan Lan was my research assistant during the revision phase; a tireless worker with an eye for detail, she was responsible for keeping my bad clerical skills in check.

Nancy Abelmann carefully read several chapters and was a generous mentor in teaching and research. Lisa Lampert also read parts of the manuscript, and as the consummate medievalist that she is, pointed out the undercurrents of Catholicism in the sensibilities of my informants. Matti Bunzl gently but firmly prodded me to let go of the manuscript. Cathy Prendergast was a great neighbor, a baking enthusiast, and an excellent source of provocative ideas.

Most of all, Dara Goldman was the indefatigable spirit who showed me the intellectual and social possibilities beneath the bucolic surface of "Chambana." She is responsible for prodding me out of my so-called writer's block and procrastinating ways by providing me with great insights and cracking the whip at times. She read the final draft of the manuscript with an eye for the Spanish undercurrents in Philippine culture.

I started my academic explorations at the University of the Philippines. My friends and colleagues, Eufracio Abaya, Celia Antonio, Ponciano Bennagen, Kiko Datar, Leticia Lagmay, Violy Pallera, Realidad Rolda, Laura Samson, and Mike Tan, may have lost all hope of my eventual return, but I have always seen my work and my life here in America as intrinsically linked with some form of homecoming. Maybe someday. Hopefully soon.

Richie Zarragoza shared with me his wicked wit and the joys of experiencing the connections between life and language, especially when hanging out in the streets of New York that are (as he asserts) "the runways" of his life. Gerry Cuachon taught me about the fabulous yet dignified air of the cross-dressing queen and remained a steadfast supporter of this project.

Oscar Campomanes brought his treasure trove of Filipiniana and his truly interdisciplinary knowledge to bear upon my work. I have always admired Gayatri Gopinath's work, which resonates with my own. I have benefited from Gayatri's elegant arguments and cogent ideas about queer diasporas.

My good friends in the Philippines, Ariel Reyes, Bobby Abastillas, Bebon Gatuslao, and Manolo Tanquilut, have remained the truest of friends. After fifteen years of being away from the Philippines, I came back to visit in 1998; I found that the bonds that had originally brought us together more than twenty years ago at Lourdes School were still strong. Thanks to Caring Lahoz for being part of my extended family in the U.S.

Ricky Bonus was my phone therapist and my long-distance comrade in book manuscript "hell." Both of us know all too well the pain and pleasure of writing that "thing" and of family members' and friends' well-meaning but irritating questions such as "Aren't you finished yet?" I will always be thankful for his humor, critical thought, and generosity, especially in the last stressful stages of writing this book.

Unlike other people's dissertation advisors, Tom Gibson encouraged me to explore and go off on my own course. I will always be thankful for his support. Ayala Emmett gave me a much needed boost at crucial periods of fieldwork and unselfishly shared her own experiences as an immigrant intellectual in America.

Deb Amory was my devil's advocate and patient editor. She gently nudged me into finishing and more than anything made this book and my stay here in America possible in many ways. I will be indebted to her for the rest of my life.

Ken Wissoker was a great editor who was sensitive to the intellectual demands of book writing and expressed a true love of scholarship that I have found compelling. Leigh Anne Couch shepherded the project with sensitivity and professionalism. Judith Halberstam and Lisa Lowe were the most generous series editors. They remain staunch supporters of my work, and their own brilliant works are a constant source of inspiration. During times of uncertainty, they opened my eyes to my project's possibilities and gently shepherded it to completion. Lisa has been instrumental in my coming back to academia after years of AIDS work and unselfishly mentored me despite my erratic institutional affiliations. Judith patiently went over the manuscript with me and unfailingly believed in my ideas.

Finally, I would like to honor and thank my biological family. Like Gerry, Rene, and other informants whose families of birth were critical networks of support, my own family has continued to be here with me despite my long period of absence in the Philippines. My parents, Martin Jr. and Francisca, my siblings, Winnie, Doda, Jovy, Paolo, and Earl, and siblings-in-law, Sasa and Binky, were my rock and refuge against many storms. My nieces, Nikki and Samantha, and nephews, Pio, Ira, and Joshua, continue to provide me with the poignant joys of witnessing lives just beginning and the excitement of journeys yet to be taken.

Some sections of the individual chapters were published previously in different versions. I thank the publishers for permission to reprint and the anthology editors for their advice in the writing of these articles: "(Re)locating the Gay Filipino: Resistance, Postcolonialism and Identity." 1993. *Journal of Homosexuality* 26 (2/3): 53-73; "Disorienting the Body: Locating Symbolic Resistance among Filipino Gay Men." 1994. *positions: east asia cultures critique* 2(1): 73-90; "In the Shadows of Stonewall: Examining Gay Transnational Politics and the Diasporic Dilemma." 1995. *GLQ: A Journal of Lesbian and Gay Studies* 2(4): 425-38. A revised version appeared in Lisa Lowe and David Lloyd, eds., *The Politics of Culture in the Shadow of Capital*. 1997. Durham, N.C.: Duke University Press; "Performing Filipino Gay Experiences in America: Linguistic Strategies in a Transnational Context." 1996. In *Beyond the Lavender Lexicon: Authenticity, Imagination, and Appropriation in Lesbian and Gay Language*, edited by

William Leap. New York: Gordon and Breach; "Speaking of AIDS: Language and the Filipino Gay Experience in America." 1996. In *Discrepant Histories: Translocal Essays in Philippine Cultures*, edited by Vicente Rafael. Philadelphia, Pa.: Temple University Press. Published simultaneously in Manila by Anvil Press; "Diasporic Deviants/Divas: How Fillipino Gay Transmigrants 'Play with the World.'" 2000. In *Queer Diasporas*, edited by Cindy Patton and Benigno Sanchez Eppler. Durham, N.C.: Duke University Press; "Biyuti in Everyday Life: Performance, Citizenship and Survival among Filipinos in the U.S." 2001. In *Orientations: Mapping Studies in the Asian Diaspora*, edited by Karen Shimakawa and Kandice Chuh. Durham, N.C.: Duke University Press.

Introduction

Points of
Departure

The effect of mass migrations has been the creation of a radically new type of human being, people who root themselves in ideas rather than place, in memories as much as material things; people who have been obliged to define themselves — because they are so defined by others — by their otherness; people in whose deepest selves strange fusions occur, unprecedented unions between what they were and where they find themselves. The migrant suspects reality: having experienced several ways of being, he understands their illusory nature. To see things plainly, you have to cross a frontier. — SALMAN RUSHDIE, *Imaginary Homelands*

I left the Philippines for America to become the international beauty queen that I was meant to be. I thought everything will be like the movies and TV shows that I have seen when I was growing up. Well, I have had some disappointments. I still wonder what would have happened if I were still back home. Would I still be the exotic beauty of my childhood or the blond bombshell that I am today? I am very happy to be here [in America], but once in a while, memories of Manila and my wild days come rushing like a typhoon — and I get a little nostalgic. — MARIO

No Borders?

It was 4 o'clock on a Sunday afternoon in Greenwich Village. In keeping with urban gay weekly rhythms, gay men were converging for tea time, or tea dance. This ritual has nothing to do with the British custom of drinking the brew and eating fancy sandwiches. This is the moment when gay men who have been up the previous night carousing go off to their favorite bars or dance clubs for one last chance to cruise or hang out before the much-dreaded Monday morning. Exotica, my main informant, and I were in a gay bar, which at that time (August 1987) was the in place to be on a Sunday afternoon.

We were doing what most of the natives were doing — S&M, or "standing and modeling," that is, trying to appear nonchalant while attentively appraising the crowd. Suddenly, Exotica nudged me and said, "Tingnan mo, isang pang Miss Philippines." [Look, another Miss Philippines.]

In the middle of a small group of white men was a seemingly uncomfortable Asian man who would approximate what I would consider a Filipino (on the basis of my extended experience). Exotica suggested that we approach him. After some initial greetings and small talk, Arturo (the other Miss Philippines) started to warm up to us. He mentioned the fact that he had been in America for more than five years and that he lived in Jersey City, New Jersey.

Exotica asked, "Atche, ang ganda-ganda mo e bakit ka parang napapaso. Parang hindi ka nag-eenjoy." [Big sister, you are so beautiful, but why do you look uncomfortable? You don't seem to be enjoying yourself.]

Arturo said, "Ay hindi matake ng biyuti ko ang drama dito sa bar." [Oh, my biyuti (I) can't take the drama in this bar.]

"Vakit?" [Why?] Exotica and I both chorused.

Arthur countered, "Puro mga bakla este gay ang mga tao dito, walang totoong lalaki. Kung hindi lang ako pinilit ng mga puting ito, hindi ako pupunta dito." [This place is full of bakla. I mean gays. There are no real men here. If these white folks didn't cajole me into going, I would not be here.]

"E saan ka naman nanghahagip ng min?" [Where do you go to pick up men?] I asked.

Arturo mentioned a section of Jersey City that is home to a large number of Filipino immigrants and even has a street called Manila Avenue. He said that among his Filipino neighbors he had found his one true love.

Then he described his boyfriend/lover as "Totoong lalaki, 'di tulad ng mga tao dito—macho! May asawa pa!" [A real man, unlike the people here—macho! He even has a wife!]

Exotica gushed, "Ay mamà, talagang orig pa rin ang drama mo, made in the Philippines!" [Oh, mamà, your drama is still original, made in the Philippines!]

Arturo said, "Parang hindi nagbabago pero iba na rin ang drama ko ngayon." [It seems to be unchanged, but in fact, my drama is different now.]

This conversation occurred in what can be considered the quintessential space for gay identity and culture everywhere—the New York City gay bar. For many lesbians and gays, this space evokes a sense of community and solidarity. Activist Simon Watney (1995: 61) suggests that the gay bar is the site for ubiquitous homecomings for gay men and lesbians around the world, the one place where despite divergent origins and agendas, queers readily feel at home. He writes, "Few heterosexuals can imagine the sense of relief which a gay man or lesbian finds in a gay bar or a dyke bar in a strange city in a foreign country. Even if one cannot speak the local language, we feel a sense of identification. Besides, we generally like meeting one another, learning about what is happening to people 'like us' from other parts of the world" (ibid.).

Watney's statement resonates with the popular view that gay identity and space are intrinsically and organically linked. By this logic, Arturo is not quite "like us" and thus not included in the "we" of Watney's vision of the modern lesbian and gay world. Instead, in these terms, Arturo occupies an anachronistic pre-gay if not pre-modern state of being. Others might go so far as to fault Arturo for being "internally homophobic" or self-hating or for being an ignorant immigrant who is "fresh off the boat." Their logic goes this way—given time Arturo will be as comfortable in and assimilated into the American mainstream as Exotica and I. For this book, however, I draw on the contradictions, discomfort, and disparities between the three of us in the bar to complicate the popular and hegemonic tableau of a world turning gay or of queerness going global.

The idea of a global lesbian and gay culture has become part of most popular discourses around queer visibility. Consider this specific example. The theme for the New York City Lesbian and Gay Pride Month celebrations in June 1996 was "Pride without Borders." The official guide to the different activities and parties read:

> We are so different from one another. The places where we live, the colors of our skin, the possessions and beliefs we hold dear all conspire to divide us and remind us of our difference, but all over this city and in this state, in these 50 states, and in provinces, cantons, parishes and hemispheres so convenient for maps and for separating us, the one thing that we are is gay and lesbian. And queer. And homosexual. . . . We are so different. And we are everywhere. . . . And we are dykes and fags and pansies and patas and sissies and so butch we're questioned in the ladies' room at rest stops. . . . We know we are everywhere and that we have always been everywhere, and that knowledge should make all of us proud. We are strong because our love and our struggle draw us together. Our Pride, our desire to celebrate what we have made for ourselves and our determination to achieve everything that we deserve erases all the borders and makes the differences meaningless. We are so different, and yet we must work as one. (New York Lesbian and Gay Pride Guide 1996: 12)

The text begins and ends with difference and yet is permeated by political exhortations of its elision. The 1996 theme not only implies an engagement with diversity, but also idealizes the globalization or universalization of lesbian and gay identity. At the same time, it engages with a popular "McDonald's" notion of the global as a homogenizing process that emanates from above. Thus, while there is a perfunctory gesture toward differences, the final act is to break down these potential barriers to community. The rainbow flag (a flag with horizontal stripes in the colors of the rainbow), an important symbol of gay and lesbian identity and community, is an example of some of the ways by which the lesbian and gay "community" has attempted to recognize diversity. Seemingly separate bands of color are fused into a unitary amalgam and one single cultural emblem of queer togetherness and belonging. While these important symbols and meanings of unity provide a potent impetus for community efforts, they at once obscure contradictory and uneven queer spaces. As in the case of Arturo in the gay bar, fissures and borders crisscross the seemingly placid terrain of queer communities. How do we understand these differences in the face of the global dispersal and movement of people beyond a teleological narrative of the movement from tradition to modernity, and from discomfort to settlement into gay and lesbian life?

Globalization is often seen in extreme terms either as a foreboding specter of a catastrophic future or as a cause for a celebratory jubilation over the resolution of local repressions (Giddens 2000). In queer discourses, redemptive narratives of the global abound and are deployed in various venues such as gay pride parades, mass media, gay rights groups, and most notably in the twenty-fifth anniversary celebration of the Stonewall rebellion held in New York City in 1994 (Manalansan 1995). On the other extreme, various nation-states forestall what is perceived as a contaminating global flow of Western queerness as a means to erect and resurrect legal, cultural, and politico-economic barriers (Alexander 1997). Indeed, ideas about diaspora and globalization have invaded even the most mundane aspects of queer lives. Such words as *globalization* are used to index or mark sophistication and cosmopolitanism in queer culture. At the same time, skeptics have used the words as ominous signs of more insidious processes such as Western capitalist expansion and queer cultural imperialism and exploitation.

These facile yet dangerous ideas have necessitated what has been called a "transnational turn" in lesbian, gay, and queer studies (Povinelli and Chauncey 1999). This shift in lesbian, gay, and queer studies in the past ten years recognizes the limitations of place-based queer politics and at the same time conveys the complications brought about by migration and travel of queer peoples and cultures.

Queering the Diaspora and the Global: Whose Gaze? Who's Gay?

The transnational turn in lesbian, gay, and queer studies has not produced a singular mode of inquiry. One group of scholarly works focusing on the global and transnational has insistently examined gay and lesbian transnationalism as symptomatic of the proliferation of gay and lesbian social movements and their growing strengths within specific national and regional contexts.[1] These works often suggest that globalization can best be gleaned in the activities of established and institutionalized social movements and negotiations with state institutions and processes. This leads to a rendering of diaspora and migration, if mentioned at all in these works, as insignificant after-effects or vestigial processes of queer globalization. At the same time, diaspora and migration stand in for the idea of America as a monolithic and powerful center of queerness, ready to spread its influence all over the world. Unfortunately, these studies unwittingly posit a *white* gay male gaze—namely an omniscient, unreflexive observer whose erotic and practical politics are based on an imagined level playing field for all queers. Within this framework, queer globalization is primarily a privileged form of "optic"[2]—or a vantage point that allows a certain kind of ownership of global gayness or lesbianness in various locations and thus enables the right to claim queer spaces everywhere as "home."

Competing with these scholars are practitioners of what I call the "new queer studies."[3] While the now established works and scholars in queer theory, including Eve Kosofsky Sedgwick, Michael Warner, and Biddy Martin among others, have emerged out of disciplinary concerns of reading canonical works or popular media texts, the scholars of the "new queer studies" have come out, so to speak, from the intersection of established disciplines and formerly marginalized terrains of the American academy such as ethnic studies, postcolonial studies, women's studies, and gay and lesbian studies. The new queer theorists critically locate themselves and their works in local and global processes to produce scholarship that Gayatri Gopinath (1998: 117) aptly describes as "a more nuanced understanding of the traffic and travel of competing systems of desire in a transnational frame . . . and of how colonial structures of knowing and seeing remain in place within a discourse of an 'international' lesbian and gay movement." This body of work can best be examined in terms of the political stakes in positing a particular understanding or vision of the global. In other words, these bodies of works that constitute the transnational turn in queer studies can be exemplified by what Appadurai (2000) has called the "optics" of globalization. Who gets to *see* globalization and in what way? For whom and to whom does this vision of queer globalization speak?

To illustrate this contention, let me relay a particular moment in queer globalization scholarship. In a jointly authored introduction to a collection of works (Cruz-Malave and Manalansan 2002), Arnaldo Cruz-Malave and I recalled a particular moment in a 1998 conference on queer globalization which we had co-organized and which had been held at the Center for Lesbian and Gay Studies of the City University of New York Graduate Center. At the penultimate plenary, a white scholar deemed it appropriate to ask the panel consisting of queer scholars, including Geeta Patel, Norma Alarcon, Michael Warner, and Kobena Mercer, what he could have done in a particular encounter that occurred that same afternoon. He had been sitting in Bryant Park across the street from the CUNY Graduate Center building when a "Latino" man who was distributing born-again Christian literature approached him. The scholar informed the "Latino" man that he was gay and did not need the literature. The "Latino" man then informed the scholar that he had been gay but had changed when he "found" Christ. The white scholar then asked the panel what he could have told the "Latino" man. The panel members were noncommittal, but as Cruz-Malave and I pointed out, rather than answering the scholar's question, it was critical to interrogate the presuppositions of his own question and narrative of the event. To what extent is the story of this scholar in question another instance of ideological re-colonization or more appropriately another example of the unequal and hierarchical structure of knowledge around the global, the transcultural, and the transnational? Why does the scholar assume that the "Latino" man would even be interested in what he has to say? To bring it to another level, how can scholars of queer globalization not repeat such moments of colonization and privilege like that of the queer scholar in his response to the "Latino" man? How do works like this book refuse a recapitulation of one-sided communication and omniscient observations?

I suggest that one way to undertake and respond to these kinds of dilemmas is to take seriously the genealogy of the "new queer studies," particularly its investment in a progressive understanding of globalization and transnationalism. This book and the works of the "new queer studies" owe a clear intellectual debt to feminist scholars of the "politics of location." In the mid to late 1980s, several feminist thinkers, among them lesbians, Third World women, and women of color, began a critique of the prevailing feminist construction of *woman* as a universal category and called for the recognition and analysis of the particularities and divergences in experiences of women in various parts of the world. Adrienne Rich (1986) is popularly cited as the first theorist to use the term "politics of location" to acknowledge her own position as a white woman within U.S. national and international relations of power. Rich identified the body and the nation as important sites for the provenance of critical insights around identity, location, and difference. Therefore, she suggested that race, class, and ethnicity, among other categories, complicated the facile "sisterhood" that was often assumed in feminist circles.

Chandra Talpade Mohanty (1990, 1991a, 1991b) and others [4] have insisted on the interrogation and destabilization of long-held "natural" categories such as "woman" and "gender" and have focused their attention on understanding the politics of difference as inflected by various hierarchical arrangements brought about by colonial and postcolonial processes. Chicana feminists, specifically Gloria Anzaldúa (1987) and Chela Sandoval (1991), have highlighted race as an important vantage from which to mount a more fruitful critique of the complexities of geography, identity, and struggle. More recently, the works of Caren Kaplan and Inderpal Grewal (1994) have extended the views of these women from more traditional perspectives of the local into a more transnational perspective in which seemingly bounded experiences and struggles are implicated in relationships that go beyond national and state lines within a globalizing world. Indeed, Kaplan (1996) goes on to critique the "politics of location" scholarship for not being more mindful of the displacements caused by global migration and travel.

These feminist works are clearly relevant for queer scholars who are responding to the vicissitudes of the intensified movement of people, capital, ideas, and technology across borders. The works of the "new queer studies" are questioning the universal gay/lesbian subject but *at the same time* recognizing the ways in which gay and lesbian cultures in specific localities inflect and influence the growth of alternative sex and gender identities and practices. In other words, the useful step that these new queer scholars are making is not in denigrating gay and lesbian identity categories and cultures but rather expanding and troubling their seemingly stable borders by illuminating the different ways in which various queer subjects located in and moving in between specific national locations establish and negotiate complex relationships to each other and to the state. In the face of so-called mobile queers, it is also necessary to expand the notion of "mobility" and to talk about the ways in which cosmopolitanism is not always privileged.[5] Immigrant queers of color in particular demonstrate how mobility is not only about the actual physical traversing of national boundaries but also about the traffic of status and hierarchies *within* and across such boundaries.

At the same time, important books on globalization and transnationalism have disregarded or decentered the place of gendered and sexual subjectivity.[6] In fact, Povinelli and Chauncey (1999: 445) bemoaned the tendency of "the literature on globalization . . . to read social life off external social forms—flows, circuits, circulations of people, capital and culture—without any model of subjective mediation." *Global Divas* addresses this gap by presenting an ethnographic case study of how processes of globalization and transnationalism are negotiated through the processes of identity formation and everyday life of Filipino gay immigrants in New York City. I trace the historical and cultural parameters of Filipino immigration in general and the issue of Filipino gay immigration in particular as way to offer a window on how these supranational elements and processes are not creating generic "McDonaldized" lives but rather intricately woven lives that are at once global and local. This ethnography, while based in New York City, is far from the traditional view of a local picture of a group of people. Rather, this book presents a complex picture of interconnections and disjunctures faced by this group of men. As such, the lives of these men are historically and culturally counterposed to the networks and movements of people, ideologies, technologies, capital, and the whole enterprise of diasporic travel in the late twentieth and early twenty-first centuries.

"Belonging to the World":
The Transnational Sites of the Filipino Gay Immigrant

Dapat ka bang mag-ibang bayan?
Dito ba'y wala kang mapaglagyan?
Tungkol sa babae, dito'y maraming okey.
Dito ang lalaki ang kulang.
Bakit pa iiiwanan ang lupang tinubuan?
Dito ka natuto ng iyong mga kalokohan.
Baka akala mo ganoon lamang ang mamuhay sa ibang bayan.

At kung ikaw ay magaasawa, ang kunin mo ay Pilipina.

Mas magaganda ang mga Pinay.

Sa bahay man sila'y mahuhusay.

Minsan ay selosa rin ang Pinay

Sapagkat ang selos ay tanda ng pagmamahal ng Pinay

At kung umibig ay lalong okey ang Pinay.

Do you need to go to another country?

Don't you have your own niche here?

In terms of women, there are a lot of okay ones here.

Here, the guys are outnumbered.

Why do you have to leave your homeland?

You learned all your mischief here.

Don't you know that it is not that easy to live in another country?

And if you were to get married, get a Filipina!

Pinays are more beautiful.

They are even well skilled in the house.

Sometimes they are also the jealous type

Because jealousy is the sign of the Pinay's true love

And the Pinays are even better when they are in love.

Sometimes the Pinay is the jealous type

Because jealousy is a sign of love.

And when they are in love, the Pinays are even more okay.

—FLORANTE DE LEON, "Pinay"[7]

In the 1970s, the song "Pinay" became the anthem for a predominantly
male migrant labor flow from the Philippines to the Middle East. *Pinay*
is a Tagalog slang term for Filipina, or a Filipino woman. The song's
initial mournful invocation of national belonging is coupled with the
sexualized and gendered dimensions of the nation. Indeed, the song
prescribes heterosexual marriage and desire to be the saving grace for
the potential male migrant worker. Moreover, the song strongly suggests that the female body and the Pinay's excellent domestic skills
should be more than enough reason for the potential migrant to stay
home in the Philippines.

The song constructs the space outside the nation as dangerous for
heteronormative masculinity.[8] This song's viewpoint has been supported by gossip and stories about life outside the homeland. Stories
about Arab men preying on beardless and relatively hairless Filipino
men were rampant and included episodes of homosexual rape. Fur-

thermore, narratives of Filipino overseas workers succumbing to the perils of murder, rape, and/or diseases such as AIDS further amplified this view. However, although these stories strengthened the heteronormative underpinnings of Filipino male patriotism, they did not diminish the allure of economic benefits brought about by dollar remittances and other material rewards of life abroad.

The Filipino diaspora in the last two decades of the twentieth century reached astronomical proportions. Labor migration has become a highly institutionalized practice in the Philippines with the state functioning in more than a facilitating role together with private and nongovernmental/nonprivate organizations. This has lead to the Philippines becoming the "world's largest exporter of government-sponsored labor" (Tyner 2000: 132).

Anthropologist Jonathan Okamura summed up the far-reaching range of the Filipino diaspora when he wrote, "Filipinos can be found in more than 130 nations and territories throughout the world including both developing and developed countries" (1998: 101). Computer programmers, nurses, doctors, construction workers, domestics, entertainers, and sex workers are a huge part of the mobile labor power leaving the Philippines.[9] Epifanio San Juan, a prominent Filipino literary theorist, eloquently described the Filipino as "belonging to the world," meaning that Filipinos when they migrate "become assets, 'human capital' . . . exchangeable commodities" as part of the global labor market (1998: 7).

However, in the past twenty years, Filipino labor migration has become increasingly female.[10] Thus, in many ways, the song "Pinay" may seem to have become an obsolete paean in that the Filipina, or the Pinay, has become the paradigmatic migrant laborer coming from the Philippines and not the one who stays put. Filipinas work in such jobs as domestics, entertainers, teachers, and nurses in various countries in Asia, the Middle East, and North America. This gendered transformation did not alter the heteronormative underpinnings of nationhood, however. Rather, many discourses about several tragic situations that have befallen these women abroad have intensified the normalized and naturalized positions of women. At the same time, there is a strong acknowledgment among Filipinos of the global demand for female labor and despite particular misgivings about women leaving their families, these women are almost deified by the government and mass media to the point of martyrdom or heroism.

Despite the global dimensions of the Filipino diaspora, the United States has remained the ideal destination for Filipino immigrants. The largest Filipino overseas community is in the United States and numbers about 1.4 million (Okamura 1998: 101). After independence from U.S. colonial rule in 1946, the Philippines maintained close cultural, economic, and political ties with its former colonizer. These relationships have forged popular imageries that normalize and naturalize the links between the two countries.

Imaginary topographies that construct the United States and the Philippines as physically contiguous are part of many Filipino immigrant life narratives. Roberto, one of my informants, told me that while he was growing up he had always thought that America was just an hour bus ride away, hidden by the mountains of his home province. As a child, he had watched gray buses containing dozens of young American men with crew cuts running down the main highway near his home on their way to some spot in the mountains. It was only when he was eleven and he took a trip to Olongapo City that he learned that the America he thought was in the mountains was in fact only a military facility and that America was indeed very far away.

In the novel *Umbrella Country*, Filipino American author Bino Realuyo weaves a gay coming of age story set in the Philippines, where the persistent background image of America propels personal yearnings and an imagined future. A bittersweet tale of a young boy aptly named Gringo amid the lower middle-class mayhem of a Manila neighborhood, *Umbrella Country* is punctuated by scenes and dreams of America. At first glance, this story may be seen as a mere echo of a million other dreams and aspirations of would-be immigrants to America from all over the globe. However, as many scholars have argued, Filipinos occupy a unique position among diasporic groups owing to their colonial and postcolonial relationship with America.[11]

Some commentators such as Pico Iyer (1988: 151–93), a popular travel writer, suggest that the Filipino is a sad, almost pathetic, copy of the American, an empty cultural shell devastated by Spanish and American colonialism. He further suggests that while Filipinos are virtuoso performers of American culture, they are left with the dubious heritage of disco, rock and roll, and the beauty pageant. In other words, Filipinos have nothing substantive to show except the shallow features of American popular culture.

However, more astute observers such as the anthropologist Fenella

Cannell (1999: 252) conjure up the image of contemporary Philippine society as a palimpsest where colonial and postcolonial elements bleed through layers of history and culture.[12] Cannell further suggests that Filipinos, particularly the rural poor of the Bicol region that she studied, are constantly negotiating with the image of America and various imagined "others" in order to displace power and hierarchies, and to create a sense of self (ibid.). For Cannell, what Pico Iyer and others have considered to be the pathetic imitative nature of the Filipinos is not constitutive of a barren tradition but rather of an "alternative modernity."[13] Therefore, Filipinos' modernity is established not through a rejection of "tradition" but rather through complex amalgamations of cultural and historical elements. In this book, I extend and complicate Cannell's incisive analysis by examining the predicament of Filipino gay men within the contradictory and uneven sites of transnational migration and global cultures. Queer immigrants, like the Filipino gay men I consider in this book, perform between competing ideologies of belonging and citizenship to offset the multiple forms of displacements of life away from the homeland. Carrying the baggage of colonial and postcolonial cultures, the Filipino gay immigrant arrives in the United States not to begin a process of Americanization but rather to continue and transform the ongoing engagement with America.[14]

Performing Selves and Transforming Citizenship: The Filipino Gay Immigrant in the Modern World

The processes of globalization and transnationalism have complicated, if not transformed, the ways subjects create a sense of belonging and identity.[15] Notions of being Filipino, American, or gay cannot be easily apprehended in static, essential terms alone. While nationhood is no longer the primary anchor for creating a sense of citizenship and belonging, the situation is far from a simple dismissal of the nation. Despite what many herald as the demise of the nation, the contemporary moment has created a "crisis of citizenship" (Castles and Davidson 2000). Place, identity, and belonging can no longer be regarded as logically connected in the midst of globalizing tendencies (Gupta and Ferguson 1992), but at the same time people on the move are not just free-floating monads or cultural vagabonds who are unmoored to specific spaces and identities. In the face of these realities, queer diasporic subjects, particularly those from the Third World, who are confronted with multiple displacements, are faced with the monumental tasks of creating and refiguring home.

I argue that Filipino gay men are not typical immigrants who "move" from tradition to modernity; rather, they rewrite the static notions of tradition as modern or as strategies with which to negotiate American culture. Immigration, therefore, does not always end in an assimilative process but rather in contestation and reformation of identities.

The juxtaposition of performance and citizenship is based on the anthropological notion of cultural citizenship. Following Rosaldo (1994), Ong (1999), and Rofel (1999), I consider the process of citizen formation not as a mere political process but one "in which culture becomes a relevant category of affinity" (Rofel 1999: 457). Here, I take these scripts of belonging to include the "right to be different and to belong in a participatory democratic sense" (Rosaldo 1994: 402; see also Ong 1999). Cultural citizenship, therefore, is constituted by unofficial or vernacular scripts that promote seemingly disparate views of membership within a political and cultural body or community. Citizenship requires more than the assumption of rights and duties; more importantly, it also requires the performance and contestation of the behavior, ideas, and images of the proper citizen.[16]

I am interested in the way in which performance in diasporic queer communities is part of Filipino gay men's attempts to write or rewrite scripts or modes of behavior and attachments. As May Joseph (1995: 6) aptly puts it, the conjunction of performance and hybrid subjectivities in this context "[makes] possible competing epistemologies of mutually afflicted, dissonant, and contesting narratives of empires, bodies, localities, and nations." Ella Shohat and Robert Stam (1994: 42) argue convincingly that Third World transmigrants or, as they call them, "hybrid diasporic subject[s]," are "confronted with the 'theatrical' challenge of moving, as it were, among the diverse performative modes of sharply contrasting cultural and ideological worlds." The immigrant is continually made aware of the performative aspects of survival so much so that he or she is continually compelled to move or "travel" (albeit discomfittingly) between various codes of behavior. The immigrant has a heightened consciousness of the importance of having a *bricoleur*'s sense of the right or appropriate conduct. Such valuations of conduct continually change depending on who is (over)-

seeing the situation, which could be anyone from an older family member to immigration authorities.

Performance as a paradigm in the humanities has been seen as a universalizing process that is inherent in such matters as gender (Butler 1990, 1991, 1993).[17] More importantly, the intersections of performance with race, class, and ethnicity have remained largely unexplored. I suggest following Rosalind Morris's lead, that in order to understand both these situations, the interpenetration of the everyday with spectacle and theater must be placed in the center of the analysis. As Morris brilliantly notes, "Gender [and sexuality] may not be the primary object[s] of identification. . . . We need a conceptual vocabulary that permits discussion of engenderings that are multiply refracted in and through other categories of identities that are not reducible to gender. . . . We still need ethnographies that explore the constitution of racialized and ethnicized genders and/or genderized races and ethnicities" (1995: 585). To accomplish this task, one needs to locate performance within various hierarchical relationships, which implies divergent engagements of actors with so-called "scattered hegemonies" (Kaplan and Grewal 1994). In other words, performance is constituted through and contextualized by power and history.

My preoccupation with performance as part of citizenship developed from consistent themes that arose from fieldwork encounters with Filipino gay men. In many instances, informants' discourses and behavior have presented a persistent performative view of the world.[18] This is evident in the pivotal idioms of *biyuti* and *drama*. As I have briefly explained in the preface, both idioms pertain to aspects of personhood, demeanor, and self-fashioning. *Biyuti*, unlike Cannell's (1999) transliteration, is not the same as the English word *beauty* but extends to other realms of social and personal life. I have deliberately changed the spelling to reflect the difference in meanings as well as the pronunciation and speaking situations among Filipino gay men. I deploy the idioms *biyuti* and *drama* from Filipino gay men's language to encapsulate a self-conscious notion of performance that is embedded not only in gendered phenomena but in the exigencies of everyday life, including those of kinship and family, religion, sexual desire, and economic survival. These idioms serve as a means of understanding the world, and, more importantly, assessing proper conduct and action.

However, as Arturo and Exotica's words imply, the dramas of Filipino gay men's lives are full of complex and difficult navigations and negotiations of bakla and gay traditions. The cleavages and differences that exist within the so-called gay community, as exemplified by Arturo's discomfort, should be seen not as temporary irritations or momentary lapses on the path toward becoming full-fledged gay citizens, but rather as part and parcel of the diversity of performances of selves in the gay public arena and in everyday life. Cultural citizenship then is not about monolithic constructions of identity and belonging, but rather about competing cultural traditions and ideologies of self and personhood.

My work highlights the ways the everyday lives of Filipino gay men inform and are informed by the idioms and processes of religion and theater. In other words, I want to explore the dramaturgy of Filipino gay men's lives not only as an aesthetic exercise, but also as a way of understanding the articulation of their identities and the conditions under which they live. The primacy of the everyday provides an ethical basis for considering the theatrical aspects of social life. Performance in this book, therefore, is not only a matter of just "acting," but rather is about the aesthetics of Filipino gay men's struggles for survival. They are agentive sexual subjects who defy their representations in either mainstream films or in gay male porn (Fung 1991a, 1991b). They move beyond the stereotypes of houseboys, farmers, feminized sexual vessels, innocent waifs, and other "Oriental" icons in both genres (Ogasawara 1993).

This book is an ethnographic study of how Filipino gay men, most of whom are immigrants or long-time residents, negotiate between hegemonic American/Western and Filipino/Southeast Asian sexual/gender ideologies. Bakla is concerned with the manipulation of surface appearances in such a way that a singular consistent self is not suggested. Rather, bakla self-formation involves a range of possible scripts and the scripting of divergent selves, each of which is embedded in a specific social situation and network of social relationships.

Filipino gay men construct their sense of self and citizenship through negotiations between bakla and gay traditions that occur in quotidian and spectacular arenas. In the next five chapters, performances of these negotiations and engagements are portrayed in the interpenetration of time and place, images and memories, actions and counter-reactions of both "staged performance" and performance in everyday life. While American/Western sexual ideology is not totally foreign to Filipino gay men, the colonial and postcolonial ties with America have created hybrid amalgamations of practices and beliefs. This book attempts to re-imagine this highly contested terrain by releasing seemingly static concepts such as *bakla, gay, Filipino,* and *American* from their incarceration within specific places and ideas. By doing so, I open up the possibility of rethinking these identities, practices, and ideas within the grounds of history and culture, and I lay out the possible ways Filipino gay men create a sense of cultural citizenship amid and despite economic, political, and cultural spatial constraints.

As such, Filipino gay men's experiences with modernity and with America are suffused with the ambiguity and ambivalence of immigrant life. Filipino gay men's experiences in a drag beauty contest in Manhattan or in riding the New York City subways reveal the instability of boundaries and at the same time portray how, in many instances, such boundaries can also be experienced by these men as essential, fixed, and unchanging nodes of difference and/or affinity. While most accounts of postmodern or late modern travel and diasporas articulate a kind of mournful, if not listless displacement, the narratives in these chapters complicate this rather one-sided view. Consider the words of Leilani, who said, "Coming to and living here in America may be difficult at times, *pero* [but] I think it is all worthwhile. I think you can't forget the good and bad side of immigrating here. But consider the things that opened up for me when my biyuti arrived here." I submit that together with experiences of alienation and displacement come the experiences of a rebirth or a second chance, or more succinctly, experiences of pleasure and settlement. The ceaseless dialectic between unbounding and fixing, displacement and emplacement becomes apparent in the narratives and life events of these informants in the next five chapters. Furthermore, I argue that experiences of immigration and displacement guide Filipino gay men's "readings," or interpretations, of gay cultural events and identity as well as shape their reactions to and engagements with these phenomena.

The succeeding chapters present a nuanced and complex tableau of experiences that both demarcate and unbound the borders between the bakla and gay ideologies. These experiences, I would argue, are mediated not only through the trappings of Western modern elements such as a gay consumer lifestyle, but also through the vigorous process of vernacularization. This process occurs not only at the level of language but also on the level of cultural practices, which include the pervasive and vigorous undercurrents of family and folk Catholicism. While some people may apprehend these elements as either anachronisms or vestigial aspects of homeland culture, I argue instead that such elements are vital symbolic and material anchors for these men's lives and are instrumental in the creation of a particular form of modernity that is constructed by multiply marginalized peoples.

Filipino gay men in the diaspora are not mere members of a "post-Stonewall" generation that emerged out of the ushering in of modern gay identity. As immigrants and as queers, Filipino gay men are destabilizing the idea of "generation" and geography. I veer away from a strict chronological conception of "generation" as a temporal or cohort marker. Instead I recast the term as constituted by cultural displacement and temporal-spatial intersections. By doing so, these men's lives are seen to be complicating the ways gay, lesbian, and queer histories and cultural studies can be written and new queer activism forged. Positioned at the intersection of LGBT (lesbian, gay, bisexual, and transgender), ethnic, global, area, and postcolonial studies, this book pushes the boundaries of queer scholarship by going beyond nationalist and disciplinary restrictions.

The Book: An Itinerary

Global Divas is marked by a nonlinear trajectory. As Clifford (1992: 105) rightly describes it, an itinerary can offer a "way into" the various chapters of a book by presenting them not as a series of tightly chained ideas but rather as a more dispersed "history of locations and a location of histories." In this vein, every chapter in this book speaks to and against the others.

Chapters 1, 2, and 3 map out the linguistic, cultural, and geographic spaces in which Filipino gay men's border crossings take place. These three chapters in fact set up the stages on which enactment of crossings, contestations, resistance, capitulation, pleasure, and survival are played out. These chapters describe and analyze institutions, identities, practices, and persons that constitute the material and symbolic borderlands in the lives of Filipino gay men. Linguistic, cultural, and geographic borderlands are necessarily contingent and always in flux, particularly in terms of how gay and bakla traditions are marked, reconfigured, and realigned with other experiences and practices in the lives of Filipino gay men living in New York City.

In chapter 1 I describe and analyze the borderlands between *bakla* and *gay*. While maintaining their permeable cultural boundaries, *bakla* and *gay* also have concepts and ideas that do not "travel." Foremost among these is the idea of coming out, which is crucial to a gay self-formation and which does not translate to a particularly meaningful bakla category.

Chapter 2 discusses swardspeak, or the queer vernacular/code spoken by Filipino gay men, and especially focuses on the pivotal roles of the idioms of *biyuti* and *drama*. It describes how queer language functions as the medium through which Filipino gay men in the diaspora create new meanings and worlds to negotiate between the promise of transnational migration and experiences of displacement. The processes of vernacularizing and translating diasporic experiences are rendered in swardspeak terms and strongly demonstrate the continuities and discontinuities of queer immigrant life.

In chapter 3 I describe the organization of gay life in post-Stonewall New York City. This chapter interweaves narratives about the various ways in which gay places, practices, and images inflect and demarcate race, class, and gender. I then move into a discussion of the place of Asians and more specifically Filipino gay men in New York City gay life. Far beyond a description of an ethnographic setting, the chapter argues that an examination of queer spaces in New York from a particular marginalized gaze can provide a complicated yet positioned view of gay urban landscape in the late twentieth century.

Chapters 4, 5, and 6 are the heart of this book and provide thick descriptions of Filipino gay men's negotiations between bakla and gay traditions. In each chapter, Filipino gay men's crossings and transgressions between the two traditions are marked in particular spaces such as everyday life, ritual or stage spectacles, and the AIDS pandemic. Filipino gay men's performances are located or positioned in the aforementioned spaces and are placed against experiences of immigration and displacement.

Chapter 4 narrates/unravels the dramaturgical dimension of everyday life among Filipino gay men. Discussions of various spaces and practices, such as domestic space and weekly routines, are provided in order to present issues of race, class, and other forms of social relationships (i.e., religion, family) as part of Filipino gay men's negotiations with various instances of differences and exclusion. This chapter argues that everyday life is an arena for contestation and resistance against as well as acquiescence and capitulation to the experiences of cultural displacement and marginality. Moreover, Filipino gay men's quotidian struggles are in fact part of a drama of survival that goes beyond performances of gender and sexuality, and that brings into focus the predicament of being an immigrant of color in the late twentieth-century United States.

In chapter 5 I consider the Santacruzan, a traditional Filipino religious ritual that is performed by a group of Filipino queers and becomes the context for an examination of Filipino gay men's negotiations in the public arena. A specific performance of the ritual in 1991 by a group of Filipino gay men in New York City is presented to lay bare the issues of race, gender, and class, and the tensions between bakla and gay traditions as they are manifested in the contested practice of cross-dressing.

Chapter 6 explores how AIDS has transformed or affected the lives of Filipino gay men, who have the highest number of HIV cases among Asian Americans. Conversely, it examines the discursive practices Filipino gay men have employed to confront and indeed transform AIDS. Using life histories of both Filipinos with and without AIDS, the discussion centers on *Tita Aida,* the idiom Filipino gay men have coined for AIDS and the concomitant practices and beliefs that surround it. I demonstrate how such an idiom connects various Filipino ideas about homosexuality, gender, religion, cross-dressing, death, family, and illness, as well as the whole enterprise of immigration and transnational lives. The relationship between AIDS and immigration among Filipino gay men illustrates how the intersections of place and time are highlighted, particularly in trying to come to terms with the suffering involved in the pandemic and the struggle for some kind of transcendence.

In the conclusion, I reflect on the various themes encountered in the ethnographic chapters, particularly focusing on the location or position of Filipino gay men's performances or articulations of being and belonging within a global and transnational context. I explore the dialectic of arrivals and departures as a means to nuance the implications of this work in terms of possible academic and political routes to the future.

One

**The Borders
between *Bakla*
and *Gay***

Immigration is typically rendered in terms of multiple modes of movement and mobility. Often, stories of immigration are told as a coming of age narrative or a bildungsroman. The plots of these narratives are constructed along the line of progression from an early point of innocent youthfulness to a mature self-realization. These teleological plots usually are framed in terms of contrastive pairs, such as youth to adulthood, traditional to modern, and (in this case) from *bakla* to *gay*. As I have previously discussed, *bakla* is not a premodern antecedent to *gay* but rather, in diasporic spaces, *bakla* is recuperated and becomes an alternative form of modernity (Ong and Nonini 1997). In this chapter, I map out the border between *bakla* and *gay* not in terms of self-contained modes of identity but as permeable boundaries of two coexisting yet oftentimes incommensurable cultural ideologies of gender and sexuality. This cartography in turn contextualizes the negotiations and experiences of Filipino gay men living in New York City that are featured in the next five chapters.

The Contours of Gay Identity

Barry Adam (1990) characterized the emergence of gay identity as part of a "modern homosexuality" that arose more distinctly at the turn of the twentieth century and was formalized in the Stonewall Rebellion in New York City in 1969.[1] This watershed historical moment, which marked this shift, consisted of a series of events precipitated by several weeks of police raids in several gay bars, one of which was the Stonewall Inn in Greenwich Village. It culminated with confrontations between the police and groups of gay men. The features of this "modern gay" homosexuality are as follows:

> 1. Homosexual relations have been able to escape the structure of the dominant heterosexual kinship system. 2. Exclusive homosexuality, now possible for both partners, has become an alternative path to conventional family forms. 3. Same-sex bonds have developed new forms without being structured around particular age or gender categories. 4. People have come to discover each other and form large-scale social networks not only because of existing social relationships but also because of their homosexual interests. 5. Homosexuality has come to be a social formation unto itself, characterized by self-awareness and group identity. (Adam 1990: 24)

The first emphasis of Adam's definition is the escape from the biological familial bond. This emphasis in fact exposes other kinds of ideas, such as individualism, that go beyond the same-sex practices that helped shape gay identity. In *Habits of the Heart,* Bellah and his cohort of scholars (1985) interviewed Americans (none of whom were identified as gay) and they noted that in American society the sense of self is predicated on issues of individuation, separation, and leaving home. While the first two, individuation and separation, are confronted by most human beings, "leaving home in its American sense is not universal" (ibid.: 57). The American cultural landscape, premised on this specific kind of cultural, physical, and emotional distancing from the family, is the same one in which gay identity is founded. I am not suggesting that gay identity is based on an anti-familial rhetoric. Rather, I am arguing that gay identity and the cultural practices around it heighten anxiety around family and kin, and this anxiety in turn is enhanced if not further validated by mainstream American cultural values around individualism and commitment.

This same anxiety fuels gay discourses where secrecy and the closet are paramount idioms. Coming out, a liberation from the closet, is founded on a kind of individuation that is separate from familial and kin bonds and obligations. This kind of individuation is also predicated on the use of verbal language as the medium in which selfhood can be expressed. More than anything, discourses on coming out are about verbal narratives and confrontations with friends, families, and significant others.

The other defining characteristic of gay identity is the focus on sexual object choice, or who you have sex with, as the primary and singular defining factor. In other allegedly antecedent forms such as those in Latin American and Asian countries, participation in same-sex acts is not the crucial standard for being labeled homosexual or identifying as gay; rather, gender performance (acting masculine or feminine) and/or one's role in the sex act (e.g., being anal inserter vs. insertee) form the standard.

Gay identity then is defined by a conscious acknowledgment of a "man" who desires to have sex with other "men." While gender and age-based homosexualities are often seen in scholarly and popular media as primordial phenomena, gay identity is a kind of liberation from these "anachronisms."[2] Chauncey (1994) argued that the post-Stonewall era ushered in massive changes in the structure of gay life in New York City. Among such changes was the shift from a kind of gendered homosexuality to one that valorized the hypermasculine ideal.

More importantly, gay identity has become more than just homosexuality, same-sex desire, and sexual acts. In the three decades since Stonewall, it has become evident that gay identity has meant all these things and more. Gilbert Herdt and Andrew Boxer observed changes in the gay category after Stonewall and differentiated it from the homosexual category. They suggested that *gay* is perceived as "a distinct cultural category. . . . [Gay] represents more than a sexual act. . . . It signifies identity and role of course, but also a distinctive system of rules, norms, attitudes, and yes, beliefs from which the culture of gay men is made, a culture that sustains the social relations of same-sex desire" (Herdt and Boxer 1992: 5). The rise of cultural institutions, images, and practices has formed the idea of a singular gay culture that interfaces with other cultural systems in American society. These contradictions and anxieties about family, leaving home, and individuation are also dilemmas confronted by Filipino gay men, but as I would argue throughout the book, these dilemmas are articulated in terms of different cultural expressions and idioms, most notably within the semantic realm of the bakla.

Mapping the Space of the Bakla

By using the Tagalog term *bakla,* I do not assume that Tagalog adequately addresses the internal social and linguistic differences within Philippine society. However, Tagalog (or Pilipino, as it is officially designated) is spoken in most, if not all, of the islands (apart from English and the regional languages). *Bakla* has a wider circulation than terms from other Philippine languages owing to the popularity of Tagalog films. I submit that the bakla is an enduring social category for Filipinos. These linguistic and cultural realities justify formulating the discussion on the concept of the bakla. As the chapter on swardspeak will show, my usage of the term does not preclude any cross-fertilization between regional languages and cultures with Tagalog language and Manila-centric culture.

My non-usage of the transgender identity category is due to the dissonance it creates vis-à-vis the bakla, but also as I have mentioned before, cross-dressing and effeminacy, which are the conceptual core of the social construction of the bakla, are not necessarily encompassing realities for all my informants. The majority of my informants did not cross-dress, but they drew on the bakla as a social category and as a pool of meanings in analyzing everyday events in terms of the intersection of race, gender, and sexuality. In some situations, *bakla* symbolized Filipino queerness while *gay* symbolized white queerness.

In most instances, *bakla* is an emotionally laden as well as a potentially derogatory term. It does not have the political implications of *gay* as an identity, although scholars and writers have translated the term bakla as homosexual (Whitam and Mathy 1986), queer (Itiel 1989), and gay (Mathews 1987). This translation distorts the term's social dynamics. By understanding the social construction of the term, one is better able to understand the travails and struggles of the being called bakla.

Bakla is a problematic Tagalog term. Its etymology is popularly seen to be a result of the contraction of the first syllable of the word for woman *(babae)* and the first syllable of the word for man *(lalaki)*. Tagalog dictionaries define bakla as hermaphrodite. In addition, it is also seen in terms of the in-between, or *alanganin* (which was also another term for Filipino male homosexuals in the 1950s and 1960s). The interstitial and epicene quality attributed to the bakla illuminates the social script. Indeed, while *bakla* conflates the categories of effeminacy, transvestism, and homosexuality and can mean one or all of these in different contexts, the main focus of the term is that of effeminate mannerism, feminine physical characteristics (i.e., small, frail bodies, delicate facial features, and so on), and cross-dressing.

Most of the discussions of the term construct it as non-condemnatory and descriptive (Hart 1968; Mathews 1987) except for a lone Filipino scholar who started her article by describing *bakla* as an emotionally charged word (Raquiza 1983). Phonetically, *bakla* ends with a glottal stop, which makes for the very abrupt and harsh pronunciation usually associated with disparaging words.

According to popular lore, the bakla possesses what is called the "female heart" *(pusong babae)*. This idiom encapsulates what is perhaps the core of the social construction of the bakla — that of the male body with a female heart. The yearnings and needs of the bakla are seen to be similar to women's. This construction explains why some bakla, such as Arturo in the previous chapter, would say they are looking for a "real" man. By "real men," they mean straight (being married and having a girlfriend boost the masculinity of a man). There are very few reported cases of sexual relationships between baklas. It is seen as incestuous, unnatural, and weird. Some baklas view the act in cannibalistic terms (*kumakain ng sariling laman* — "eating one's flesh") or as lesbians doing it (*lesbiyanahan* — verb form of the word for lesbian). When a bakla discovers that his boyfriend is also a bakla, he is said to have been fooled or *natanso* (which literally means "bronzed" and is used to describe the treachery involved as opposed to "real" golden masculinity). The humorous saying goes that if a bakla has sex with one of his own kind, he will be hit by lightning (*tatamaan ng kidlat)*, as if such an act goes against the divine order of things.

This idiom of the "female heart" is further elucidated by the problematic category of the "masculine" bakla. Indeed, there are baklas who do not cross-dress or exhibit effeminate mannerisms. The masculine bakla is the anomalous category in the Philippine taxonomy of sexual behavior. The popular notion about the bakla is that there is a "real" screaming queen beneath the masculine facade. While the Filipino public seems to be disinterested in the masculine bakla, it is because there is no social discourse by which to discuss these kinds of men. These baklas are met either with puzzlement or suspicion.

Thus unlike his American counterparts, the bakla's predilections are seen to be focused on the straight male population. This is manifested in a thriving tradition of male prostitution. Whitam (1990) suggests that about 80 percent of men from working- and lower-class origins have participated in some kind of prostitution with a bakla or baklas. The majority of gay bars in Manila and other tourist spots are hustler bars. It must be noted that outside Manila and the tourist areas there are no organized male prostitution rings. There are mostly informal transactions between baklas and seemingly straight males. The flow of money and gifts goes from the bakla to the call boy or boyfriend.[3]

This preference for seemingly straight men is further clarified by the ideal type of male prostitute the bakla would interact with as opposed to the gay foreign tourist. Mathews's (1987) study of male prostitutes focused on those who catered to foreign tourists. Most of his informants presented effeminate mannerisms. In contrast, Filipino clientele of male prostitutes insist on masculine acting and looking men. Indeed, for the bakla, the male prostitute or the call boy should represent the paragon of masculinity. Call boy-bakla relationships are not the same as the Latin American *activo* and *pasivo*, which are based on the roles each are presumed to play in anal intercourse (Stephen Murray 1987). Actual sexual practices by both parties (bakla and call boy) can vary according to whim, negotiation, and the bargaining abilities of those involved. Despite being in a country where more than 80 percent of the people are living in poverty, it is expected that the bakla will fare better economically than the rest of the population. This is the social script of the bakla. In order to fulfill his inscribed role, a bakla has to slave away at work in order to survive and get what he is told he should desire — the "straight" macho man. He is told to suffer and not expect to have his needs filled. The ideological rationale for this situation is that, like a woman, he must suffer, but unlike a woman — being a pseudo-woman — he must pay. The complicated relationship of bakla to social class is discussed further below.

Coming Out and Coming Over: Do Closets Travel?

As a way of introducing the themes of the succeeding chapters and complicating the understanding around *bakla* and *gay,* I want to discuss two parallel issues that propel and situate these narratives, issues of coming out and the immigration/migration process. This discussion attempts to act as a bridge between the previous section, which dealt with describing the gay and the bakla, and the following discussion, which gestures to movement and crossings between these two categories.

The most pivotal rite of passage in the life cycle of a gay man is the coming out event. While most people realize that coming out is a process and not an isolated situation, the popular conception still remains that it is a singular moment. A gay man's life is turned from a life of secrecy and careful manipulation of behavior and images to one of a public avowal of identity. "I came out when . . ." punctuates these stories with a sense of rebirth and transformation into a person endowed with the sensibilities and desires of being gay. [4]

In many gay men's discussion groups in the United States, the coming out story is perhaps the most familiar topic. However, many Filipino men, even those who came here as children (the one point fivers), have problems with the notion of coming out. When I asked these men about coming out, they seemed to look at the practice of coming out as a particularly American idea and behavior. One of the informants said:

> Iba ang mga afam 'day. Puro coming out ang drama nila. Noong nagaaral ako sa ( ) wala nang pinagusapan ang mga bading kung hindi coming out. Siguro, ang mga pamilya nila masyadong malupit. Sa atin, queseho. Magagalit ang mga motherhood at fatherhood . . . pagkatapos, wala na. Pero ang mga puti, diyusme, puro mga iyak, may-I-escape ang pamilya, Puro mga malulungkot ang story, please lang, itigil yan. . . . In short, mga puno ng crayola to death.

> [The Americans are different, darling. Coming out is their drama. When I was studying at (a New England college) the queens had nothing better to talk about than coming out. Maybe their families were very cruel. Back home, who cared? But the whites, my God, shedding tears, leaving the family. The stories are always sad. Oh please, stop that. In short, (the stories were) tearjerkers.]

The term *coming out* has been translated in swardspeak as *pagladlad ng kapa,* or "unfurling the cape." I find this translation to be at once illuminating and problematic. The swardspeak term reveals the performative element of the bakla. Many Filipinos, including scholars, believe that the clothes the bakla wears are external signs of the inner core, of essential qualities of feminine sensibility and emotion. As I have indicated below, the *loob* (inner) and *labas* (outer) dimensions in this situation are not monolithic constructions; therefore, the act of "unfurling" does not actually reveal a secret self but rather an unfelt or unapprehended presence. I suggest that undisclosed homosexuality is not analogically or metaphorically represented as being "in hiding" or being "inside."

Some informants reported very positive responses from families when they did come out. Many informants, however, felt that they didn't have to come out because they thought that their families knew without being told.. Here, the "feeling out" *(pakikiramdaman)* of situations and truths is very important. In this context, many Filipino gay men believe that silence is in fact a part of the discourse and that verbalization is superfluous, as Danny's experiences attest:

> Wala akong sinabi sa kanila. Wala silang tinananong sa akin. Basta alam ko alam nila, Nararamdaman mo naman e. Noong magkasama pa kami ni Dan, inuuwi ko pa siya diyan sa parents ko sa Jersey. Pinagluluto pa ng nanay ko ng sinigang. Type ni Dan ang sinigang. Pero hindi na namin pianguusapan kung ano si Dan o kung ano ako. Para que pa?

> [I did not tell them anything. They did not ask me anything. I know that they know. You can "feel" it anyway. When Dan (his Caucasian lover) and I lived together, I took him to my parents' home in Jersey. My mother cooked him *sinigang* (a tamarind flavored stew). Dan loved sinigang. But we never discussed what Dan was (to me) or what I am. What for?]

In a discussion I participated in with Filipino gays and lesbians in Manhattan, one gay man agonized over why his mother, after he revealed his homosexuality, refused to talk about it during family gatherings. Several people in the group asked him why he thought it was necessary for his mother to talk about it. He said, "By talking about it, it would let me know that my mother thinks it is okay. If she is silent, I get the feeling that she is still not accepting it."

His comment started an interesting discussion about coming out and the need to verbalize and talk about one's gay or lesbian identity in the Filipino family. More significantly, the participants talked about the importance of silence. Carlo, who grew up in a town in a rural area in the Philippines, noted:

Naku 'day, may nakitulog sa amin na isang grupong basketbol players. May isa sa kanila, napaka-BY Natulog sila sa kuwarto naming mga lalaki — kuno. Isang hilera kami sa banig. So nang matulog na kami — si Bert yata ang pangalan niya, katabi ko [laughter]. Siyempre, pinagtabi ng tadhana — etching. Kinalabit ako, nagkalabitan kami — so ayun, nangyari ang mga malalagim na pangyayari. The next day, eto na ang daldalero at pinagkalat sa mga teamates niya na di-nu ko siya. Hanggang malaman iyon ng parents ko. Galit na galit sa akin at hindi ko raw binigyan ng hiya ang pamilya namin. Hindi naman ako sinermonan ng husto pero alam kong galit na galit ang tatay ko. 'Wag daw akong babakla-bakla — magpamin daw ako. Ako naman — may I bow and kiyowet ang biyuti ko. Ayun, after that, hindi na namin pinaguuusapan ang mga kalandian ko. Pagkatapos noon, kapag mga kabarkada ko inuuwi ko sa bahay, nagtitilian kami. Minsan lang kami pinagsabihan kami na huwag daw kaming masyadong maingay pero, hindi naman ako pinagsasabihan na huwag maging bading. Alam na nila 'yon. Hindi na nila mapapalitan ang buhay ko. Ganito na ako. Kiyowet na rin ang biyuti nila.

[Oh dear, a group of basketball players stayed overnight at our house. There was a nice looking one. They slept in the boys (not!) room. We slept in a row on the straw mat. When we were asleep, Bert I think his name was, slept beside me — but of course! We were thrown together by fate (not!). He nudged me. We nudged each other, and so there, the harrowing experiences happened. The next day, this gossip told all his teammates that I did him. This gossip reached my parents. They were so angry; they said I brought shame to the family. They didn't scold me too much, but I knew that my father was really angry. (He said) I shouldn't act like a bakla, I should be masculine. I just maintained a docile and quiet biyuti. After that, my gang and I would go home and we would be screaming. Once, we were told not to be too noisy, but I was never scolded about being a *bading* (another more polite term for bakla). They knew it. They could not change my life. I am this way. Now their biyuti is silent.]

Here, the silent biyuti of Carlo's parents was seen neither as being homophobic nor as the parents' unwillingness to talk about it. One of the participants in the discussion said that silence was to be taken neither as denial nor complete acceptance. While ambivalence may permeate this kind of silence, he argued, it is also indicative of a kind of dignified acquiescence and, more importantly, of abiding love.

A Filipina lesbian talked poignantly about silence in terms of language or the gulf between languages. Having been born in the United States, she never learned her mother's native tongue, Waray. She disclosed that when her mother was dying and in the throes of her illness, she stopped talking in English and instead talked in her native Waray. She was unable to understand her mother and grew frustrated, but at the same time, she realized that there comes a point in people's lives when it is too late to learn another language or, for that matter, to deal with particular forms of sexualities and identities. Then, she addressed the gay man who bemoaned his mother's silence by saying that the mother's silence was in fact her way of communicating with him. She recalled how when her own mother learned about her lesbian identity, her mother asked her to bring her "friend" over for a home-cooked meal.

Here, silence stands in sharp contrast to the kinds of discursive norms of coming out. It has a kind of quiet dignity and carries multiple meanings that can be further explained in the narratives I turn to now.

The two texts that follow further illustrate how ideas of coming out and politicized gay identity are interpreted by Filipino gay men in New York City. The first is an excerpt from a life-narrative interview with Mama Rene, who participated in the riots at the Stonewall Inn. The other text is from a conversation between two Filipino gay men, Rodel and Ron. In both texts, the meaning of Stonewall is translated and configured by the life narratives of these men.

I met Mama Rene in the summer of 1992 when my other Filipino gay men informants told me that he was one of the few remaining Filipinos who took part in the Stonewall Rebellion. As one of my informants told me, Mama Rene is one of the "pioneers" among the Filipino gay men in New York. He is an affable man of about fifty to sixty years (he refused to state his age). He immigrated to America in the mid-1960s to study at New York University. We talked for about two hours before he even mentioned being arrested in 1969. When I asked him to narrate that moment, Mama Rene nonchalantly said:

It was one of those nights. It was so hot. I was wearing white slacks — dungarees I think you call them, and I was really sweating. I knew that there had been a police raid several nights before, but I didn't want to be cooped up in my apartment so I went to the Stonewall Bar. Anyway, I was standing there in the bar and I was trying to look masculine — it was the thing then. All of a sudden, the lights went on and the police barged in. They told us that they were arresting everybody there — I don't know why — I guess I forgot why they were doing that. Of course it was harassment, but anyway . . . So . . . we were led out of the building to the streets. And you know what? There were lights, huge spotlights, and all these gay men clapping. I felt like a celebrity. The police took us in, booked us, and then we were released. We were supposed to appear a week later I think to be arraigned or tried, but the charges were dropped.

When I asked him how he felt about being part of that historic event, Mama Rene just shrugged. Echoing the previous discussion on silence as part of bakla discourse, Mama Rene contemplated his role and said, "They say it is a historic event; I just thought it was funny. Do I feel like I made history? People always ask me that. I say no. I am a quiet man, just like how my mom raised me in the Philippines. With dignity."

Mama Rene rarely goes out to watch Gay Pride parades. He said, "Too many people and quite chaotic." He insisted that he was not an "activist" like most of the white gay men he knew. He had nothing to say to the public nor was he particularly interested in speaking to them.

Ron's and Rodel's ideas parallel those of Mama Rene's. Both of them immigrated in the early 1980s and were, at the time of the interview, in their thirties. We were comparing our plans for the next several weeks when the conversation turned to the Stonewall celebrations. I moved to the back seat, poised as a listener. The following is a transcription of what transpired.

RODEL: Ang martsa sa June 23. Watch lang ba ang biyuti mo o join ka ng float naka-mu? [The march is on June 23. Are you going to watch or maybe join a float in drag?]

RON: O please, bakit ko gagawin yan? Besides, bakit ginagawa ng mga utaw yan. Ano pa ang ipu-prove nila? [Oh please, why would I do that? Besides, why do people do it? What do they (these gay men) have to prove?]

RODEL: Totoo 'yan. Pero sobra na. 'Yang mga mujerista sa mga floats at mga maskuladong pa-min na halos hubad na. Parang karnabal. [Yes that is true. It is too much. All these drag queens in floats and macho muscle men wearing almost nothing. It is like the carnival.]

RON: Taon-taon na lang meron tayong celebration, hindi ba titigil na 'yan. [Every year we have these celebrations—will it ever stop?]

RODEL: Hoy, hindi ba nag-mumujer ka? [Hey, aren't you the one who likes to go around in drag?]

RON: Hindi naman ang pagmumujer ang grabe kung hindi paglalan-tad ang sobra. Iba naman kapag nagpupunta ako sa mga club at bar at rumarampa, pero iba ang pagpaparada sa Fifth Avenue naka-high heels. Nawawala ang mystique mo, ang mystery. [It isn't the drag part that is awful, it is the spectacle. It is one thing if I go to clubs and cruise in drag, but it is another thing to parade on Fifth Avenue in high heels. You lose your mystique, your mystery.]

RODEL: Napaka-true niyan. Para kang baklang karnabal. [That is so true. It would seem like you are a bakla of the carnival.]

While class elements may partially underlie these attitudes toward Stonewall, further conversations with these three informants indicate that class issues (they come from different class backgrounds in the Philippines) are subordinated to the immigrant experience. For Ron and Rodel, the experience of coming to America to start a new life was both exciting and traumatic. When I asked Ron and Rodel about the symbolic meaning of Stonewall, Ron answered, "I am an ordinary bakla. I have no anger. I have no special joys. Other gay men have so much anguish. I came here to America to seek a new life. I have been successful. I don't have too much drama."

Several Filipino gay men believe that public spaces such as the streets (as in the Stonewall slogan, "Out of the bars and into the street") are not spaces of pride, but rather potential arenas of shame and degradation. These informants' views are not the result of homophobia, but are racialized and classed readings of the gay world. The kinds of exclusions and boundaries involved in the immigrant experience form the parameters for these ideas. The term *baklang karnabal* carries over meanings from Filipino traditions to illustrate the difference between the three Filipino gay men and politicized gay men. For these men and some other Filipino gay men I have interviewed, American gay men practice a kind of spectacular and scandalous cross-dressing that runs counter to the mode of several of my informants, which emphasizes dignity and attempts at verisimilitude. In other words, these informants apprehend this public display of identity to be inappropriate, reminiscent of the kind of carnivalesque vulgarity of a particular type of lower-class bakla. I illustrate and extensively discuss these views in chapter 5.

Ron's recuperation of the idiom *baklang karnabal* is not only an instance of this kind of reading, but an implicit suggestion of multiple possible "performances" of "baklaness." He differentiated himself from other gay men by calling himself an "ordinary bakla." In doing so, he exposed a specific mode of bakla self-fashioning that resists and renounces the inelegant and churlish low-class public performance of gay identity. Ron's words exemplify the kinds of translations and transvaluations of the closet and the process of coming out articulated by Filipino gay men.

Public visibility, canonized in the mainstream gay community, is questioned and held at bay by these men. In my conversations with many Filipino gay men, coming out, or more properly the public avowal of identity, is not necessary for their own self-fashioning. In a discussion group that involved members of Kambal sa Lusog, a Filipino gay and lesbian organization based in New York that was in existence during the early 1990s, several individuals expressed their concern about the usefulness of coming out narratives based on their experiences as immigrants or children of immigrants. One person in the group actually declared that coming out is a "foreign thing — totally American and not at all Filipino."

For my informants who self-identify as gay, notions of the closet and coming out become fragmented and are realigned with other experiences of being an immigrant in America. I asked one informant whether he felt that coming out as a gay man was an important issue for him; he reminded me that to declare oneself publicly as a homosexual or as a gay man was a cause for the denial of entry visas, permanent residency, or citizenship until very recently. Until the late 1980s, U.S. immigration laws categorized homosexuality together with membership in the Communist party and being convicted of a crime as grounds for barring individuals from entering the country. However, my informant went on to say, "When you are an illegal alien, you have other things to hide apart from being gay. It [being gay] is actually the least of your problems." Another informant said that he would rather declare he was gay than say he was a Filipino, since he was here illegally. He said, "I had no qualms about acting like a queen, but I would lie and tell people I was Hawaiian since there would not be any questions about citizenship."

Therefore, the process of coming out and the notion of the closet are not culturally constituted by Filipino gay men in the same way as the mainstream gay community. As one informant said, "I know who I am and most people, including my family know about me—without any declaration." Filipino gay men argue that identities are not just proclaimed verbally, but are also felt (*pakiramdaman*) or intuited. The swardspeak term *ladlad ng kapa* suggests how identity is something "worn" and not always "declared." It is this act of "wearing" identity that makes public arenas for gay identity articulation superfluous for many of my informants. This idea of identity is what spurred Ron to declare himself an "ordinary bakla." This particular phrase was echoed by several other informants, who spoke about how their identities defy coming out's implied narrative of moving a hidden, secret self from the private domain to the public realm. One informant, Joe, encapsulated their opinions when he said:

> Here in America, people always talk about everything, including those [things] that you don't really need to or necessarily want to divulge. Isn't it all obvious anyway? Talking is a luxury. A lot of us [Filipinos] don't have that luxury. Besides, I don't think we need it [talking about sexual identities]. When I see another bakla, he does not need to say anything. I don't have to say anything. Instantly, we know. Or with my friends and family, they know . . . They have known way before my *kapa* [cape] ever unraveled or I would have stepped all over it. I have been wearing it all my life!

Informants who came here as immigrants considered narratives about success and making it in America to be more important than coming out. Here class and its translation in a diasporic setting are very telling. Some of my informants who came here illegally were well educated and hailed from privileged backgrounds, but they were forced to take working class or lowly jobs as janitors, sales clerks, or domestics, among others. As one informant would say, "That is part of coming to America." I describe how this sublimation of class runs parallel with Americans' discomfort with notions of class and the rhetoric of equal opportunity more extensively in chapter 4. Many of these Filipinos imply that in order to survive in America it is necessary, at least provisionally, to relegate class to the background. This does not mean, however, that class does not figure into their narratives. Rather, class loses its central location in identity articulation and is reinscribed within other important nodes of identity such as race.

The narratives of these diasporic Filipino gay men point to how the closet is not a monolithic space, and coming out or becoming publicly visible is not a uniform process. Filipino gay men in the diaspora have, to use their own rhetoric, a different drama, that is, a particular performance of coming out and identity articulation that is emblematic of their experiences of the gay community, of America, and of bakla culture. While Fenella Cannell (1991) argued that the bakla in a rural area of the Philippines negotiate their identities with images of America, I argue that Filipino gay immigrants like Ron make sense of their existence through a complex deployment of experiences in and symbolic practices from both the Philippines and the United States. This particular performance, afforded by the diasporic experience, enables the contestation of long-held beliefs about the translation and transfer of modern gay technologies of the self. For example, Mama Rene's refusal to valorize the historic importance of Stonewall can be seen as an alternative diasporic reading of the event. The words of Mama Rene, Ron, and Rodel rewrite the public, visible, and verbalized gay identity against the grain of the bakla.

These everyday revisions of bakla/gay identities have been engaged by contemporary scholarship to which I now turn.

Bakla and the Search for Modernity

The windfall of recent writings on homosexuality in the Philippines during the early to late 1990s has been in part a response to the "flowering" of gay and lesbian studies in the West and the spread of the AIDS pandemic. In this new crop of scholars, notable works by Tony Perez, Jomar Fleras, Michael L. Tan, and J. Neil C. Garcia present crucial positions on the bakla. These scholars provide not only the most vibrant engagement with issues of gay identity and politics (*qua* liberation) in the Philippines today, but at the same time they propose varied critiques of the exigencies of the bakla as a social category.

Tony Perez published a collection of his short stories and poetry in a book entitled *Cubao 1980*. Cubao is a commercial district in Quezon City that is part of metropolitan Manila and is known for (among other things) male hustlers hanging around specific places in the area. The book is subtitled *The First Cry of the Gay Liberation Movement in the Philippines* (my translation from Tagalog).

The ideas in the book were crystallized in a poem called "Manipesto" (Manifesto), an injunction to transform the image of the bakla into the gay man. In the poem, Perez provides a kind of call-to-arms to eradicate the stereotypical notion of the bakla as a gossip, an unambitious, bitchy, and effeminate queen. He said that unless the illusion is destroyed and the mistake corrected, there can never be any attainment of rights. Writing from a self-conscious "gay liberationist" perspective, Perez's view of bakla salvation is thoroughly conditional and contingent upon an unquestioned set of universal values and qualities, which Nicanor Tiongson, a Filipino cultural historian, emphasizes in the book's foreword (translation mine):

1. The *bakla* needs to accept that he was born biologically male and that he should stop feminizing his feature or behavior.
2. "Gay" are not some cheap impersonators in some "mice race" but are honorable laborers, soldiers, priests, professors, businessmen, and athletes.
3. The right partner for the *bakla* is another *bakla*, otherwise the relationship would be unequal.
4. The gay relationship will never be the same as a heterosexual relationship that has the blessings of church and society.
5. Being *bakla* is not an illness that one can become well from or that should be treated. (Perez 1992)

Jomar Fleras's (1993) essay, "Reclaiming Our Historic Rights: Gays and Lesbians in the Philippines," extends Perez's argument into a historical one. Writing in the latest edition of the ILGA (International Gay and Lesbian Association) Pink Book, Fleras traces the rationale for the fight for gay and lesbian rights to male pre-Spanish religious shamans called *babaylan* who cross-dressed and reputedly indulged in same-sex practices. Significantly, these babaylan occupied honored positions in the community. Fleras uses Mt. Pinatubo, the symbol of the once-dormant volcano and its recent spectacular eruption, as a temporal marker as well as an apt metaphor for the emergence of Filipino gay men from historical slumber and invisibility into the light of gay activism.

Although Fleras is not alone in this view (a gay group at the University of the Philippines is called Babaylan), he disputes his own assertion of linkages with the cross-dressing shamans and follows Perez's views by disparaging the cross-dressing practices and transgender behavior of some Filipino gay men. He asserts that these practices and behaviors are historical remnants or anachronous artifacts:

> While the Stonewall riots gave birth to gay liberation in the U.S., in the Philippines, homosexual men and women were still perpetuating the feudal stereotypes. Gay men portrayed themselves in the media as "screaming queens" who did nothing but gossip, act silly and lust after men. . . . To legitimize their existence, homosexual men and women came out with the concept of gender dysporia: The gay man thought of himself as a woman trapped in a man's body while the lesbian envisioned herself with a trapped male soul that phallicized her. (Ibid.: 74)

Fleras pathologizes the bakla and prescribes the debunking of this "false" image. He asserts further that gay liberation consists of gay men and lesbians "deconstructing and breaking away from the feudal stereotypes imposed upon them by society" (ibid.: 76). According to Fleras, the future of the gay liberation movement in the Philippines is extremely bright:

> Plans are even under way for a Gay Pride week, which will feature an international lesbian and gay film festival, a theater festival, mardi gras, and a symposium. Soon there will be a gay press. Gay men are now banding together to battle the spread of AIDS. . . . Gay and lesbian activism [in the Philippines] is in practical terms just starting. . . . Gay men and lesbian women [sic] will assert their personhood. They will fight and eventually win their historic rights as leaders and as healers. (Ibid.: 78)

Fleras's nativist attempt to situate historically the fight for gay and lesbian rights in the Philippines falls apart when he unconditionally takes the Western model of sexual object choice in characterizing gay identity and repudiates the gender-based model of the bakla. Together with Perez, Fleras falls into a kind of conceptual trap while aiming to show the particularities of the Philippine experience of gays and lesbians. He does not interrogate the notion of visibility/invisibility and instead portrays the fight for rights in terms of public cultural productions such as parades, films, and books. He dichotomizes between the bakla identity of the Philippine traditions and the gay identity of the international cultural network. Indeed, like the ILGA constituency for which he writes, Fleras unwittingly prioritizes a Eurocentric model of liberation.

Tan (1995) argues that MSM, or "men who have sex with men," an epidemiological category coined during the AIDS pandemic, is in fact a better term to use than *bakla*. He claims that in many cases, the term has been adopted and used by men who have attended safer sex workshops in Manila. He further illustrates the limitation of *bakla* by creating a taxonomy of groups of men who comprise the homosexual population in the Philippines.

1. Call Boys. These are male sex workers, whose clientele includes MSMs from different subcultures, as well as middle-aged women (matronas). Most call boys come from urban and rural poor families. . . . Call boys are an important segment of the MSM population. In cities outside Metro Manila, there are no gay bars but there are many free-lance male sex workers. . . .

2. Parloristas. This is a generic term for low-income MSMs, many of whom work in beauty parlors although there are also those working as domestic servants, small market vendors, and as waiters. For the average Filipino, the parloristas, who are found throughout the country, represent the entire "homosexual" population, defined as *bakla*. . . . The parloristas rarely patronize "gay" establishments and tend to organize their own activities, usually drag beauty pageants, through neighborhood associations.

3. Gays. This group has become visible in the last two decades in Metro Manila. Many self-identify as "gay," "homosexual," or "bisexual," and in contradistinction to the lower-class bakla/parlorista. This group is far from homogenous, and can basically be divided into those with middle-class origins and those from high income groups. It is the middle-class group that has been actively organizing the country's gay men's organizations. This gay population remains partly in the shadows, socializing in gay establishments in Metro Manila but keeping its sexual orientation discreet at home and in their workplace. The middle-income group, far more vulnerable to economic dislocation, tends to remain in the closet, even as they become active in gay groups. . . . These three visible populations have varying linkages with the large shadow MSM pop-

ulation consisting of individuals who may not self-identify as homosexual but are not "out" as well as others who self-identify as bisexual or heterosexual. (Ibid.: 87)

Tan rigidly conflates class, self-identification, and other social dynamics by specific "sub-culture." The difficulty with this formulation is in part with the conceptualization of *class* and with Tan's inability to account for the fact that bakla as he himself mentions in the end "dominates the rhetoric" of homosexuality in the Philippines. While *bakla* does evoke particular class notions of being tacky beauticians or female impersonators, these evocations do not easily or unproblematically translate into actual "real" persons or "populations." In addition, Tan hints that with the growing awareness of gay politics and actual political organizing around AIDS and gay issues, there is an increasing shift from *bakla* to *gay* both as a mode of identification as well as a system of cultural practices and norms. In this light, Tan, Fleras, and Perez provide a simplistic understanding of the dynamics between bakla culture and gay culture. All three, in varying degrees of explicitness, valorize *gay* over *bakla,* and despite some limited notions of "native" or "nativist" responses, portray bakla culture as eventually dying off.

Of the four, Garcia is the only one to reflect on the exigencies of bakla culture vis-à-vis the emerging politicized gay culture. His essay appears in an anthology called *Ladlad* (Unfurling), which he coedited. In his close reading of a play by another Filipino gay author, Orlando Nadres, *Hangang Dito na Lamang at Maraming Salamat* (Up to This Point and Thank You Very Much), Garcia focuses on the two main characters, the seemingly masculine, respectable Fidel and Julie, the screaming, vulgar queen, or the stereotypical bakla. Garcia argues that the author in the end causes Fidel to identify with Julie and demonstrates the startling realization that it is Julie who rises up from the chaos. Garcia writes, "Nadres then depicts the political and strategic desirability of using Julie for the gay movement, when he makes Julie emerge from the floor of Fidel's childish rage and frustration, in tatters yet brimming with pride. For this short and noble moment . . . [the play] is finally a celebration of gay resistance and pride, pure and simple" (Garcia 1994: xvi).

Garcia advocates going beyond a monolithic construction of a gay community. He argues that "the urgency of forming a community that embraces all kinds of homosexuals — be they the selectively 'out' Fidel or the unabashedly and uncompromisingly open Julie — is clear in *Ladlad,* where themes on *kabaklaan* (being bakla) intersect, if not merge, with the homoerotic self-avowals of those 'other gays' whose primary anguish concerns their desire and the difficulty of pursuing it to fulfillment" (ibid.: xviii). The multivocalic nature of Garcia's conception of a gay community is an attempt to reconcile the strength of traditions, attitudes, and practices in relation to outside influences. Instead of uncritically transferring the technology of gay and lesbian politics from the outside, Garcia proposes a syncretic move toward intersecting models of homosexuality and politics.

Garcia's proposal fails to examine critically notions such as coming out, visibility, and most importantly — the closet. What kind of a space is the closet? Why are those who refuse to conform to highly politicized and self-conscious forms of homosexual identification relegated to its supposedly dark and forbidding terrain of homophobia? How and why does the bakla refuse to follow the narrative of coming out of the closet?

One way to get around these questions is to examine bakla ontology or the formation of the self. Gay scholars and activists writing about bakla selfhood revert to using what they see as indigenous concepts. Garcia (1996) is a prime example. He advocates for a coming out process and a gay politics based on his understanding of the dimensions of the Filipino bakla and the process of self-formation. He notes that the bakla, as the dominant pattern of homosexuality, is in fact a "psychosexual inversion." This "fact" suggests that in order to locate the bakla properly within a cultural context, Garcia must take the logical and necessary step of deploying prevailing ideas about Filipino selfhood, which primarily consists of an inner domain and a "outer body."

> I make the effort to locate a comparable organizing structure in the native culture's model of selfhood that has facilitated and made possible this implantation. In this respect, I speak of the duality of selfhood in the dichotomy of *kalooban* [inside] and *panlabas na katawan* [outer body], and its predication of local identity on psychospiritual depth. Hence, it may also be said that with the Catholization of the Philippines, the metaphysical opposition between the two has almost been completely guaranteed. (Ibid.: xx)

Garcia's formulation is premised on a narrow view of the inner and outer dimensions of the Filipino self. This formulation is in fact a strategic move to create a space within which to prescribe a public and visible gay politics, but it carelessly imposes the notions of the closet, gay identity, and coming out. Garcia seems to take an unduly literal and liberal approach when utilizing Philippine scholarship on selfhood.

Two leaders from this body of works are Reynaldo Ileto (1979) and Vicente Rafael (1988). Both Ileto and Rafael suggest that selfhood and self-making is primarily about locating oneself in a circle of social relationships and obligations. Thus, both of them focus on the notion of *utang na loob* (debt of gratitude), which is an idiom used to define the circulation of reciprocal relationships and debt obligations. However, they differ in the kind of formulation they provide in understanding this dichotomy between the inner and outer self. Ileto, writing on Philippine millenarian movements, suggests an actual bifurcation between inner and outer dimensions of the self. According to Ileto, Filipino peasant revolutionaries utilize Catholic doctrinal rituals and native values and idioms as a way to cultivate the loob. The subsequent failed peasant revolt against authorities is in fact the process of bringing out or realizing the cultivated loob. Rafael, on the other hand, refuses to resurrect the symbolic dichotomy and instead constructs the loob not as a vessel or an actual domain but as part of the social map of reciprocal relationships and obligations.

I find Garcia's (1996) position to be untenable, and Rafael's (1988) ideas on this matter to be more relevant in reference to the bakla. I base my assertions on informant interviews and observations and on the astute and subtle insights of anthropologists Mark Johnson (1996) and Fenella Cannell. Focusing on a poor rural area in Bicol, Cannell (1991, 1995a, 1995b, 1999) suggests that Filipino selfhood is negotiated with an Other, usually a cultural or economic superior. Mimicry in such situations as amateur singing competitions and gay beauty contests reveals the ways Filipinos or specifically lowland Christian Filipinos implicitly acknowledge the "power of appearances" in the conversion of their subordinated relationships with imagined others, such as America (1995b: 248–56). Unlike other scholars on the Filipino self, following Rafael (1988), Cannell (1991) brilliantly argues that selfhood in the Philippine context is articulated in terms of an "outside" and a mastery of prized cultural capital such as the "goods, gestures, and language" of America as well as the persistence of the process of transformation.

> Bicolano [the region] people of all classes are in fact extremely interested in thinking about the Philippines with reference to somewhere else. Usually, that somewhere is America, and usually, the comparisons stress that the "outside" or distant place — the imagined America — is a place of power, wealth, cleanliness, glamour, and enjoyment. . . . The central point, I think, is that people see the imagined "outside" as one source of power and as the key source of wealth. Making a voyage to America as a migrant worker is thought of as one of the only ways in which one can transform life at home, becoming wealthy, prosperous, and freed from the burden of subjection which poverty brings. (1995b: 225)

Cannell focuses on the notion of beauty as the site of transformation not only in amateur singing contests and gay beauty contests but also in spirit mediumship, healing, and folk Catholic ritual. Here she departs from the popular bifurcation of the inner and outer dimensions, and like Rafael (1988) argues for a self embedded in a field of social relations and always in process. This processual notion in fact defies the notion of the inner, or loob, as the hidden source of power or truth.

For Cannell, the bakla is the mimic par excellence (1995b: 224). Through cross-dressing and makeup, the bakla facilitates the transcendence of difference. Baklas are "often seen to assimilate their identity to a language of visibility and hyper-visibility, referring to themselves as an *apir* (a word seemingly derived from the English *appearance*) and talking about their power to seduce as 'exposing ourselves' " (ibid.: 242). Heavily influenced by Cannell, Mark Johnson further notes that this rhetoric of appearance or exposure points to an important juncture between gay beauty contests, the notion of beauty, and the self:

> "Exposing" one's beauty in the beauty contest . . . is similarly seen to signal this active process of transformation. Exposing one's beauty is neither uncovering to reveal something hidden, nor simply a process of covering to conceal that which must remain hidden, but is rather an active process of objectification which through literal application of layers upon layers of signs of beauty enacts an ontological transformation. (Johnson 1996: 100)

Both Cannell and Johnson construct Filipino *bakla/bantut* self-formation in terms of a struggle for and power over meaning. By becoming adept in the skills of mimicry, these men are able, at least in specific moments, to gain power over others and their surroundings. Additionally, their ideas suggest how the notions of the closet and coming out, premised on the idea of a truer inner self, may be culturally untenable.

My informants' views support both scholars' ideas. Some informants suggested that the bakla's body is not his own. An informant from Quezon province, in the southwestern part of Luzon, told me that another euphemism for bakla in his hometown was *manyika ng Panginoon* (doll of God). While the drag paraphernalia forms the outer shell of the bakla, his physical self is the plaything of God. Again, the images of the bakla as a spectacle and as a passive object for somebody's amusement are elevated into divine fate.

This notion can actually explain how *bakla* can also be used as a verb. *Nababakla* can loosely be translated as "baklaness" happening or descending on somebody as opposed to *nagiging bakla,* that is, "becoming bakla." The first verb actually suggests that *bakla* can also be an essence that can be transferred to or can descend upon a person like a trance or a fever. Thus, in some aspects, bakla behavior is seen to be not a product of something inside a person, but rather as a product of an outside force or forces.

I complicate and extend Johnson's and Cannell's ideas by focusing on several issues, including the use of the nonverbal modes of communication, the primacy of everyday life, and diasporic struggles. Filipino gay men utilize and deploy various modes of nonverbal or implicit communication. These practices revolve around the idea of "feeling out" (pakiramdaman) things and situations. In addition, there is a prevailing notion among Filipino bakla that what is said is not always what is true as encapsulated in different turns by the idioms of *kiyeme* (which Cannell limits to nonsense), *charing,* and *etsing,* which I discuss in my description of swardspeak in chapter 2. I am arguing for the importance of the nonvisible or unexposed, implicit or "hidden transcripts" (Scott 1985) of communicative styles mostly found in the bakla's everyday life. In short, there may be power to appearances, and yet appearances may be deceptive.

In addition, I explore how everyday life and the vicissitudes of immigrant life create a space for rearticulating and translating the practices around power that Cannell in particular has so convincingly argued. Her (1995a) analysis of practices around the "imitation of Christ" and her nuanced study of folk Catholicism in lowland Christian culture provide one of the more foundational ideas in my own study of Filipino gay men in the diaspora. As mentioned before, instead of seeing the immigration of Filipino gay men as a movement from religiosity to American secularism and modernity, I am looking at the ways in which Filipino Catholic imagery and meanings permeate and persist in the daily lives of these men. More importantly, I am examining how these images and meanings are reappropriated not merely to show indigenous difference or even exhibit a ludic attachment to the past but actually to present a modern figure of the Filipino bakla in the diaspora. The succeeding chapters will expand on these assertions as I move from conceptual mappings to the actual cultural practices and everyday experiences of my informants.

Two

**Speaking in
Transit: Queer
Language and
Translated
Lives**

Migrants always inevitably undergo a process of cross-cultural translation when they move from one place to another, from one regime of language and culture to another. — IEN ANG, *On Not Speaking Chinese*

"Translation! Translation!"

Asian and Friends, an organization of Asian and non-Asian gay men, held a beauty pageant in 1995 at the Lesbian and Gay Community Center in Manhattan. I attended the occasion together with two informants, Rene and Exotica. The emcees during this event were a Caucasian man and an Asian drag queen named Coco Le Chine, whom we first thought was Chinese.

The first part of the show was the presentation of the contestants. One of them was named Anna Pinakamaganda. The Caucasian emcee immediately admitted that Anna's last name was so difficult that he was not even going to try to pronounce the name, but Coco Le Chine took over and gave it a flawless Tagalog pronunciation. Coco further added, "Pinakamaganda means the 'most beautiful.'" It turned out, from conversations with Rene and Exotica, that Coco was not from Le Chine but was actually a Filipino of Chinese parentage.

Anna proceeded to walk gracefully to the microphone at the center of the stage to give the requisite introductory remarks. Instead of speaking in English, Anna addressed the Filipino gay men in the audience and spoke in swardspeak and Taglish. The Filipinos in the audience, including Coco, started laughing and applauding. The white men in the audience were visibly miffed and started shouting, "Translation! Translation!" Neither Coco nor Anna attempted to fulfill this request or more appropriately, this command. As Anna traipsed along the ramp spanning the center of the auditorium, he turned to the group of Filipinos seated in several rows and, with a wink, started giggling to his countrymen's thunderous applause.

This situation locates the issue of language, particularly queer language in the diaspora, within divergent and competing frames.[1] This chapter explores the contours of swardspeak, which I first mentioned in the preface with one informant's play on the word *diva*. Swardspeak is the vernacular language or code used by Filipino gay men in the Philippines and in the diaspora.[2] The word *swardspeak* comes from *sward*, a Cebuano word for homosexual and/or sissy.[3]

The discussion that follows below sets up the stage (so to speak) in which various quotes, outbursts, bits of gossip, confessions, and declarations by Filipino gay men can be properly located. The purpose here is not to provide a laundry list of words but to connect and contextualize the role of language with Filipino gay men's articulations of selfhood, immigrant experiences, and the gay world at large in the rest of the book.

Swardspeak is not a mere bundle of words but actually reflects the politico-historical and cultural experiences of multiply marginalized men from a former Spanish and American colony.[4] Furthermore, swardspeak appropriates elements from dominant Filipino, American, and Spanish codes, and rearticulates their symbolic meanings. I argue that Filipino gay men use swardspeak to enact ideas, transact experiences, and perform identities that showcase their abject relationship to the nation. At the same time, the practice of swardspeak highlights

Filipino gay men's complicated struggles in negotiating their sense of belonging, or citizenship, and self-identity.

Throughout this book, direct quotes in Tagalog and/or swardspeak by Filipino gay men are followed by English translations. However, these translations are not meant to capture fully exact meanings or the spirit of the moment. Swardspeak, more than anything, goes beyond this simplistic idea of translation and unravels the multiple, divergent, and sometimes conflicting deployment of the act of translating.

Translation, as the situation of the beauty pageant above illustrates, is an act of power. People, such as immigrants of color, who are usually from less powerful positions, have to translate and assimilate into particular regimes of dominant languages, such as English. The white gay men at the pageant were demanding a translation and felt that they were entitled to one. The refusal to translate by either Anna or Coco was an act of resistance to assimilation to the various cultural and linguistic regimes.

At the same time, translation is also a creative negotiation between languages and cultures.[5] In their use of swardspeak, Filipino gay men in the diaspora deploy translation as part of their attempts to claim a space for themselves as queer citizens in both the homeland and in the new place of settlement, the United States. By staking a space for Filipino gay swardspeakers, Anna and Coco were creating a temporary world that pulled Filipino gay men together within a mainstream gay arena of the Lesbian and Gay Community Center in Manhattan. This situation indicates how language is a means to resist total assimilation or capitulation within a transnational context. The use of swardspeak suggests that the processes of becoming gay and becoming American need not happen in a linear and totalizing manner. More importantly, as the linguistic practices below illustrate, Filipino gay men claim pleasures and attempt to work out miseries and disappointments by utilizing idioms and linguistic practices that capture these men's search for modernity, the itinerant quality of immigrant life, and the sometimes elusive cosmopolitan ideal of living life away from the homeland.

A Mobile Language

Swardspeak is a crucial marker of "being bakla." As one informant said, "Ay, mukha siyang macho, pero nang ibuka niya ang bunganga niya — oh my — parang paroparo at nagsward language. Isa siya sa atin manash." [Oh, he looked so macho, but when he opened his mouth—oh my—his mouth fluttered like a butterfly and he spoke sward language. He is one of us, sister.] As an indicator of bakla identity, swardspeak is a code full of seemingly contradictory elements, including mobility, cosmopolitanism, rootedness, and nostalgia.

Language is a crucial component of identity and self-formation. Self-presentation and biographical experiences are revised, rehashed, and refigured through particular strategic uses of language. In my life history interviews with Filipino gay men, Tagalog, English, Taglish (which is English-Tagalog code-switching), Pampango (a regional Filipino language), and swardspeak were used depending on the informant's choice. However, it is precisely this choice and the circumstances around it that provide glimpses of how language mediates identities and selves. For example, during one interview an informant claimed to be from a rich family in the Philippines. When he realized that he and I knew a common group of people, he started to converse in a specific form of Taglish used by urban, upper middle-class Filipinos who had been educated in private schools. Another Filipino started the interview in Tagalog/Pilipino and then shifted to English when the questions focused on sexual behavior and relationships. These examples suggest how language choice is in fact a way to create social and personal affinity and distance.

Unlike the code-switching system of Taglish, which is used by many Filipinos in mainstream discourses, swardspeak immediately marks the speaker as queer. Informants have told me about situations in which men whom they originally thought to be heterosexual had slipped in a swardspeak term or two, which caused these informants to suspect that the speakers were not exactly straight after all. Taglish, itself, is not a monolithic system. There are styles of speaking Taglish that index particular class or gender status. For example, there is the *kolehiyala* or coed Taglish, which is stereotypically seen as being spoken by female students in exclusive, mostly Catholic, private schools in Manila. Swardspeak on the other hand, while definitely encoding gender and sexuality in the speakers, has a blurry if not contradictory relationship with class. Some people contend that swardspeak is a communication style prevalent among lower-class queers who work mostly in beauty parlors. However, most informants, who are neither from the lower classes nor work in beauty parlors, consider swardspeak as a more democratic system of linguistic practice.

One informant, who proudly announced that he had recently become an American citizen, insisted on conducting the interview in English despite the fact that he could barely converse in this language. As he said, "We are in America now. We need to speak English." But he was punctuating his sentences with " 'di va?" [isn't it?] and " 'day" [sister]. When I pointed this out to him, he laughed and said, "No matter what you do and how hard you try, the bakla in you will come out of you."

Archie, who immigrated as a child and was raised in America, makes it a point to punctuate his sentences with Tagalog and swardspeak words. He tries to speak swardspeak as much as possible but knows he will never be fluent. He does this to prevent other Filipinos from thinking that he is not one of them or that he has a bad attitude. Archie believes that swardspeak is one of the more important elements that differentiate Filipino queers from other gay men. He said, "When you use swardspeak, you create this world that only you and other badings inhabit."

The conversations and dialogues between swardspeakers create worlds, no matter how fleeting. These worlds are made and remade in a speedy, often dizzying, manner because swardspeak, according to many informants, is always on the move. The vocabulary and various syntactic transformations are so rapid that the very idea of writing words and sentences down in this chapter goes against the spirit of swardspeak. Many of my informants tell me that they always ask friends in the Philippines or those who are visiting New York City from the Philippines about the latest trends in the swardspeak.

"Ano va ang bago?" [What is new?] is the question most of my informants ask of their friends. "Parang pasalubong!" [They are like gifts from home!] one of them said. This comment implies a popular view about the Philippines as the source of innovation and the site of authenticity. This is particularly instructive since swardspeak in the Philippines is seen to be more "outward" looking or as having a reliance on American culture for its innovations. A good number of the Filipino gay men I talked to believed that all "new" things about swardspeak come from the Philippines. They said that their linguistic skills have diminished because they do not get to practice swardspeaking as often as they would in the Philippines. However, the same people also admitted that in fact there were certain innovations that they could trace to "here," that is, the United States. These U.S.-based innovations had more to do with culture, politics, and other aspects of American life that are not popular in the Philippines.

Some speakers often talk about needing to be always on your "toes" because the language changes from "under your feet." At the same time, this elusive quality is part of the allure of swardspeak. Many informants talk about the exasperating and at the same time exhilarating, swift transformations inherent in the lexicon. The fast pace of this code is due in part to several reasons. First, swardspeakers acknowledge how language should mirror the changes in popular culture; thus the search for the new and the modern becomes the propelling force for changes in the language. Second, swardspeakers acknowledge that this language can be seen as a code for queer people, an "open" secret for people "in the know."[6] Changes are therefore seen to keep up the exclusivity and maintain the communal aspect of this linguistic practice.

The aim of the speaker is to be au courant, to be modern and to be aware of the latest and newest word or the twists and turns of the new verbal acrobatic act — be it in terms of syntax or bodily movement. Most Filipino queers who will read the collection of words herein will find it dated. Despite this condition, this chapter makes evident how swardspeak is indeed a vagabond tongue that drifts and moves from one place to another, moving always toward the new, the cosmopolitan, and the modern.

The obsession with the "new" is something that many of the men reported to be not only part of Filipino gay men living in the diaspora but also of those in the Philippines. The changes in the code are usually seen as very rapid, so much so that conversations almost always contain lexical or syntactic innovations. As one informant quipped, "Ay ang linguwahe ng mga bading sing-bilis ng jet, kung hindi matalas ang pandinig mo, maiiwan ka ng biyahe." [Oh, the language of the bading is as fast as the jet; if you do not have a sharp ear, you will be left behind.] This chapter then is already a failure by attempting to inscribe what is essentially a spoken code that rapidly changes. The glossary at the end of the book is entitled "An Elusive Glossary" because many informants who have looked at the list have commented that a good number of the words are obsolete. The terms below are indeed dated and placed; that is, the temporal and spatial markers of the terms are evident not only in the terms that have traveled to or from America or the Philippines, but also in the ways cultural icons and images from both places are reformulated and reinscribed in the act of speaking.

Hart and Hart (1990: 29) note that swardspeak derives many of its elements from different languages, such as English, Spanish, Tagalog, and Cebuano. New lexical items from French and other languages have also been reported. Swardspeak marks and reinscribes the historical and biographical histories of colonialism, postcolonialism, and diasporic displacement and settlement.[7] Apart from the Philippine languages, English and Spanish are the colonial languages that are the source of lexical and syntactic practices in swardspeak. This situation points to the divergent history of these two languages in the Philippines. Spanish did not become a lingua franca; instead, it deteriorated into a four-semester requirement for all college students in the Philippines. English, in contrast, became the medium of instruction in all levels of education and is usually the second if not the first language for most Filipinos. Bringing these two languages together in a code is not just a recapitulation but rather a reappropriation of Philippine linguistic history and the hierarchical relationships between the three languages with the colonial languages having the upper hand.

For Filipino gay men living in New York City, swardspeak is not only a source of nostalgia but also a means to cross linguistic and cultural borders that are part of living in a transnational space such as New York. As one informant told me, "Whenever I hear the words and tones of swardspeak, I feel like I am back in the Philippines." For others, the ability to find other speakers of the queer vernacular is testimony to how New York provides a wide array of opportunities, including those of escape as well as refuge.

Therefore as a mobile code, swardspeak moves through imagined spaces, across borders, and beyond restrictions of travel to arrive at some semblance of cosmopolitanism, modernity, and in the case of these men, a sense of survival and continuity. Swardspeak therefore is a quintessential queer code that is constituted by border crossings between languages and cultures in a rapid and purposive manner.

"It Has to Do with the Shape of Your Lips and the Swish of Your Hips": Performing Swardspeak

Speaking the code involves more than just knowledge of the vocabulary and certain sentence constructions; more importantly, it involves performance and bodily movement.[8] Arthur, a man in his fifties, told me that a swardspeaker needs to have a flexible, if not wild, mouth that enables him to make the verbal flourishes that are involved in the code. He mentioned the swardspeak practices of substituting the v sound for b and the f sound for p in Tagalog words. First, this substitution creates a certain kind of cosmopolitan air, since the v and f sounds are not part of Tagalog phonetics but rather are "obviously" from English. According to Arthur, the fact that one's lips form these sounds makes one appear more knowledgeable of the glamour of America or things "abroad" (that is, outside the Philippines). Second, it transforms the speaker and releases him from the confines and constraints of proper speech, thereby giving him more freedom in linguistic and corporeal behavior.

The use of the eyebrows is usually an important component in the performance. "Pakitaas nga ang kilay ko!" [Can you please raise my eyebrows!] is used to express incredulity or shock at a particular situation. Taking a finger to push an eyebrow up is one way to express these sentiments without even uttering the words.

Another practice in the early 1990s had to do with the term *kiyeme* and the use of the finger to glide across any surface, such as a piece of furniture or a body part. Kiyeme and its corollary terms, *charing* and *etsing*, can variously mean artifice, inauthentic, nonsense, exaggeration, artfulness, to fool, to joke around, and to manipulate social situations in a playful manner. For example, when a swardspeaker hears something he believes to be false or to be too much of an exaggeration, he can say, "Charing" or "Kiyeme" and swipe his finger on a tabletop. Dodi, after being told that another Filipino gay man was telling people that he was thirty years old, shrilly exclaimed, "Charing! He is fifty, my dears! Kinekeyeme kayo" [He was trying to fool you] and proceeded to glide his finger along one of the walls of the room. Another way for speakers to use these words as a commentary on matters at hand is to feign a sneezing attack and say "Etsing!"

Kiyeme, charing, and etsing are crucial in what I found to be the attitude of many Filipino gay men toward truth and the "real." Once I asked Carlo, an informant who had been joking throughout the interview, if what he had just finished telling me in the past hour and a half were lies. He replied that it was not a matter of truth or untruth, but rather how one manipulates situations and facts. He said that the best way to control a situation or to gain mastery over things is to treat everything as dissimulation or as artifice. Artifice and dissimulation, according to Carlo, have enabled Filipino gay men to survive in situations where they did not have proper immigration papers. Carlo further asserted that one had to "make kiyeme" because otherwise immigrant life becomes untenable.

Changes in the speaker's tone also mark the performance of swardspeak. David, a bank teller who arrived in the United States in the 1970s, admits that talking in swardspeak with a "straight" voice and demeanor does not work. By "straight" he means the regular way in which any speaker will use any mainstream language, be it Tagalog or English. He said that when one uses swardspeak, "Hindi puwedeng hindi sumayaw ang mga labi mo at mag-gumamela ang boses mo." [It is impossible not to have your lips dance and your voice become like a hibiscus.] When I asked David what he thought about situations when non-Filipinos heard him talking swardspeak, he replied that they would probably think he was speaking in some Asian tonal language and would not think in terms of changes in the registers of gender and/or sexuality.

Lexical Crossings: The Biyuti and Drama of Transformation and Shifting Identities

The social construction of the bakla revolves around gender crossing and transgression. As I have mentioned above, these crossings are based on a mercurial self that undergoes transformation depending on situations. While there are noticeable categories for male and female, in swardspeak the feminine dominates the discourse around the self. Let us take an example of a conversation with an informant (R = researcher; I = informant).

R: Papaano mo i-dedescribe ang sarili mo? [How will you describe yourself?]
I: Well, isa akong mabuting tao . . . teka, isang biyuting tao . . . este, babae. [Well, I am one nice person . . . wait, one beautiful person . . . er, woman.]
R: Babae, ibig mong sabihin e babae ka? [Woman, do you mean you are a woman?]
I: Girl na rin! Mujer 'day . . . kapag gabing madilim [laughter]. [A girl too! Woman, sister . . . when it's a dark night.]

In the last line, the informant uses a euphemistic line *(na rin)* that suggests the inclusion of the self in the female category. Notice the use of the English word *girl* and the Spanish word for woman (*mujer*). Both of these words are used to describe real women, and many of my informants also use these words to describe themselves or other Filipino gay men. While there is humor ingrained in this kind of discourse, many of the Filipino gay men acknowledge the contradictions in the language's use of the feminine. I suggest that this hybrid assertion of the female as an interstitial character is crucial to the construction of the Filipino gay self. This assertion is further illustrated by the creation of separate categories for male and masculine within the language. An example would be the words *lalique* and *baccarat*. Both are brands of crystal, but the language's play of sounds transforms lalique to stand for *lalaki*, or male/man, and baccarat to mean bakla.

The use of words that index the body further extends this point about gender. Several informants (who are not transsexuals) would use the female sexual organ when referring to their own.

I: Pagkatapos ng date namin, inuwi ako ng min, tapos nang papasok na ako sa pinto, may I sunggab niya ang aking pekpek. [After our date, the guy brought me home (min is swardspeak for man or guy), then as I was about to enter my door (may I) he grabbed my pussy.] ("May I" is part of a popular phrase pattern with swardspeak and is thought to be derived from the game, "Mother, may I?")

R: Pagkatapos, ano ang nangyari. [Then what happened?]

I: Di anu fi, nilapastangan niya ang puri at biyuti ko. [What else? He transgressed/raped my dignity and beauty.] ("What else?" which is usually *ano pa* in mainstream Tagalog is changed to *anu fi*: changing the consonant "p" to "f" is another popular form of swardspeak.)

In this excerpt from a longer dialogue, the informant continually used nouns and adjectives that indexed him as a female in the encounter. Swardspeak's lexical items for sexual acts provide another way of categorizing the speaker or the informant as female or pseudo-female. The phrase for blowjob is *lumuhod ng walang belo* or "to kneel without a veil," which irreverently alludes to the tradition (no longer practiced) of Catholic Filipino women of wearing veils to church. The phrase for mutual fellatio, or sixty-nine, is called *kainan ng matris* or "the eating of the uterus."

As mentioned above, cross-dressing is the quintessential core of the social construction of the bakla. Drag or cross-dressing among gay Filipinos contains a self-consciousness that is very revealing of the dynamics of the bakla tradition. Words from English such as drag and transvestite are transformed into *dragon* (a play on drag and the mythical monster) and *tranvestita*. The Spanish word *mujer* is changed to *mujerista* or "one who goes as a woman."

CONSTRUCTING THE OTHER

In constructing the Filipino bakla self, multiple alterities and identities are implicated. As has been mentioned above, the categories male and female as classified by swardspeak are not stable closed systems. The Filipino gay man assumes many feminine attributes and creates numerous syntactic and lexical strategies that extend these attributes.

In constructing alterity or otherness, swardspeak and its practitioners have created many lexical items that provide degrees of closeness or distance from the self. Family is an important element in this category. Kinship terms are used for relatives and friends. For family members, some popular terms for mother and father are *madir* and *padir* (sounding like the English words) and *mudra* and *fudra* for motherhood and fatherhood. Kinship terms, particularly those used for female kin, are used for friends, both gay and gay-friendly. Such terms include *tita* (aunt), *ate* (older sister), *manash* (sister), *lola* (grandmother), and *nanay* (mother).

Lovers are called *asawa* (spouse) or *jowa* or *jowawis* (the last two are a play on the first). Other terms include *churot* and *juwiwing churlilus*. Lesbians are called tomboy, *t'boli*, *tunggis*, and *portugesa* (a linguistic play on geography and sound since the capital of Portugal is Lisbon). Informants who had butch-acting Filipino lesbian friends were called by male kin terms such as *kuya* (older brother) or *pars/pare* (ritual/fictive kin).

Class is an implicit boundary marker for many Filipino gay men. Gay men who seem to lack proper breeding or have uncouth, "common" ways are often called *baklang talipapa* (bakla of the fish market), *baklang parlor* (bakla of the beauty parlor), or *baklang squatter* (bakla from the slums). Somebody who has a lot of money is called *datungera* or *madatils* (from *datung*, the Tagalog slang for money). Somebody who does not have money or is poor is called *purita*. This is a female name and if speakers want to be dramatic about somebody's poverty they may say, "He/she is Purita Kalaw Ledesma," which is the name of a prominent woman in Philippine society.

Physical attributes are integral to the language. As mentioned earlier, biyuti is seen as a physical attribute as well as a state of being. Together with its variation such as BY and BYU, biyuti can be seen as a central core of other physical and personality attributes. Filipino movie stars or beauty queens have been the icons for biyuti or lack thereof (Nora Aunor for a dusky beauty, Vilma Santos for a *mestiza* or a more Caucasian looking beauty, Charito Solis for a chubby beauty, and so on). *Shonget* (a play on the Tagalog word *pangit*) or *ukray* (which has other meanings mentioned above) are words for ugly. Penis size is seen in terms of big *(dako, Dakota, Dakota mansion, Dakota Harrison),* regular (*Reggie Regalado* — the name of a couturier), or short (*dyutay,* duty free).

Words about personality attributes are played against the standpoints of reality and biyuti. *Ilusiyonada* (someone full of illusions) and *pantasyadora* (someone full of fantasies) are people who do not deal with reality. For example, when informants intend to insult someone who thinks he or she is beautiful or has a lot of money, they use a metaphor of drinking coffee (*Magkape ka!* literally means "Drink coffee!") as a way to tell the person to "Wake up and smell the coffee!" *Imbiernadora* are people who destroy one's emotional balance, sense of being, or biyuti.

While race is not an elaborate discourse in the Philippines, skin color and ethnicity are part of the development of diasporic swardspeak in America. In swardspeak, the racial other is contrasted with the concept of biyuti. In this context, *biyuti* utilizes a more Caucasian-centered standard for physical attractiveness. A word used for ugly is *chaka,* from the black singer Chaka Khan. Even other Asian gay men are seen as radically different from Filipinos. For example, the Chinese are also called *shonga,* which is a play on the name of a Filipino comedian, Ponga (who used to play stereotypical renditions of the Chinese on Philippine television shows).

White Americans are called *afam* even in the Philippines. In the Philippines, there is no need to delineate diversity among Caucasians, whether they are from America or not. However, in New York, ethnic diversity is very apparent even in what is seemingly a monolithic white population. For example, Jews who are *Hudyo* in Tagalog are called "who do you know" to approximate the Tagalog pronunciation. Latinos, a category that does not exist outside America, are called *mantika* (grease), *Espangoles, cha-cha,* or España Extension (a street in metropolitan Manila). Puerto Ricans specifically are called *purico,* which is a contraction of the name as well as a brand of lard in the Philippines, or *paro-paro* (butterfly). This latent racism in swardspeak practices is extended to words for African Americans. Instead of the Tagalog words *negro* or *negra,* which can cause some furor if they are over-heard, swardspeakers call blacks *jutim,* which is a phonetic play on the Tagalog word for black *(itim).* Chinese are called *chinois* from the French. Indians (from the subcontinent) are called *bumbayic* (from the city Bombay and the Tagalog term for them, which is *Bumbay).* The categories Asian and Oriental have become important as the terms *asiatica* and *orientalia* are now part of the lexicon.

CONSTRUCTING GAY EXPERIENCES

One of the important features that informants have reported about gay life in America is its amazing diversity. They are particularly struck by leather or S&M. Terms like *mahilig sa balat* (one who likes leather) or *mahilig manakit* (one who likes to hurt) are used for this particular gay tradition. Gay bars are an important component of gay life. Rice paddy, or *palayan,* rice bar, and rice bowls are terms incorporated into the lexicon to designate places where Asian gay men and the Caucasian men (rice queens or *mahilig sa kanin*) who desire them congregate. Bar names are also given specific names, Twilight is called Twirlili, Rounds is called Bilog, Club 58 is called Klabing (which is another word for bakla). Bathhouses are called bahamas or *baños* (Spanish for baths).

As I will discuss in chapter 6, AIDS has an enormous impact on informants' construction of gay life in America. AIDS is called Tita Aida (Auntie Aida) in swardspeak. There have been a plethora of dis-courses surrounding AIDS among Filipino gay men, which I discuss more fully in chapter 6. However, it is sufficient to say that the idiom for this epidemic reproduces the kind of interstitial feminized figure prevalent in swardspeak. *Drogas* (drugs), which are part of gay night-life in New York, are also given female or feminized names. Some Filipinos have reported using some of these drugs and have coined new words for them, such as *tasing* (a female name) for ecstasy and *mari gunggong* (a play on a female name coupled with a slang word for "stupid") for marijuana.

One informant who had AIDS talked about the perils of using drugs and the possibility of contracting HIV in this way: "Ang sey ko sa aking mga amiga e mag-ingat kay Tita Aida. Wag nang magcoca at baka ma-tsug ang biyuti nila." [I told my friends to be careful of Tita Aida. They should stop using cocaine otherwise they (their biyuti) might die.] In this context, *biyuti* refers to the physical health of the person. In fact, several HIV prevention pamphlets in California that have utilized swardspeak have used the notion of biyuti as a metaphor for health.

Biyuti acquires a different dimension when referring to the hyper-masculine world of the gay white community. Many swardspeakers refer to the practice of going to the gym as going like the *barako* (a big lizard native to the Philippines that also signifies machismo). One informant said (with obvious disdain) that his Filipino gay friend had stopped being a dragon (drag queen) and was now a barako. Thus when this friend turned barako *(barako ang drama niya* or *barako ang biyuti niya)* his biyuti crossed gender and racial lines. The standard of the T-shirted and muscled (usually Caucasian) gay man replaces the feminized cross-dresser.

CONSTRUCTING THE IMMIGRANT EXPERIENCE

Immigration problems, icons, and symbols permeate Filipino gay men's discourses, and this reality is reflected in the lexical items that dominate the language. In New York, the most prevalent Filipino immigrants and residents are nurses and other medical professionals as well as those who work in the United Nations (where Filipinos occupy the biggest number of non-American and non-career diplomat positions). Nurses, particularly male nurses, are called *narscisa,* which is a female name, while UN employees are called "Miss International" or "Miss United Nations."

Tita Imee, or Aunt Imee, is the name given to the Immigration and Naturalization Service. Imee is the name of the eldest daughter of former Philippine president Ferdinand Marcos. This federal agency is the one feared most by Filipino undocumented immigrants. Several informants who were undocumented talked about being TNT *(tago ng tago,* or in hiding) or described hiding their biyuti from the INS because they had no legal working papers *(walang papeles)* and feared being deported *(madeport ang biyuti).*

A: Hoy, narinig mo ba si ( ) ay dinampot ni Tita Imee. [Have you heard? (Name of a person) was picked up by Tita Imee (INS).]

B: Ha? Baket? [Why?]

A: Ano fi? E di wala siyang berde, hindi siya Amerikanang tulad ko . . . TNT lang siya 'day! Kaya ayun, deported ang biyuti niya. [What else? He did not have the green (card), he was not an American (girl) like me . . . he was in hiding, sister! That is why his biyuti was deported.]

Biyuti in this context refers to the physical person forcibly removed from U.S. soil. Illegal immigrant status is held secret for fear of being discovered, but it is also a demeaning condition that some Filipino gay men use for bitchy slurs or threats. Once at a party, a fight broke out between two Filipino gay men, and one of them said, "Hoy, walanghiya ka, wala ka namang papeles, illegal ka, malandi ka! Isumbong kita sa immigration makita mo!" [Hey you shameless person, you don't have any (legal) papers! You are illegal! You whore! I will squeal on you to the INS!]

If a person is a new immigrant or acts like one, he is called *promdi* (short for from the islands or from the provinces) or *f.o.b.* (fresh off the boat). A person who is Philippine-born is called *local* while someone who is American born is called *stateside* or *born in the U.S.A.* (from the Bruce Springsteen song). If somebody is denied a visa, a green card, or citizenship, he is called a *denial queen* (which is also used to describe people who deny their baklaness).

Biyuti in the immigration context straddles several dichotomies, such as citizen vs. non-citizen, American vs. non-American, legal vs. illegal. In such a context, biyuti not only points to physical being, but more importantly to the legal and cultural personhood of the individual. Biyuti and drama, as has been shown above, are shifting and contingent concepts that are used in virtually all contexts from the construction of the self to that of the immigrant experience. I choose to focus on these concepts because of their importance in all levels of Filipino gay experiences. More importantly, their mercurial character metaphorically reflects the plasticity of the immigrant experience and the ways in which Filipino gay men create meaningful worlds through linguistic and cultural negotiations. These negotiations will be discussed in the next three chapters.

Queers on the Go and Language on the Move

Translation as a process of cultural assimilation need not be, as Ien Ang (2001: 4) suggests, inevitable among migrants. In fact, as Filipino gay men's use of swardspeak has shown, the space for the refusal of this form of translation is possible in the diaspora. Swardspeak, as a vagabond tongue and an itinerant code, refuses any fixed space and contexts. Switching and shuttling between languages, the sward-speaker acquires a cosmopolitanism that is sometimes denied him else-where because of economic, racial, ethnic, and cultural hierarchies and exclusions. This kind of cosmopolitanism is not always and already a privileged one but rather comes close to what Louisa Schein (1998: 293) terms as "oppositional cosmopolitanism" or non-elite "worldly" negotiations with "the nexus of privilege and constraint." Therefore, Filipino gay swardspeakers in the Philippines and in the diaspora, de-spite being excluded from numerous arenas, are creating alternative worlds and localities by their rapid and creative rearticulation and appropriation of various images, meanings, and practices.

Swardspeak, then, resides in what Alfred Arteaga (1994) calls the "linguistic borderlands," a contestatory arena where marginalized peoples attempt to find a voice and a grammar to confront power. Therefore, Filipino gay men living amid the colonizing power of En-glish and mainstream gay culture are able to navigate the semantic seas by developing and deploying new linguistic and cultural regimes.

The idioms of biyuti and drama as explained above and elaborated in succeeding chapters are crucial sites of articulating and creating new meanings for Filipino queer diasporic survival. Both idioms are charac-terized by constant shifts and transformations. Biyuti and drama, like all other elements of the swardspeak code, are not about passive mimi-cry of colonial languages, nor can one trace their provenance from the West. Keeping in mind the complicated politics of postcolonial mimi-cry (Bhabha 1992), the idioms point to the unsettling and unsettled nature of the code. This reality further exemplifies Filipino gay men's struggles against the homogenizing tendencies of *gay* and attempts to "inscribe heterogeneity, to warn against myths of purity, [and] to show origins as always already fissured" (Niranjana 1994: 50).

The rapid shifts and changes in swardspeak lexicon and syntax reveal how the search for belonging and citizenship need not be based on fully taking on or assimilating into the majority culture's regime of meaning. If language is a constitutive element of an imagined commu-nity,[9] Filipino gay men's use of such swardspeak idioms as *biyuti* and *drama* unravel the vexed relationship between their sense of belonging and citizenship with the idea of the nation. Swardspeak then creates a dissident form of citizenship that refuses incarceration to a specific geographical, cultural, and linguistic space but instead enables speakers to be "mobile" as it were by appropriating cultural and linguistic items and imbuing them with specific local meanings.

Shuttling between linguistic and cultural landscapes, the Filipino gay man living in the diaspora does not represent valiant homelessness but rather a constant struggle for survival as well as moments of pleasure and settling in. As the succeeding chapters will highlight, these men are not passive consumers but rather are "translating agents" who with the wildness of their lips, tongues, and bodies are able to lay claim to a space no matter how fleeting or limited in the transnational setting of New York City.

Three

**"Out There":
The Topography
of Race and
Desire in the
Global
City**

The city, the contemporary metropolis, is for many the chosen metaphor for the existence of the modern world. In its everyday details, its mixed histories, languages and cultures, its elaborate evidence of global tendencies, and local distinctions, the figure of the city, as both a real and an imaginary place, apparently provides a ready map for reading, interpretation and comprehension. Yet the very idea of a map, with its implicit dependence upon the survey of a stable terrain, fixed referents and measurement, seems to contradict the palpable flux and fluidity of metropolitan life and cosmopolitan movement. . . . Beyond the edges of the map we enter the localities of the vibrant everyday world and the disturbance of complexity. Here we find ourselves in the gendered city, the city of ethnicities, the territories of different groups, shifting centers and peripheries — that city that is a fixed object of design (architecture, commerce, urban planning, state administration) and yet simultaneously plastic and mutable: the site of transitory events, movements, memories.
— IAIN CHAMBERS, *Migrancy, Culture, Identity*

New York permits homosexuals an unparalleled chance to assemble a mix-and-match life. — EDMUND WHITE, *States of Desire*

Kakanta na ba ako ng 'New York, New York'? Parang nasa sentro ako ng mundo. Noong lumalaki ako sa Maynila, ang Amerika para sa akin ay Manhattan, Empire State, Statue of Liberty. O 'di va ? Ang baduy Ko 'no para akong turistang fresh off the boat.

[Shall I sing "New York, New York"? I feel like I am in the center of the world. When I was growing up in Manila, America for me was Manhattan, the Empire State Building, and the Statue of Liberty. Isn't that tacky of me as if I were a tourist fresh off the boat?] — ARTURO

Homo Xtra or *HX*, a weekly gay guide to New York City, includes a section called "Out There." In contrast to the other parts of the guide, which enumerate the gay offerings of various Manhattan neighborhoods or districts (e.g., the Upper East Side, Chelsea, and the West Village), this section lumps together all the various gay bars and events outside Manhattan. The "Out There" section exemplifies a typical and popular topographical rendition of New York City with Manhattan as the cosmopolitan center and the surrounding areas as the less sophisticated peripheries. Most of Manhattan below Harlem is popularly seen as the modern gay "white" metropolis with Chelsea, the East Village, and more recently Hell's Kitchen as the prime gay neighborhoods. In contrast, the other boroughs are more often than not seen as peripheral, decrepit immigrant enclaves as well as premodern and anachronous queer sites. These two spaces are separated not only by bridges and tunnels but more importantly by racial, class, and ethnic cleavages. The "B and T" or "bridge and tunnel," which is a disparaging term used for the general population living outside Manhattan, is also deployed for queers of color from the "outer" boroughs who are seen to frequent the venues in and inhabit the spaces of the "out there."

To further illustrate the ways this imagined geography operates in daily life in the city consider this particular vignette. I was walking with my friend Ernesto down Christopher Street one cold winter day in 1995 when a gay white man coming out of a bar wobbled toward us. Visibly drunk, he accosted us with the question, "Are you two Orientals?"

We were too shocked to answer immediately. He proceeded to declare, "Well, I have never seen two Oriental homos before." My friend

Ernesto, who was in fact Chicano, had a sharp tongue. Facing the drunken man, he blurted, "Excuse me, but we prefer the word *ornamental*." Ernesto and I looked at each other and started laughing, and we left the man speechless.

This vignette and the "Out There" section demonstrate the fissures around race and other forms of differences that shape the contours of gay spaces in New York City. Both point to the kinds of "grids of difference" (Pratt 1998) that crisscross the urban terrain. To understand these grids, it is necessary to think of them not as serendipitous but rather as products of the structural processes of a global city. Saskia Sassen (1994, 2001) was among the first proponents of the global city as a "contested terrain" (1996: 151) and as a highly differentiated space. Mollenkopf and Castells (1991) suggested and critically analyzed a useful model of the global city as an uneven landscape on the one hand and a structured duality on the other. This structured duality is made up of a superstructure consisting of modern technological and financial industries that are buttressed by a service sector made up mostly of immigrants, people of color, and women. In other words, the gleaming modernity of New York City's financial, commercial, and cultural centers with highly educated, mostly white personnel is supported by a gendered, ethnicized, and racialized substratum. This model is useful in enabling us to understand the myth of a monolithic gay community but also to see the divergent racialized spaces as overlapping realities (Parker 1999: 54; Chauncey 1994: 2–4) that transgress and/or intersect with each other. Therefore, despite its reputation as a gay mecca and the persistence of queer subcultures, new communities have formed in New York City that are only partially recognizable as gay (Parker 1999: 224).

This chapter takes a traditional component of ethnographic texts called "the setting" and recasts it into a shifting narrative of places, peoples, and events that implies not a static geographic area but one that is made and remade by specific kinds of observers and participants. In this case, I take myself and my informants as roving eyes and itinerant feet walking the gay city — somewhat like and unlike the figure of the *flaneur*. The French poet Charles Baudelaire (1964) first posited the figure of the flaneur, whose adventuresome character sets out to map the twists and turns of modern urban life. Walter Benjamin (1983) further elucidated the flaneur as one who, untrammeled by convention, casts a knowing eye and, unwittingly, a lustful heart to a city waiting to be possessed by his omniscient knowledge. Critical studies of the flaneur have argued that the figure is a white upper-class heterosexual male who is able to gain access to and possess the various scenes and personages of the city. Accordingly, feminist and queer scholars have explored the possibilities of other marginal people walking the modern city and laying claim to its spaces. For example, cultural theorist Sally Munt (1995) offered a critical reflection on the lesbian "flaneur," or *flaneuse,* while the gay fiction writer Edmund White (2001) presented a more biographical rendition of the gay flaneur in his own traversing of Parisian gay spaces. This chapter goes beyond these formulations by attempting to answer how queers of color strive to map out the gay city as they stake out their own spaces. What follows is less of a systematic cartographic exercise and more of a series of loosely interconnected stories and events that produce a partial and highly specific topography. Therefore, the mapping of gay New York City is not only about the physical layout of the queer landscape but is also about hierarchical and uneven spatialized imaginings where particular queers are socially and symbolically located.

Gay New York: Beyond / In Black and White

For immigrants and other mobile people, the city represents the coming together of "worlds" and "nations" into one geographic area (Hannerz 1996). For many queers, urban space is the site for constituting selves and communities (Bech 1997; D'Emilio 1983).[1] Many people, my informants included, perceive these interlocking worlds of New York City as a unique milieu in which to create a gay sense of self.

Filipino gay men marveled at the infinite variety of activities, events, and places marked as gay or queer in the city. One informant said that this variety is emblematic of everything "American," in which everything is always seen as bigger, more plentiful, and wider ranging. Many of my informants described this variety in terms of products to be bought and consumed.[2] As one informant put it, "Gay life in New York was like a big vending machine." Indeed, by the late twentieth century, New York City gay life had mushroomed into a plethora of groups and events that catered to almost every possible political, cultural, economic, physical, and social need. The pages of gay travel and entertainment guides, directories, and other gay-oriented publications show how gay men in the city are able to join and access groups that have a variety of agendas, including those that focus on the political (e.g., Gay Republicans), ethnicity (e.g., Irish Lesbian and Gay Association), religion (e.g., Dignity or "Gay Catholics"), occupations (e.g., Firefighters Lesbian and Gay of New York, Inc.), self-help (e.g., Gay Alcoholics Anonymous), support (e.g., Gay Circles), and law (e.g., Lambda Legal Defense and Education Fund).

This enumeration of places, groups, and people is necessary to provide the backdrop for how Filipino gay men talk about gay life in the city to their friends back in the Philippines. At the same time, many of my informants would talk about race, as would most people in America, in terms of black and white. However, this bifurcation more often coincided with Filipino gay men's stereotypical views of race and of gay spaces. I would ask various informants to sketch verbally the locations of an array of gay venues in the city. Most of them would talk of places in terms of the racial composition of the bars and neighborhoods.

The mappings of racialized queer spaces come in many genres. Notable among these are two ethnographic studies that highlight the stark racial and cultural boundaries between black and white gay men in New York City. The ethnographies of two Manhattan-based groups of gay men by Martin Levine (1990, 1992, 1998) and William Hawkeswood (1996) represent critical forays into the divergent reactions to the emergence of a gay culture. These two geographically bounded groups are not only culturally distinct but are also racially differentiated. Therefore, to modify my earlier statements about Manhattan, this borough-island is not in itself a monolithic gay enclave. In fact, these studies show that people living in Harlem or upper Manhattan have created a gay niche that is quite different and separate from the world renowned gay neighborhoods located downtown.

Levine's (1990) ethnographic study of the gay macho "clone" examined a loose group of predominantly Caucasian men who dominated and set the tone for the post-Stonewall New York City gay scene in the 1970s and early 1980s. Levine studied the culture, social organization, and behavior of a cohort of men that was among the first to be affected by the AIDS pandemic; it was, in fact, the generation to be devastated and, in a way, decimated by the disease.

Gay clones rejected the effeminate stereotypes prevalent during the pre-Stonewall era and went to the opposite extreme. This generation of men presented a hypermasculine series of images in their manner of dressing, in the sites where they gathered, and in the symbols they utilized. For example, the clone usually donned working-class outfits, particularly those worn by lumberjacks, construction workers, the military, and police. These outfits also provided other coded messages to other clones. The colors of handkerchiefs and their placement in either the left or the right back pocket sent a message about the wearer's favored sexual act and the position (top or bottom) that he assumed in that act. Other coded clothing styles included key chains, leather chokers, and ropes. Most men sported mustaches and had muscular, buffed bodies.

The organization of clone social life centered on the "clique" (Levine 1990: 80–90). The clique included men whose lives were dominated primarily by the fast life of parties, dances, drugs, and easy sex. These men participated in a routinized and ritualized series of events, parties, and other seasonal gatherings called the "circuit" (ibid.: 92). The circuit events were highlights in the gay clone's social calendar and were important cultural events.

Clones also maintained clear boundaries in their representation of family and other "straight" institutions. Most of these clones were from other states and had migrated to New York for economic as well as sexual opportunities. Levine noted that gay clones generally anticipated reproach and chastisement from heterosexual kin, friends, and colleagues and attempted to escape this by living in gay enclaves and substituting the clique for these other social relationships as their main social network (ibid.: 98). Levine suggested that the clone socially isolated himself and created a social world mostly populated by others like him (ibid.: 80). This was made possible because of the relative privilege enjoyed by these mostly Caucasian men and, more importantly, by a rhetoric of individualism that pervades mainstream gay identity politics, which I discussed in the previous chapter.

In contrast, Hawkeswood (1996) focused on a specific group of African American gay men who lived and socialized in Harlem, and preferred other African American men for sexual partners during the late 1980s. This group of men had little significant contact with the mainstream gay enclave in downtown Manhattan. Within this relatively self-contained group of gay men, cultural practices, codes, and folklore differed from most of what is largely considered to be the New York City gay lifestyle.

These men did not live separately from their non-gay African American neighbors. Rather, they participated fully in Harlem community life and were accepted as full members. Religion and family were important components of their lives unlike most of the men from the clone culture, which veered toward secular issues. Religion, particularly in largely black congregations and denominations, is an arena for gay socializing and the formation of what is called the "church girl" network (ibid.: 111).

While the gay clone projected the ultra-masculine look, Hawkeswood's informants continued to present themselves as ordinary men without special clothing styles in everyday life. Drag, however, was very popular as an annual drag ball was an important event in the social calendar for this group of men. In fact, vogueing or house culture, a particular drag/cross-dressing cultural practice among African American and Latino gay men, is an integral part of many of these men's lives (ibid.: 85–87, 188–89). The vogueing ball, which I describe in detail below, is not only a statement about a different engagement with images of gender, homosexuality, and gay identity, but is actually a performance of class and the racial components of the class hierarchy. In these balls, black and Latino men and women dress up as Wall Street executives and as gangsters, or banjee (street) men, as private school coeds and as runway models, as street prostitutes and welfare queens.

Caucasian gay clones have an ambivalent relationship with discourses on class. The fetishization of working-class clothes comes together with images of opulence. Mainstream gay events are almost always imbued with glamour and images of what is seen as upper-class taste (which may vary according to each person). Many of the gay men I have met from various ethnic and racial groups would admit that they have "good taste." Gay men, according to popular, stereotypical lore, are bearers of "good taste," but the specifics of what constitutes "good taste" and who are its arbiters vary widely despite its heavy class underpinnings. Good taste, therefore, despite its material manifestations from furniture and art to houses and clothes, is naturalized in many ways as an intrinsic part of being gay. I would suggest that class is always sublimated in most gay discourses and subsumed not only under the cloak of good taste but also under a rhetoric of same-sex desire and the image of the valorized (white) gym-buffed body. Moreover, as the discussion in chapter 4 will show, Filipino informants report that Americans in general seem to be totally ill at ease with the question of class.

Most importantly, the irony behind white gay clones' dis-ease with class is the fact that mainstream gay cultural events and lifestyles are suffused with class demarcations, which, in turn, hide racial boundaries. Consider the following entry from *Circuit Noize,* which was a bible/guide for gay men who wanted to become part of the circuit in the 1990s.

> The circuit is a series of queer parties that are held around the world. A circuit party gives us the chance to escape the pressures of our day-to-day existence and to enter the altered world where man-to-man sex is not only accepted, but is celebrated. . . . From gay ski weekends to an escape to South Beach [Florida] in the middle of winter. From a party at the Olympic Stadium in Montreal to a spring celebration in the middle of the desert. (Circuit Boyz Productions 1996: 6)

Major American, Australian, and European cities become the venues for this series of parties. The circuit party, among other queer events, has caused the notion of homogenizing queer culture. But what is left unsaid is that many men are excluded from such events despite a desire to be part of the scene; many are unable to travel either because of money problems or lack of documents. The circuit, more than anything, showcases the tension of class and mainstream (white) gay identity. With class comes the concomitant racial question in the face of the economic and culturally marginalized positions of gay men of color. Who among gay men of color may be viable members of the circuit even if they were welcomed into it? Certainly not Hawkeswood's informants from Harlem nor many Filipino gay immigrants.

Most importantly, while gay clones largely decentered racial or ethnic identity in relation to gay identity, the African American men Hawkeswood studied were concerned about black identity and black expressive styles. These men's preference for residence and social life within a black environment "further serves to explain the perception they hold of themselves as being primarily black men" (124).

The tension between urban queer spaces and race is more vividly explored in sites where various racial and ethnic groups meet. A recent work on the racialized and sexualized spaces of Times Square by the celebrated gay writer Samuel Delaney (1999) examined a section of the city that is known as a racial and ethnic crossroad and goes beyond the racially circumscribed sexual spaces of the city. In *Times Square Red,*

Times Square Blue, Delaney described in both biographical and ethnographic terms the various sexual emporia, theaters, street corners, bars, and other places in the midtown Manhattan district where queer men met for sexual and social purposes. He chronicled the changes in which hustlers and clients of various racial, class, and ethnic backgrounds converged in the area while seeking sexual pleasures and entertainment. He lamented the intrusion of giant corporations and stores and the eventual "cleaning up" of the district under the auspices of Mayor Rudolph Giuliani. While he unflinchingly exposed the gritty side of the pre-Giuliani years, including the harsh realities of queer public sex, he is equally unflinching with the horrors and violence of gentrification and normalization of Forty-second Street and its environs.

"Where's the Gay Bar?": Shifting Sites and Selves

Having mapped out the broader range of gay spaces in the city, I shift attention to what is considered to be the quintessential gay space — the gay bar. It is the most prominent space for socialization and, for many, authentic belonging to the community. Going clubbing or bar hopping is one of the typical preoccupations of many gay men. In fact, one way to differentiate oneself from the rest of the gay population is to declare that one is not into the bar scene. The New York City gay bar is epitomized in works of fiction, cinema, poetry, and other cultural forms. However, this section is an exploration of the more mercurial if not elusive aspects of queers of color spaces that defy the usual and popular renditions of the gay bar.

There are particular types of gay bars. According to my informants' informal taxonomy of gay bars, there is a diversity of bars that cater to particular sexual tastes and more often are demarcated by ethnicity and race. There are leather bars for people who like leather and slapping (mahilig sa balat at sampal). Then there are Western/cowboy bars, which focus on country music and cowboy attire. Then there are sports bars, which possess a more casual atmosphere with a lot of athletic decor and without a rigid dress code. This type of bar was described by one informant as "totally pa-min" [ultra-masculine or masculine appearing]. Then, there are piano bars, which many of my informants would describe as places where gay men can participate in sing-alongs. There are TV bars, which cater to cross-dressers, transvestites, transsexuals, and other transgendered individuals and their admirers. Here, many of my cross-dressing informants found a veritable home especially since these are places where they can, as one informant quipped, "go all the way with kabakalaan" [being bakla]. Finally, there are the racially delineated bars, such as Latino or cha-cha bars, black or *dinge* or *madilim* (dark) bars, and Asian or rice bars (which are discussed further below).

Gay bars are assumed to be unambiguous spaces in terms of marking its target clientele and sensibility. More specifically, New York City gay bars are seen to be stable sites in terms of maintaining the sensibility of a "gay space" at least over a particular period of time. Gay travel guides feature maps where gay bars are indicated as points within various grids. However, this kind of mapping is too simplistic and does not take into account the various ways in which public spaces, particularly those "out there" can be inflected by other identities. Two bars in the Queens immigrant neighborhoods of Woodside and Jackson Heights reveal the prevalence of ambiguity and malleability of queers of color spaces.

In one bar, located in the Latino neighborhood of Jackson Heights and a block away from the elevated tracks of the no. 7 train, the clientele, staff, and music are primarily straight until 7 P.M., after which everything changes; from the people drinking to the ones serving the drinks to the music being played, it becomes a gay bar. When I visited the place with two other Filipino gay men, I was skeptical about what I had been told about the bar. Before 7 P.M., the bar, which was a one-room affair, had fifteen clients. Several male and female couples sat around drinking to a tear-jerking ballad in Spanish. Sure enough, it was indeed like clockwork. The bartender started counting his money. The couples and other single people in the bar started putting on their coats. And at 7:01 P.M., the new bartender stepped in, placed a tape in the stereo system, and started playing a dance song by Madonna. Soon, several men arrived; some, at least to us three Filipino observers, seemed gay or as one of my companions said, "queenly."

Dodi, one of my companions, said that he had gone to several gay bars in the area, and he complained that he needed to have a visa in order to enjoy being in these places. He admitted that the people in the bars, including the bartender, were very friendly, but Dodi was frustrated at his lack of Spanish language skills. In fact, he said that being in these bars reminded him of his much dreaded Spanish classes when he was in college in the Philippines. Dodi regretted not having been serious with his language studies. As he lamented, "Who knew that those irritating Spanish classes were going to be useful in my later life? At least, I can still remember basic things like 'Me llamo Dodi' and 'Voulez vous couchez avec moi.'" When I reminded him that his second phrase was in fact French, he exclaimed, "See, it is so hard to socialize in this neighborhood, especially if you are not Latino."

At the New Manila (a fictitious name), which was a Filipino restaurant in Woodside, there was a big Friday night event every week. Woodside is a large immigrant enclave with a significant number of Filipino residents and Filipino-owned business establishments. The pageant was organized by Miss Saudi, one of my informants who once worked in the Middle East. He said that Miss Java, one of my other informants and a famous figure among Filipino gay men, was judging the contest. I arrived at 7:30 P.M., and I was expecting to be confronted by a nightclub or pub-like atmosphere. Instead, I was surprised to see a family-style restaurant with big round tables and various families seated and eating Filipino food. Except for one or two Caucasians, most of the people in the place were Filipinos. In the middle of the din of people talking, eating, and walking around, I heard someone singing at one end of the stage. A middle-aged man was crooning quite convincingly to the karaoke machine's rendition of Frank Sinatra's ballad, "My Way." I thought I had come on the wrong night when Miss Saudi called my name. He rushed to me saying, "The pageant is a bit delayed. Tonight is karaoke night, also." I asked if the pageant would be held after the non–queer-looking clientele had left. He said that the pageant was part of the night's entertainment. "It is like the Philippines. Somebody lip-synching and then you have a drag beauty contest. Somewhat like the karnabal [carnival]." There's more on pageantry and Miss Saudi in chapter 5.

It is clear from both sites that queers of color spaces are no more essentially queer than any other space. These sites display and invoke intersections of temporalities and places. They are not intrinsically separate from their own mainstream immigrant communities, but are somewhat integrated into the geographic layout of diasporic life. Gay bars "out there" are no more gay bars in the stereotypical sense than they are places in which immigrants participate in claiming their own location in the city.

The Drama/Cultures of the Racialized Queer Body

An informant told me that to be gay in New York was to be confronted and in fact visually and "pleasurably assaulted" by images of the male body. One informant, after witnessing his first gay pride parade, said, "Ganito pala ang pagiging gay, parang karnabal, puro karne." [So this is what it means to be gay, like a carnival, full of meat.] Another informant quipped, "Katawan, katawan, at katawan pa rin . . . Hindi ka makaescape sa drama ng katawan." [Bodies, bodies, and more bodies . . . you cannot escape the drama of the body.] Many informants shared this opinion. Indeed, one need only read any gay-oriented magazine or attend any gay function to know that being gay is to live what one informant termed the "drama of the body." This drama involves diverse cultural practices that construct the body according to various groups. For example, a group of gay men (mostly Caucasians) are called bears because they are mostly husky, hirsute, and bearded. However, despite this diversity, Filipino gay men acknowledge that the most valorized corporeal image among gays is almost always a young muscular Caucasian body.

In gay-oriented magazines, most of which are based in New York City (e.g., *Homo Xtra, Next*), the cover images are usually naked or half-naked white men. Advertisements directed to a gay audience include pictures of naked men. In fact, ads for services such as dermatology, podiatry, chiropractic medicine, and other auxiliary medical services primarily serving gay men often feature the image of the valorized somatic type.

Gay videos and magazines are a veritable smorgasbord of racialized bodies. While the buffed male body is still the central focus of most of these magazines, there have also been specialized magazines catering to people who desire other corporeal types. Still other magazines focus on different ethnic and racial types such as Latinos, Asians, and African Americans. However, most of these magazines and videos that depart from the norm of the gym-buffed white body are "ghettoized." The merchandise on magazine racks and in porn video shops is often organized according to a racial and corporeal typology. For example, in one Greenwich Village video porn shop located on the main gay thoroughfare, Christopher Street, the main shelves feature videos with a mostly Caucasian cast, while videos with an obviously Latino (e.g.,

'Rican Meat, Latino Hunks), African American (e.g., *Black Stallion*), or Asian (e.g., *Oriental Boy*) cast are displayed and grouped separately. Another illustrative set of porn taxonomy included "Heterosexual," "Gay," "s&m," and "Oriental," which points to the combined racialization and sexualization of Asians (both male and female).

The gym, alongside the bars and discos, has become a quintessential gay space. There are several gyms, particularly in the Chelsea and Greenwich Village neighborhoods in Manhattan, that are overtly directed at gay male clients. A significant number of gay men that I have met often talk about the gym as an intrinsic part of their everyday routines. For many gay men, the gym is as important as three square meals a day. One Caucasian gay man told me, "There isn't enough time in the day to really squeeze in a good workout. It needs careful planning of your life and strict discipline." In addition to transforming bodies, the gym facilitates social contacts. "Oh yes, he goes to my gym," was a frequent statement made by gay men about others to assert some kind of mutual links. According to several informants, the gym parallels the church in mainstream society as a social institution for the creation of affinity and comradeship. As Exotica wisely put it, "Dito iba ang iglesia ng mga bading—sumsamba sila sa katawan." [Here the gays have a different church—they worship the body.] This statement is less an informative one and more that of an outsider looking into a distant culture. While several of my informants do go to the gym, bodybuilding practices nevertheless provided another node of difference between themselves and the mainstream. This is not to say that Filipino gay men are hypocritical but that they have a vexed relationship to this and other mainstream institutions of gay sociality.

Apart from the gym, there are other social organizations and institutions that cater to the communal obsession with the body. If one were to peruse the monthly events calendar of the Lesbian and Gay Community Center, one could glean examples of such organizations as the New York Physique Team, Knights Wrestling Club, and other sports-oriented clubs. *Homo Xtra* and *Next*, two of the leading weekly guides to events in the New York City gay scene, include not only personal ads but also ads for groups that focus on tactile experiences (not limited to massage), meditation, and alternative health philosophies (e.g., Reiki).

The baths and sex clubs are important if not ubiquitous institutions in the mainstream gay community. The late 1990s have seen the resurgence of these institutions after several years of dormancy owing to the AIDS epidemic. During the late 1980s concerns expressed by some AIDS activists and city health officials focused on how these institutions promote unsafe sex and the transmission of HIV. Other activists argue that these places celebrate gay liberation, particularly from the dominant codes of conduct. Despite these conflicts, these institutions and the "culture" of anonymous sexual encounters still persist. In all of these places, one pays an admission, or "cover charge." Most if not all are dimly lit, and encounters are conducted either in small cubicles/booths or in public "orgy" rooms. One informant said, "There is a proper way to behave in these places. One can touch, but not too aggressively. The slightest disinterest should make one aware and act accordingly." The blatant public display of bodies leads to anxiety for some of my informants. One of them said, "There [the baths and sex clubs] there is no way one can hide the fact that one has *bilbil* [love handles]; the minimal lighting helps, pero [but] once the *hombre* [man] touches you — bingo — *luz valdez ka* [you lose]."

Like the gay clones of the 1970s, the new clones of the 1990s — the Chelsea clones — believe that wearing proper attire is a good way of asserting one's identity. Clothes, for many gay men, are not meant to cover the body but to accentuate it or call attention to it. According to my informants, the ultra-masculine style favored by mainstream Caucasian gay men has specific sets of rules for presenting their dressed selves. Like the 1970s clone attire, there is an emphasis on working-class wardrobes of tight-fitting white (plain) T-shirts, work boots, and jeans for the new clone. Tattoos, earrings, and/or pierced nipples are additional accoutrements. However, most of my informants were wary of the uniforms and clothing styles of the clones. According to Romuel, clothing cannot totally remake the person, there is still a body — a racialized one that is "carrying the clothes." Exotica, one of my wise main informants, commented on one of the fashion trends of the early 1990s — the "grunge" style where the look was disheveled and unkempt. He said, "You know that is fine for the white folks, but if one of us [Filipinos] started wearing that style we would not look stylish — just dirty and poor!" Thus, to walk the streets of the city in these styles of the moment does not guarantee membership in the community; rather, as many of my informants confided, these styles of dressing actually heighten the differences between themselves and other gays.

The Tale of Two Parties

To exemplify further the different kinds of drama and cultures of the gay body and to propose starkly the divergent constructions of gay identity and culture, I juxtapose two events. One is an annual circuit dance that is a mainstream Caucasian production and the other is a sporadically scheduled affair that is attended mostly by Latinos and African Americans. The descriptions that follow, as I mentioned at the beginning of this chapter, are based on my observations and on the experiences of Filipino gay men. My purpose in providing descriptions of these two cultural events is to locate gay Asians not in terms of an abstract gay community, but in terms of one that is fraught with racial and class cleavages.

THE BLACK PARTY

In the mainstream gay circuit there are annual events that are seen as cultural high points. Apart from the Gay Pride Parade, which usually takes place on the last Sunday in June to commemorate Stonewall, there are major parties that punctuate the year in the city's gay life. One of these is the Black Party. Despite the name, the party is not for African American gay men only. As a matter a fact, only a handful of African American men attend this event. The party's revelers are mostly gay white men who come not only from the New York City area but also from different parts of the country and the world, including Europe, Canada, and Australia. The party's name tackles the color black and its concomitant symbols as its theme. There are other counterparts such as the White, Red, and Black and Blue parties, which are sometimes held in other new gay meccas outside New York such as Atlanta, South Beach/Miami, and Philadelphia. The Black Party is one of the more expensive gay affairs with tickets running from forty dollars before the event to sixty dollars at the door. Posters advertising the event can be seen in many of the gay-oriented magazines, shops, restaurants, and bars in Manhattan.

The 1995 celebration was held at a cavernous ballroom in midtown Manhattan. I was told that the "right" time to get to the party was around 2 A.M. As my informant told me, "One cannot be caught dead standing there when the gates open. We don't want to appear too overeager." The party continued nonstop until late the next evening.

The proper attire was black leather—leather biker jacket, chaps, thongs, arm bands, wristbands, caps, and boots. An occasional black or white T-shirt and denim could be spotted, but the apparel de rigueur was either black leather or exposed flesh.

For the few Filipinos in attendance, the milieu suggested something forbidding and dangerous yet at the same time pleasurable and alluring. The black leather motif and the overall sinister masculine aura of the event lead one of the Filipino gay men in my group to exclaim gleefully, "O hindi va, parang nasa impiyerno tayo?" [Don't you think it is like being in hell?]

My informants and I arrived around 2:30 A.M. and went down to the coat-check booth. Many attendees were stripping out of their coats, jogging pants, and jackets to reveal bare chests, leather shorts, and other vestments that were totally unseasonable given the wintry weather outside. Some people changed while they were in line. Others went to the men's room to accomplish the task. On the main floor where the dancing took place, there was a huge throng of people gyrating to the music.

Informants who attended the event reported a very strong sexual tension in the whole place. Many participants would casually touch and/or fondle other people's bodies, even people they did not know. On the dance floor, several men sidled up to other men they did not know and gyrated to the music. Others removed articles of clothing while dancing. There were several instances when some people danced fully naked. An informant and I observed a group of people huddled around a couple of men, one of whom was whipping the other. My informant looked at me and said, "Kakaiba talaga ang mundong ito. Palaging nakalantad ang katawan at saka kung anung type mong gawin — anything goes!" [This world is really different. The body is always on display and whatever you want to do — anything goes.]

I left around 9:30 in the morning. The place was still packed and jumping. Another Filipino informant who was present said, "Kailangan talaga, ilantad mo ang katawan — para bang nilalako mo. Look ka na nang look at baka maka-buy kang bigla." [One really needs to display one's body — like you were selling it. You may look and look, and maybe you might buy.] The main purpose of the party was not to find a lovemate, but rather to see and be seen. As one Caucasian gay man told me, "The Black Party is what most of gay entertainment is all about — flesh and voyeurism." The party, therefore, is really a public celebration of the gay body, a carnival devoted to corporeal images and pleasures.

Culture or vogueing houses are groups consisting predominantly of Latino and African American gays, lesbians, and bisexuals. Most of these houses are named after famous fashion designers or cosmetic brands (e.g., Revlon, Fields, Miyake-Mugler). The organization of a house is patterned after the familial structure, with a mother, father, and children. These roles do not follow any generational or gender hierarchy. Therefore, one housemother may be male and the father female. The social life of the houses revolves around the preparation, management, and competition in balls. The balls are the central activity of houses and essentially are fashion runway competitions. Usually one house holds a ball and different houses from around the city as well as from other cities in the Northeast come to compete. They are usually held in big halls in different parts of Manhattan.

I attended four balls sponsored by different houses. My first experience with balls was in 1991. For my initial foray into this world, I went to a huge hall off Union Square at 6 P.M. I paid twenty dollars and was frisked for hidden weapons. According to the program, the competition was supposed to start at exactly 6 P.M. I waited for a while because the activities did not start until 8:30 P.M. I later found out that this was a usual occurrence. In most balls, regulars come in with food and drinks since most of the venues do not have any refreshments for sale. I was advised by regulars that another way to survive the ball's erratic schedule was to arrive at least two to three hours late.

The typical ball starts with the "grand march" where the members of the organizing house are presented. Each member walks down the runway to the cheers and chants of the crowd. Usually the nimble, spectacularly acrobatic, or physically beautiful are the ones given the most applause. Then the competition begins.

The competitions I attended were divided into two main categories, which were themselves sharply divided into two main parts, "femme queen" and "butch queen." Femme queens were those who presented a more feminine image while butch queens were those who presented a masculine image. However, these categories were frequently crossed and transgressed with butch queens coming out in female clothing. For example, in one particular ball I attended the specific categories under butch queen included BQ Body (muscular bodies), Butch Queen in Drag, and Butch Queen Transformation (where participants were required to model Wall Street executive clothes and then change or transform into the sexy secretary).

More than anything, while some of the categories focus on the body or the face ("Face" is an actual category where the winner is oftentimes subjected to a tactile screening by judges to test for skin roughness and beard growth), many of the categories are about the social aspirations of the mostly working or lower middle-class Latino and black participants. For example, in one ball program, the Femme Schoolgirl category is described in this way: "You just got kicked out of boarding school for lack of payments. Now what do you do in your school uniform to get back in?" Then there are categories such as Wall Street Executive and Socialite Queen. Labels, Labels, Labels subjects competitors to a close inspection by judges to see whether their clothes are authentic couture outfits.

The essence of the ball's symbolic structure is glamour as exemplified by high or couture fashion, the trappings of wealth, and media conceptions of beauty. The tension between the material realities of the participants and the excessive glamour and opulence of the categories and the whole ball itself creates an arena where a mostly gay-identified group of Latinos and blacks attempts to present their dreams and aspirations visually. Moreover, these balls are in fact encapsulations of the ironies and displacements these men and women (women and transsexuals also attend these balls) experience in the outside world and are often about race and class more than sexuality and gender.

Apart from the obvious difference in the racial makeup of "personnel" or performers in these two events, I believe these two events exemplify different twists and turns in the drama of the body. The Black Party and other mainstream events deflect class and race while the vogueing ball celebrates it. The white buffed body clad in leather may in fact have some physical similarities with the Butch Queen Transformation competitor but this is also where the similarities end. The Butch Queen competitor may suddenly appear in an Armani suit to simulate a social type he may never become because of his racial and class background. While vogueing balls do celebrate the body, I suggest that they are really less about a gay body than a Latino or black body in its various social transformations on stage. Many of my informants talked about the affinity they felt with vogueing culture, particularly cross-dressing, but more important to them were the ways in which Latino and African American queers' notions of transformation and gender performance resonated with their own cultural ideas. In chapter 5, I discuss this issue further in relation to public cross-dressing performances.

Desire in the Street, Danger under the Sheets

Walking the streets of New York City is an undertaking full of perils and possibilities. Many of my informants told me that cruising in the streets can be quite fascinating because one is never really sure of what will happen. The busy, noisy, and dirty streets of New York City are sources of nostalgic moments for some of my informants. One of them said that if one were to take out the people and the stores, the chaos of New York street life roughly approximates that of Manila's. While some other informants may disagree, this attitude uncovers the deep contradictory mix of anxiety and excitement regarding the possibilities of desire in public spaces.

Vaseline Alley is not a real alley. It is a regular street located a block away from Roosevelt Avenue in the Jackson Heights section of Queens. This is an immigrant neighborhood filled with Koreans, South Asians, and Latinos. The "alley" is actually a stretch of several blocks right around a string of gay bars on Roosevelt Avenue and is known to be a major area for queer cruising and public sex.

A couple of my informants admitted going to this area on a regular basis in the 1980s and early 1990s. One of them said, "Mahirap makipag-do dito sa kalyeng 'to, hindi mo makabisa ang tao." [It is hard to have sex here in this street; you can never be sure about other people.] When queried further, he mentioned the fact that most of his encounters were with either Latino or South Asian men who mostly spoke little or no English. He later admitted that speaking while having public sex is not important, but he was nevertheless bothered by his inability to speak to his sex partners. At the same time, Filipino gay men who frequent this area have reported violent incidents involving bashings and robbery, but as many of them admitted, the danger comes with the allure.

With these violent incidents comes fear of the police. One of my informants was arrested once, and he spent two nights in jail. He said he was a victim of entrapment; the policeman who arrested him kept talking about the INS and deportation rather than jail. My informant was terrified because he was here on a working visa and could easily be sent back to the Philippines.

Vaseline Alley, according to many of my informants, differs from the queer cruising places in Manhattan, such as the piers near Christopher Street. Most of these areas are located in gentrifying sections of the city and are now mostly inhabited by white yuppies. For many of them, Vaseline Alley, while not any safer, is in fact an area where they can blend in instead of standing out.

Many of my informants compared the public cruising areas in the city with what they knew in Manila. Romuel said that he used to frequent the area called "Chocolate Hills," which was a field near the old Congress building in Manila. He said, "When you look for sex in the dark, it does not matter where you are." Other informants disagreed with him. For many of them, the major difference was the variety of bodies available in New York and the fact that the public areas at least seemed somehow to be a democratic space. As one of them said, "Sa dilim, akala mo kahit ano puwede pero kapag diyutay good bye!" [In the dark, you might think that anything goes, but if you are not amply endowed — goodbye.] More often than not, the public cruising areas are met with some kind of hesitation; this was particularly true around the time the New York City police conducted a series of arrests in Vaseline Alley and the Manhattan piers. For many of my informants, being a person of color added to the danger of being arrested.

A queer of color cannot walk with impunity in any area of the city. Even in immigrant neighborhoods, the idea of public cruising as a democratic practice is unraveled in the face of racist sexual practices. In fact, the dangers for immigrant queers of color multiplied as intense policing of the areas occurred with great regularity in the 1990s. As much as the Stonewall slogan was in part about the claiming of public space, immigrant queers of color such as Filipino gay men view the streets with trepidation and anxiety.

Rice Bars and the Space of Gay Asian Americans

The two disparate parties discussed above are in fact illustrations of racialized and class-ladened cultural expressions in New York City gay life. However, far from being a white-black issue, New York City gay life also includes practices, histories, and places for Latinos and Asians.

To delineate the spaces as well as the kind of visibility Asian gay men, specifically Filipinos, confront in New York City, I consider several texts and discourses as well as observations that provide both the background and elaboration of such spaces. In this consideration, we inevitably meet with racializing discourses of Orientalism. Orientalism, as I use the term in this book, extends both the theoretical and geographic context suggested by Said (1978) to the realm of American gay spaces. How are Asian gay men raced/racialized? How are Asian gay men classed?[3]

Rice bars are among the most overtly Asian and Orientalized gay spaces in New York. In 1996, there were two located in the Upper East Side section of Manhattan. While Asian gay men frequent other bars, rice bars, as the derisive term suggests, are gay spaces where a sizable number or a clear majority of the patrons would likely be Asian. Rice bars, according to gay lore, were popularly or stereotypically seen to be unsophisticated institutions with outdated music that catered to a clientele made up of older homely (mostly white) men and naive immigrant Asian men. In the past, efforts have been made to transform these bars into imitations of the mainstream ones. In addition to providing new sleek interiors, these bars have also made efforts to change their image from an Asian/rice one to a more international and sophisticated reputation.

Exotica, my guide, brought me to my first rice bar in the mid-1980s. It was located on the Upper East Side. The decor was rather nondescript, but the music took me back in terms of time and space. The song "Rock the Boat" was playing and a few people were dancing on a small raised platform. Here was music that was at least a decade old and which for many of the Asian men in the bar brought to mind a time when they were still in their homelands. In addition to the dated music, most of the clientele did not mirror the younger crowd of men in the downtown bars. Exotica again explained, "Mahirap talaga dito sa rice bowl, hindi mo maintindihan, kakaiba kasi Asiatika ang customer." [It is really hard here in the rice bowl (bar), you cannot really understand it. It is different because Asians are the customers.] Many Filipino gay men perceive the rice bar as intrinsically different and atypical because it is an Asian queer space. Despite the camaraderie, fun, and pleasure that can be found in these spaces, many informants also intimated to me that these same spaces were sites of alienation and exclusion.

Informants told me that in one of the two existing rice bars in the

1980s, one of the Caucasian owners would survey the crowd and would single out people—mostly Asians—who did not have a drink in hand and scold and shame them into buying one. Exotica told me that he and his friend would make a point of picking up some stray bottle to make it seem as though they were drinking something. As Tito, one of Exotica's friends, would say, "Too bad, they are trying to sell liquor to the Asiatikas (Asians) but they will not succeed." Believing in the stereotype that Asians do not drink, Tito was also trying to make a point that the rice bar did not seem to be a good and welcoming space for Asian gay men despite the fact that this was one place where they were in the majority.

Informants told me that until the early 1980s, the presence of other Asian men in most bars and at other gay activities was very rare. They further noted that interesting configurations form in bars that cater to predominantly Caucasian clientele. For example, in one trendy Greenwich Village gay bar in the 1980s, gay men of color occupied a section of the bar off to the right of the entrance, which many informants called the "Third World" section, while the white majority occupied all the different levels and sections.

Informants noted a shift in the visibility of Asian men from the 1970s to the 1980s. An informant said: "Noong mga 1970s at early 1980s, kung pupunta ka sa isang affair ng kabadingan noon, tiyak, ikaw lang ang natatanging Miss Asia. Wala kang kakumpetisyon. Ngayon, ang daming mga contenders." [During the 1970s and early 1980s if you went to any gay affair, you would be the only Miss Asia. You did not have any competition. Now there are so many contenders.]

Like other gay personal ads in other magazines, the ads in magazines oriented toward Asian gay males (e.g., *Passport* and *Oriental Gentleman*) and those written by or for Asian gay men in other kinds of magazines (*Village Voice* and *Homo Xtra*) illustrate a myriad of textual strategies. The ads can be grouped into two: Caucasians (there have been very few nonwhites who advertise) looking for Asians and Asians looking for Caucasians. Caucasians' ads often are in these forms: "Gay Oriental Male (GOM)/Gay Asian Male (GAM) wanted: slim, boyish, small, cute, young or younger-looking, and hairless." Asians, in contrast, usually construct their ads in this way: "Gay White Male (GWM) wanted: daddy, older, hairy, husky, hunk, muscular, and masculine." Most Caucasians looking for Asians are usually older, in their forties or fifties, while the Asians are considerably younger.

GAM [Gay Asian Male], 25, 5'8", slim and professional looking for GWM [Gay White Male], hairy, muscular a plus.

Gay Filipino 30s' combines Eastern mysticism with Western pragmatism looking for G W/H/A male, professional and into relationships.

Not just another Asian, I am muscular, hairy, and aggressive, looking for same or white/Hispanic hunk.

GWM looking for boyish, young Asian. Slim and not into bars.

At first glance, a majority of these texts shows how Orientalized images that tread the lines of masculine-feminine and dominant-submissive are overtly displayed. The overt physical and generational disparities exemplified in these texts are part of what is seen as the "rice queen" syndrome. In gay lexicon, rice queens are Caucasians who are older, usually economically well-off men who are attracted to Asians. Moreover, such attraction is popularly seen to come with racist and patronizing attitudes and beliefs on the part of the Caucasian, who projects Orientalized images to his object of desire. In fact, the common belief is that the rice queen preys on young Asian boys.

In a 1993 presentation to the Gay Asian Pacific Islander Men of New York (GAPIMNY), a gay Asian group in New York, Gene Chang, a student at Columbia University, transported the rice queen phenomenon into the realm of the psychopathological (Ogasawara 1993: 11). He suggested that the rice queen's desire for Asian (young and young-looking) men is really a mask for pedophilic tendencies. He supported his contention by graphing the "incompatibility of physical attributes" (height, age, penis size, and so on) between Asians and Caucasians in personal ads. Chang further explored the exploitative and "imperialist" possibilities of encounters between an older Caucasian and a young Asian by examining mainstream gay porn films. He contended that the Asian gay man is relegated to passive sexual (as insertee) and social roles (i.e., masseur, houseboy, and so on). What is interesting in this presentation is Chang's leap from his "findings" of corporeal asymmetry mapped out in personal ads to the contention of a rice queen's real pedophile identity. Using statistical techniques and graphs, Chang charted the differences between Caucasian and Asian gay men in personal ads in terms of average height (two inches), weight (thirty to forty pounds), and age (fifteen to twenty years). He directly equated such difference with actual power inequality in gay Caucasian-Asian sexual politics.

Chang's views, though faulty, are the prevalent views among the growing number of politicized Asian gay men. Although I do not deny the existence of exploitative and racist interactions between gay Asian and Caucasian men, such prevalent views as those held by Chang adhere to the same dichotomous stereotypes on which Orientalist images are constituted. Furthermore, these same "radical" views construct the Asian gay man as devoid of agency.

The other texts I consider are gay travelogues and travel guides. These texts not only provide glimpses of people and places for touristic delectation, they also raise deep insights about the authors and the social milieu in which such genres are produced. In fact, the narrative I will closely examine is a gay travel guide to the Philippines. The narrative in question is *Philippine Diary: A Gay Guide to the Philippines* by Joseph Itiel. This is not so much an actual diary but a catalogue of cruising places and people for men who like Asian men as sex partners. For these kinds of men, Itiel offers connoisseur's tips in establishing, maintaining, and controlling encounters or relationships with Filipino gay men. He offers interesting insights about Filipino gay men based on his "relationships" with several of them, which he chronicles haphazardly in the book. Among such gems is his observation that Filipino gay men have unstable personalities. "Filipinos may be very patient," he writes, "but if they are pushed far enough, they snap completely and are capable of extreme violence" (1989: 15). His other observations about Filipino gay male traits include a childish fascination with telephones, an inability to manage sums of money, noisiness, a penchant for gossip, intellectual shallowness, and a disdain for any intellectual conversations. Among his other interesting assertions is the claim that behind smiling Filipino faces "lurks a deep melancholy, an unresolved sorrow that is almost always associated with their family relationships" (ibid.: 23).

Despite being a guide for rice queens going to the Philippines, Itiel extends his analysis to include Filipino gay men everywhere, including those in the United States. He maintains that there are particular immutable traits of Filipino gay men that do not change regardless of place of birth and socialization. The transplanted Filipino gay man in the United States displays the same child-like qualities he observed among his "companions" in the Philippines. Although Itiel says that the Filipino gay male may actually change some of his habits, he will only do so for survival and individual gain.

Itiel emphasizes that a Filipino gay man's family and class background do not matter. He asserts that whether a Filipino gay man is from the slums of Manila or has been educated at Harvard, he possesses specific immutable characteristics. Despite the global mobility of Filipinos, Itiel incarcerates the Filipino gay male into an essentialized and exoticized island of cultural primitiveness and pre-adult developmental limbo. Itiel's narrative connects itself to the dominant Orientalized stereotypes by asserting that any Filipino belongs and is rooted to that locale of imagined exotic alterities — the Orient.

It would be too easy to provide an ad hominem diatribe against this text. However, such is not the intention here. I take this text as a springboard for Filipino gay men's narratives about race in the succeeding chapters. Itiel's text may be an overt form of the rice queen syndrome, but the images constructed in the texts are the same ones that confront Filipino gay men when they enter the shores of the American gay community.

Itiel's text reconstructs the Orientalized notions of the Filipino and Asian male body. These Orientalized notions dichotomize East and West in female and male terms. The Oriental body is always and already female or feminized. This construction is then extended to the passive and active axes in sexual terms before turning to Asian corporeal characteristics that involve feminized, androgynous, and pedophilic dimensions. For example, popular Orientalized signifiers include hairlessness, boyish/feminine qualities, slimness, and a gentle mien. It is this fixed and static notion of the body that will be disputed by the narratives of Filipino gay men in the succeeding chapters.

Class, however, is particularly problematic in the case of Asian gay men. However, it is not so much the kinds of attitudes that Asian gay men have about the class hierarchy (from field experiences, they are more conscious and reverential of class differences) but the imputation of erroneous class assignations to Asian Americans in general. As the so-called model minority group, Asians in the United States are seen as upwardly mobile and occupy a tier just below Caucasians in economic resources and mobility.

As a mostly immigrant group, Asians in New York City face particular challenges. While they are generally portrayed as economically prosperous, their immigrant status is often interpreted as lacking or as being deficient in cultural capital such as fluency in English. Informants often told me that Asians are regularly perceived to be naive and innocent of the trappings of gay and Western attitudes and guile. These images tie into the kind of pseudo-pedophilic view of the Asian body as both feminine and childlike. In addition to being perceived as "fresh off the boat," Asians are also seen as imbued with a natural grace and exotic poise. This mix of contradictory yet connected images and discourses about class, body, and race are what Asian gay men in general and Filipino gay men in particular confront in their daily lives. In the next chapters, I will demonstrate how these spaces, ideas, and images are manipulated by these men to create new forms of belonging and selfhood.

Whose Community? Whose City?

When a senior scholar of queer studies read an earlier version of this chapter, he was so incensed at what he considered to be my voyeuristic tour of the gay (white) mainstream community that he accused me of writing like a *New York Times* journalist out to expose the evils of the community. He ended his tirade by comparing me to gay conservatives such as Michelangelo Signorile and Andrew Sullivan and with great flourish declared, "The white gay community is my community. I love this community."

While I would admit to the rather terse mode of some of the descriptions in the earlier version, I was surprised at the virulence of his accusations. Was I indeed the prototypical voyeur with an eye for grand exposés and scandal? Why couldn't a critical examination of the gay community be done without being accused of voyeurism or backwardness? More importantly, what was wrong with my kind of voyeurism? In other words, why could I not lay claim to this community through my own gaze and my informants' gazes?

Unlike Benjamin's flaneur — the paradigmatic figure of modernity who walks through all avenues and alleyways of the city with impunity — my gaze and physical presence as well as those of the informants in certain queer spaces were being questioned. The very idea of a critical eye being cast upon mainstream gay places and events was interpreted as being a malevolent if not an unsuitable preoccupation for a queer scholar. As someone who has been situated "out there," I began to realize that in many ways, the senior scholar saw me as an upstart and troublemaker who did not know his proper place.

In a city marked by overlapping and contradictory sites, New York City queers of color spaces are oftentimes circumscribed by larger forces such as federal, city, and state laws. During my fieldwork from the early to late 1990s, the New York City police were accused of harassment and cruelty against people of color. At the same time, Mayor Rudolph Giuliani promulgated a "quality of life" campaign that virtually wiped out public queer spaces in many areas of the city. What is particularly instructive is that people of color were more afraid of the risk of being arrested and/or harassed in various areas of the city. In addition, the ambivalent and mercurial quality of several queers of color spaces point to the abject and marginal status of these sites in relation to the mainstream gay topography.

For diasporic queers, spaces in the city intersect with other spaces from other times and places. In particular, Filipino gay men's memories are enmeshed with their experiences of the various queer spaces, which in turn shape their experiences of new sites. As participants in and observers of the various sites and places in the city, Filipino gay men are keenly aware of their location and acknowledge both the opportunities in and barriers to staking a claim to any of these places. From cruising the streets to entering the portals of the gay bar to trying to access gay cultural events, Filipino gay men are witnesses to and participants in the ongoing drama of racialized corporeal politics and hierarchical social arrangements. These men continually struggle to navigate their way through the contradictory landscape of the gay global city of New York.

Physical distance between queer spaces in the city may be connected by bridges and tunnels of modern urban public transportation, but social distance marked by race and class, for example, are gulfs oftentimes left open. In a gay global city marked by the "here" and the "out there," queers of color, such as Filipino gay men, find themselves continually negotiating their proper place and laying claims to spaces from which they are often excluded.

Four

The Biyuti
and Drama of
Everyday
Life

The everyday tells us a story of modernity in which major historical cataclysms are superseded by ordinary chores, the arts of working and making things. In a way, the everyday is anticatastrophic, an antidote to the historical narrative of death, disaster and apocalypse. The everyday does not seem to have a beginning or an end. In everyday life we do not write novels but notes or diary entries that are always frustratingly or euphorically anticlimactic. In diaries, the dramas of our lives never end — as in the innumerable TV soap operas in which one denouement only leads to another narrative possibility and puts off the ending. Or diaries are full of incidents and lack accidents; they have narrative potential and few completed stories. The everyday is a kind of labyrinth of common places without monsters, without a hero, and without an artist-maker trapped in his own creation. — SVETLANA BOYM, *Common Places*

I was sitting in a cramped apartment in Queens, New York in the spring of 1992. I had been talking for more than an hour with Roberto, one of my informants, when he suddenly blurted, "Look around you, this is not the glamorous life that people back in Manila think I have. They all believe I live in a brownstone or a spacious house on Fifth Avenue — like the ones in the movies and TV. They don't know the daily drama I have to go through here just to make it. Although, if you ask me whether I would exchange the struggle here with a cushy life back in the Philippines, I would say never darling, never!"

The complicated twists and turns of Roberto's declaration reveal a particular dimension of gay life that is often missed if not ignored in queer scholarship — the daily life struggles and experiences of queer immigrant men of color. I am interested in the ways the seemingly mundane activities in daily life construct a vital arena in which to investigate various under-explored issues, specifically the connections between everyday life, intimacy, and diasporic queer identity formation. While there has been an emerging body of scholarship in recent years around the travails and travels of gay identity and peoples within a globalizing word, most of these works have concentrated on social movements that provide panoramic snapshots of people and "communities" on the verge of parallel queer comradeship. While heavily influenced by the body of lesbian and gay community research, my work departs from it by centering on the seemingly private and banal aspects of queer people's lives.

Most ideas about queer community and identity formations are based on organized public enactments of gayness and lesbianness. In contrast, the focus on the everyday not only exposes the inadequacy of conventional narratives where self and community progressively unfold, it also points to the complexities of various intersections and borderlands of race, gender, class, and sexuality in diasporic and immigrant groups. The everyday also troubles if not resists the conventional time-space binary by expressing the ways in which memory is spatialized and space is entangled with intimate habits, routines, personal histories, and chronologies. Influenced by the works of the social theorist Michel de Certeau (1984) and the feminist sociologist Dorothy Smith (1987), I take the everyday as a crucial "problematic" and as a site of tactical maneuvers for creating selves and forging relationships for marginalized groups, particularly diasporic queers everywhere. In other words, the focus on the quotidian life unveils the veneer of the ordinary and the commonplace to lay bare the intricate and difficult hybrid negotiations and struggles between hegemonic social forces and voices from below.

This chapter grounds the cultural, political, and historical specificities of Filipino diasporic gay men's experiences within the uneven yet hegemonic power of global capitalist expansion. These men's experiences are anchored to the Philippines' long enduring political, cultural, historical, and economic connections to the United States, including being part of the intensification of the movement of labor and capital in the late twentieth century. Yet this contextual anchoring is a backdrop to the creative tensions between these men's individual predicaments and larger social forces.

Everyday life is a site for critically viewing and reading modernity (Boym 1994: 20). Unlike traditional historiography, which depends on grand narratives of "famous men" and great events, the narratives of everyday life reveal the rich intricacies of the commonplace and how these stories intersect or come up against modern institutions such as the nation-state. Everyday life intersects and engages with the intimate, the private, and the search for home in modern life. While these three sites are not necessarily equivalent to each other, I would argue that they meet at critical conjunctures, especially in the displaced lives of queer immigrants.

Intimacy, according to Lauren Berlant (1998: 287), is a crucial yet ambivalent practice in modern life because of its connections to domesticated and normative forms of relationships and spaces such as home, family, and privacy. If home, privacy, and domesticity are vexed locations for queer subjects, particularly those in the diaspora (Eng 1997; Gopinath 1998), then it follows that queers' struggles toward finding, building, remembering, and settling into a home, as well as the displacements brought about by migration, create a sphere that has been called diasporic intimacy (Gilroy 1993: 16). Diasporic intimacy constitutes those struggles that showcase the different ways in which the state, public life, and the world outside intrude upon and permeate those seemingly bounded, private, and domestic spaces of home and how diasporic subjects confront them. The process of creating diasporic intimacy can be achieved either through counterpublic cultural productions or through more mundane routes such as "the habitual estrangements of everyday life abroad" (Boym 1998: 501). Therefore, I would argue that everyday life then is the space for examining the creation and rearticulation of queer selves in the diaspora.

My analysis of the everyday is shaped by my understanding of biyuti and drama, two concepts I have described in previous chapters.

This chapter analyzes how these notions are deployed as filters in confronting and understanding everyday life situations and how they may illuminate the predicament of Filipino gay immigrant men as diasporic subjects. In this chapter, I explore seemingly commonplace, ordinary, or banal situations in order to examine the exigencies of identity articulation and formation among Filipino gay men, particularly in their negotiations between bakla and gay traditions. By examining space, class, family, religion, and other aspects of everyday living, I expose the usually hidden and highly nuanced processes of being, becoming, and belonging. In other words, I examine the quotidian dimensions of cultural citizenship. Identity articulation among Filipino gay men, as I will show in the sections on family, lovers, and friends, is based on idioms of complementarity and opposition. Sexual desire, gender markings, and racial difference become the crucibles through which relationships are forged and contrasted with each other.

This chapter may be faulted for being unruly, for having crisscrossing narratives that never seem to finish. I would argue that such unruliness stems in part from the rhythms of everyday life. As the quote from Svetlana Boym above suggests, linear narratives — particularly those that depend on a kind of teleological trajectory — crumble in the face of the kinds of improvisations (Bourdieu 1977) and tactics (de Certeau 1984) that constitute Filipino gay men's struggle for survival in America.

Everyday life has a semblance of being ordered into easy, predictable schedules and normative actions. Routines may in fact deceive the casual observer into thinking such experiences are easily, if not unproblematically, funneled into neatly recognizable shapes. While this chapter attempts to codify or reel in many of the themes and ideas of these narratives, the nature of the drama and biyuti of the everyday for Filipino gay men is a certain elusiveness that defies perfunctory categorizations. I argue that these narratives provide glimpses of how selves and identities are remade and recast in different situations. I critique the notion of the naturalized and monolithic construction of a gay lifestyle as discussed in chapter 3 by focusing on the intricacies and complexities of the daily struggle for survival of these men. I use the idioms of *drama* and *biyuti* as a valuable means by which to understand the Filipino gay men's shifting notions of self and identity in specific moments and, conversely, the relative experience of stability, essence, and placement.

This chapter begins with two pivotal narratives. The first is a story of an apartment and how physical space becomes an arena for the articulation of identities as well as the iconic tableau of the life experiences of a gay immigrant. The second story deals with the daily and weekly routines of one Filipino gay man. Here, routines are subjected to critical analysis to suggest how such seemingly ordered blocks of time and rigidly enforced activities are also instances of simultaneous contestation and capitulation within the frame of living in an urban cosmopolitan area such as New York. In both narratives, family ties, race, class, and religion erupt in mundane activities to saturate the words and actions of the Filipino gay men involved. These two narratives provide a kind of fulcrum for propelling or setting into motion other narratives that focus more closely on themes and issues that are otherwise only hinted at or suggested.

The Story of an Apartment: Space and the Commonplace

The first vignette is about Alden, a middle-aged Filipino gay man, and focuses on his apartment in Greenwich Village. Unlike most cinematic and televisual unreal renderings of the spacious and sophisticated "New York City apartment," Alden's small studio apartment is much more typical, with nothing really to distinguish it or mark it as different from other apartments of this type in the city. The living, sleeping, and eating/cooking quarters are situated within a space of twenty by thirty feet.

The furniture exudes a slightly worn quality that Alden acknowledged to be emblematic of a kind of bohemian lifestyle of the "old" Village that is slowly being eroded by the influx of straight white yuppies into the expensive condos and townhouses. Having lived in the same apartment since the early 1970s, Alden is one of the lucky few in the city to be in a rent-stabilized apartment, paying a mere four hundred dollars a month to live there.

This apartment, as Alden contends, is not just a place but is also a story — the story of his life in America. Alden came to America in 1971, and he first lived with a female cousin in New Jersey. His parents thought that it would be important to have somebody to look after him and serve as a surrogate parent. However, when he arrived at his cousin's house, the cousin declared that she was not about to be responsible for Alden. She admonished Alden to become more self-reliant because that was what was needed to be able to succeed in America. He was expected to carry his own weight and pay part of the rent. Alden was dismayed at first but after a while he admitted that it was "a different drama" that he had to learn.

He moved out after six months and stayed with a couple of Filipino men whom he knew from the private school he attended in Manila. After a few petty quarrels about rent, Alden moved out. He found his current apartment after a few weeks of searching. For Alden, finding something on his own was a turning point. It marked a distancing from his way of life in the Philippines, where he had lived in a big house with his parents, grandparents, unmarried sibling, and several maids. He had shared a room with his brothers until he was seventeen. Getting his own room allowed him to create a world for himself. Remembering that moment, he looked around his present studio and said:

> When I got my room [at seventeen], I did a full interior decoration. I went crazy and I really made it fabulous. She [Alden's mother] told me to throw out the loud curtains and throw pillows. She said it look like a [cheesy] dance hall. Here [in my Greenwich Village apartment] I can put in whatever I want. Look at that Herb Ritts poster [of a naked man]. I would not even think of putting that up back home; my mother would upbraid me.

He compared his life in the Village with his life in the Philippines in terms of the rooms or spaces he had lived in. Alden felt his individuality was nurtured in this Village apartment so unlike the room of his childhood. He was emphatic when he said that although his apartment may not look like his family's residence in Manila, it was nevertheless very pleasant. Despite the many rooms in the family residence, with equally as many maids to clean them, he almost always felt cramped there, even after he was given his own room. He felt he could not create a world of his own without the disruption of other family members.

Alden's apartment studio is a study in contrasts. Right across from the wall with the poster of a naked man is a corner he dubbed alternately as the "guilt corner" or his "Filipino corner." This corner is in fact a wall filled with photographs, mainly of family members in the Philippines. Occupying the central part of this wall, right next to the television set and VCR, is an altar. There Alden has placed several religious images and statues his mother made him bring to America, mostly antiques that were owned by his great-grandmother. The religious figures include a crucifix, the Virgin Mary, and the Infant Jesus of Prague. When I asked him why he called this his "guilt corner," he said that sometimes life in America can get so frenetic and stressful that he forgets to call his family back home. After an extremely busy week at work, he would sit on his sofa and stare at the pictures and statues and suddenly feel guilty. Then he would make his weekly overseas call to the Philippines. The power of the corner would also befall him after a series of sexual encounters, when he suddenly felt the impulse to pray and try to become, as he said facetiously, "virtuous" again.

Alden's apartment consists of two parts or sides, the American side with the poster and sofa and the Filipino side with the altar and family pictures. He said that by crossing the room, he traverses two boundaries of his two selves: "Ang parte ng apartment na ito, ay parang Pilipinas. O sashay lang ako ng kaunti to the other side, balik ako sa Amerika. Kasi, ganyan ang feeling ko palaging pabalikbalik kahit hindi totoong nag-babalikbayan." [This part of the apartment is like the Philippines. So I only need to sashay to the other side, and I am back in America. That is how I feel, going back and forth even if I have not gone home *(balikbayan)*.]

The ambivalence of "being home" and "at home" was emphasized when Alden spoke about visiting his family in the Philippines. The nostalgia and homesickness he felt from time to time was tempered by the realities of being with his family:

Actually, actually matagal na akong di nakakauwi. Mahirap at masarap ang bumisita sa atin. Pero naku ha, okey lang ang gastos pero pagkatapos ng mga beso-beso, eto na ang mga tanong. Kelan ka ba ikakasal? Bakit daw alone ang biyuti ko sa New Yok? Naka-kalukring 'di va? Masarap kung may party at kasama mo ang family mo — lalo na kung Christmas — pero para akong sinasakal kapag pinakikialaman ako. Para akong bata. Hindi ko lang masabi sa kanila na umalis ako para makaalpas sa kaguluhan ng pamilya doon. Don't get me wrong ha . . . kung may problema dito pag minsan, hinahanap ko ang support ng family ko, pero most of the time, I am grateful na magisa ako dito. Mahirap nga pero mas mabuti na yon kesa hindi ka makagalaw. Gusto nila akong umuwi pero marami ka ngang space sa bahay mo sa Manila pero hindi mo naman magawa ang gusto mo, para que pa?

[Actually, actually, I haven't gone home for a long time. It is both painful and marvelous to go home for a visit. But please, the travel costs are fine, but after the initial buss on the cheek, the questions come pouring in. When are you getting married? Why is your biyuti alone in New York? It is maddening. It's great to be at a Christmas party and to be with your family, but I feel like a child (there) when they get into my business. I can't tell them that I left to escape the chaos of family life there. Don't get me wrong, when there is a problem here (in America), sometimes I look for my family's support, but most of the time I am grateful to be alone. It is hard, but it is better this way than being unable to move. They want me to go back [to the Philippines]. But even if you have a lot of space back home, you can't do want you want to do. Why would I want to do that?]

Here, Alden echoed many of the Filipino men I interviewed. Despite the difficulties of immigrating to America or migrating to New York and the subsequent sense of displacement, many expressed a sense of relief and contentment with the distancing effects that their movement and travel have generated.

Alden still lives in his apartment. He does not plan to move out because of the rather prohibitive prices of new places. He is perhaps unique among other Filipinos in that he pays a very low price for an apartment in a premium, or choice, area, and has lived there for more than fifteen years. When I last visited him in December 1995, a full year after our interview, he had replaced the Herb Ritts poster of a naked man with French impressionist prints. He reasoned that he was getting old and Herb Ritts was after all quite passé. The altar was still there on the opposite wall. It still had the same arrangement of religious figures, except for a small bud vase with a yellow rose. Alden reminded me that his aunt was ailing back in the Philippines and he was praying for her.

Chores and Routines: The Rhythm of Difference in Daily Life

Let us move both literally and figuratively from this first vignette of Alden's apartment to another vignette, and another dimension of the everyday. Our move is from the meanings of mundane spaces to the meanings of banal activities — chores or routines. The second vignette is about the daily routines of Roldan, a forty-year-old informant, who arrived in the United States during the early 1980s. I followed Roldan's daily activities for two straight weeks and off and on for several months. I kept a diary where I recorded his daily, weekly, and monthly activities. The following are highlights of the two-week detailed record I made of his daily life. I knew him for five years before I asked him to allow me a voyeuristic view of his activities. Roldan said that he considered me as a visitor for two long weeks.

Every week, Roldan got up early and spent most of his weekdays at work and his weekends doing chores around his apartment in Queens. After breakfast on the first Wednesday, he put on his office garb, looked in the mirror, and said, "Nobody would guess who is under this suit and tie. They might think I am a Wall Street executive or a successful career girl [he giggles] — oh, I really need more coffee — I must still be dreaming. People will take one look at me and say — immigrant — fresh off the boat." He then sashayed and twirled around the mirror. "You know, people in the office treat me a little differently." When I asked him what him meant by a different treatment he said, "It is difficult to say. — You know my biyuti is Asian [Asiatika], so you never really know whether they think right away that I am effeminate or if they think I am gay because I am a thin, frail looking Asian. Who knows?"

When I pressed further about this issue, he said, "When I used go to bars in the Village or Chelsea, I felt left out — you know I don't look good in a tight T-shirt. But then, when another Filipino gay friend told me about these cross-dressing bars — all of a sudden I found a different world where these gorgeous white men found me attractive." Roldan then revealed how he started to go regularly to cross-dressing bars in Manhattan every weekend. He said, "Akala ko pumunta ako ng America para maging gay pero ngayon alam ko na nagpunta ako sa America para maging tunay na bakla." [I used to think that I came to America to be gay, but then I realized that I came to America to be a real bakla.] In this statement Roldan is referring to the fact that he always perceived gayness and gay culture as rooted both in the United States and ultra-masculine images and practices. He was reflecting on the fact that he has become more of the bakla than the gay man he thought he was going to be in America because of his weekend leisure activities.

At the same time he was talking about this, Roldan also talked about the dangers of being a cross-dresser in public. He was afraid of getting caught and thrown in jail. He was not worried about the embarrassment such a situation may potentially cause but about how such an incident might jeopardize his stay in America. I had known for a long time that Roldan was an illegal immigrant. His words when he confessed to me about his status were, "You know my biyuti is TNT." TNT is an acronym used in Filipino queer language or swardspeak and literally means "always in hiding."

He was proud of the fact that no one in the office knew about his immigration status. In fact, he once worked in a personnel department, and one of his duties was to check on the paperwork regarding job candidates' eligibility to work in the United States. Despite this irony, Roldan talked about the difficulty of being in such a legal limbo. He once considered a green card marriage but backed out. When I asked him why he backed out, he answered, "Do you think my biyuti can pass INS scrutiny. I don't think so sister [manash]! One look at me and they will say—oh a big fag, a big bakla!" I countered that maybe the authorities would just see him as another slim Asian man. He said, "Oh, there is too much risk to do that drama, too much . . . I am too afraid." Then he paused for a second and said, "Well, you may be right, I know through the bakla grapevine that there is this . . . [he mentions a famous female impersonator in the Philippines] who was in a green card marriage. Darling, he is now a U.S. citizen. Oh well, he is used to the stage—I am not . . . or maybe I am not always on stage." Then he laughs, this time a little sadly.

He mentioned that he really could not risk being caught in this situation. He had a family in the Philippines that was dependent on his monthly financial remittances. One weeknight, during the two-week period, Roldan received an urgent phone call from his mother. The phone call was unusual because they always talked during weekends. After talking to her for thirty minutes, Roldan hung up the phone with an irritated facial expression and breathed a long sigh. I asked him if anything was wrong. He said that his mother had just informed him that his youngest sister, whom he was sending to one of the most exclusive private schools in Manila, wanted to get married. She was seventeen years old. Roldan's mother wanted him to talk to the sister to convince her to continue her studies. Roldan was fuming mad, not only at his sister, but also at his mother, who expected him to play surrogate father via an overseas phone call. Besides, he said, his father was still alive, but because of Roldan's vital role as provider, he was by default given authority over specific family issues.

He made it clear to me that his family was not poor but rather "middle class." The money and goods he regularly sent back enabled his family to be more comfortable economically, especially during the troubled times in the Philippines. He said that he was looking forward to the day when his responsibility would end. After saying this, he shook his head and admitted that his previous statement was in fact wishful thinking. Then in a voice of surrender he said, "Ganyan talaga ang drama." [That is how the drama goes.]

Positions and Everyday Life: Some Themes

The two previous narratives portray and betray recurring themes that seem to permeate the inchoateness of everyday life, albeit in different forms. Family, class, and religion intersect with sexual desire, social conflicts, and corporeality. More importantly, these themes are really sites of difference, or categories, that position Filipino gay men in everyday life. In other words, family, class, and other categories place these men within existing hierarchies and continuous and discontinuous practices. The following narratives and descriptions attempt to flesh out these themes by bringing in other informants' stories and field observations.

FAMILIES WE CHOOSE?

The family is always seen as a social unit that exerts an enormous amount of power over the lives of immigrants or non-white groups. Discourses that purport to explain cultural differences between so-called mainstream or white communities and cultural and racial others usually focus uncritically on "close family ties" as a defining characteristic or trait. More often than not, there is a bifurcation between the somber image of an isolated nuclear family in mainstream society and the rather vibrant tones of the extended family of the ethnic/racial other. These discourses elide the diverse shades, degrees of ambivalence, and the incongruous meanings that beset familial relationships, especially among immigrants of color.

When informants talked about the early part of their lives, memories of their families permeated their stories. The invisible chain linking the present to the past was very evident in my informants' narratives centered on the family. More often than not they painted a sympathetic picture of family life. For those who were born in the Philippines and whose family members were still mostly in the Philippines, family and geography were enmeshed. Therefore, for those who migrated to America, family was also something bounded or rooted to a place.

Rico perhaps said it best when he observed, "Dito puro trabaho [sa Amerika] . . . walang kang pami-pamilya. Dito puro trabaho o kaya kalandian . . . mahirap isingit ang pamilya." [It is all work here (in America) . . . you don't have time for the family. Here it is either work or whoring around . . . it is hard to make time for the family.] When I asked Rico about his memories of growing up in the Philippines, he said that when he was growing up he always was concerned with family and that if he had not immigrated to the United States he would still be living with his family even though he was in his thirties. He said his family was a great influence in his life: "Kaya siguro ang drama ko ngayon ay masaya at walang kiyeme." [Which is why my drama is happy and with no kiyeme.] To some extent Rico considered his family to be an ideal one in which to grow up. He argued that while his family life may seem too sheltered to many of his friends in America, it was this kind of atmosphere that allowed him to succeed and survive here. In other words, it gave him a firm foundation when he was growing up.

For many Filipino immigrants, leaving the Philippines means leaving family members behind. This experience provides the most fundamental influence on the way Filipino gay men analyze, create, and reflect on ties with their biological families. Moving far away from the family is not socially expected in the Philippines. Alden, who was from a prominent family in the southern part of the Philippines, said that his mother kept asking why he would want to leave if he could get a job with his father and not bother about housework, food, or rent. He told her wanted to make it on his own.

On the other side of the coin were Mel and many other informants whose families thought that going to the United States was the most logical thing to do. According to several of my informants, the Philippines did not offer any promising future for them. Like many other Filipinos who saw a bright future in living abroad, Mel and many others had their families' blessings and hopes for a successful future overseas. Rene is a good example of how those who were born and raised in the Philippines were socialized into thinking about immigration. "Everything in the Philippines was oriented toward America," he said. "In the 1960s when I went to elementary and high school in Manila there was the 'English Only' rule. We were fined for speaking Tagalog. In my family, my parents encouraged us to speak English. The only time I had to speak Tagalog at home was to the maids."

Moving away involves ambivalent feelings, including both the heartwarming and the equally (at least to some informants) "suffocating closeness" of the extended family. The distance between the immigrant and his family promotes particular engagements and claims that complicate narratives about family relationships. The freedom that comes with distance from the family affords some Filipino gay men a chance to try new experiences and remake themselves. Much like Alden's poster of a naked muscular man, many Filipino gay men are able to do things that they would never have done under the surveillance of family living nearby. Tony, or Tonette as he was sometimes called, noted that being far way from his family enabled him to experiment with roles and personas:

Noong nasa Manila ako, kunyari pa akong pa-min ang drama ko although alam ng lahat na bading talaga ang truth. Pag-step ng aking satin shoes dito sa New York, o biglang nagiba ang pagrarampa ko. May I try ko ang pagmu-mu and also nag-gym ako. Ang sabi ng ibang Pinay na bading na parang lukresiya ako. Bakit daw ako nagpapamuscles and then nagmumujer ako. Alam mo, pag wala ka sa pakikialam ng pamilya at kaibigan mo sa Pilipinas, kahit ano puwede.

[When I was still in Manila, I was still putting on the macho drama although I know that all the badings knew the truth. When my satin shoes hit New York, I suddenly changed the way I walk the ramp *(rampa)*. I tried going in drag and going to the gym. Many Filipinos told me that I was crazy. Why, they ask, was I growing muscles and going in drag? You know, when you live far away from your parents and friends in the Philippines, anything is possible.]

The meaning of the family in all of the narratives contains notions of continuity and persistence and at the same time the translation and transformation of relationships. For example, Alden's cousin, who insisted that familial ties needed to be rearticulated in consonance with "individualistic" America, induced Alden to reevaluate his notion of family albeit with some misgivings. While Alden recognized his cousin's wise words, he nevertheless maintained a pragmatic view that this kind of "every man to himself" attitude was true only in America and that it did not apply to his relationship to his family back home. In contrast, Roldan's distance and regulated phone contact with his family enabled him to step back a bit and reflect on the difficult issues surrounding his "surrogate breadwinner" and "head of household" status.

In both Alden's and Roldan's cases, there is an explicit placement of the traditional idea of family to the Philippines not only because that was where most members of their immediate families were based. Rather, as other informants whose immediate family members lived in America would attest, the distancing allows these men to confront the demanding life in New York. In other words, except for crucial moments like phone calls or visits, Filipino gay men attempt to locate family life at a distance to enable them to engage in an individualistic way of life. Moreover, it is the rooting of the traditional meanings of family and the ambivalent feelings that accompany them that create the anxiety and pleasure of nostalgia for both Alden and Roldan. Indeed, the meanings of family are negotiated through various situations and moments. This is especially true for informants whose experiences include cross-dressing (see chapter 5) and AIDS (see chapter 6).

In the two previous narratives about Alden's apartment and Roldan's daily routines, familial ties sporadically interrupted or disrupted the blissful flow of daily life. In Alden's case, his family's influence was spatially and temporally situated when the power of the "Philippine corner" with its religious relics and family photos produced feelings of guilt after sexual encounters or pangs of homesickness during holidays. In Roldan's life, the phone calls and remittances of money and goods were his links to daily dilemmas with his family back home.

Many informants told me how such links as phone calls and remittances have become part of the routine. One informant said, "Every Saturday morning at 9 A.M., when the phone rings, I know it is my family in Manila calling." Still another informant talked about how he always had a balikbayan box that he slowly filled with canned goods, T-shirts, colognes, perfumes, and any special request from his family in the Philippines. He told me that shopping trips and the act of looking at shop windows usually yielded another item or two for the box, which he ships every other month.

For some informants, holidays are important occasions that require extensive efforts at sending gifts of money and consumer goods. Raffy, a forty-year-old man whose parents and six siblings still lived in the Philippines, noted that he still sends gifts for all occasions from Christmas to birthdays. Apart from the money he sent every month, Raffy also sent canned corned beef, which his father loved, linens, candies, and other items that are too expensive to buy in Manila. When I asked him why he did this, at first he said that it was cheaper than going on an actual visit. After thinking about it more, Raffy said, "I know many of my American friends and especially my lover think I go overboard with my family, but they *are* my family. I think that sending packages is nothing compared to the fulfillment I get from being able to do so. My lover and I went to a Christmas Eve party two years ago. There were three other couples there, but somehow, after more than ten years here, I felt very lonely. I went home and called my parents. Burt, my lover, was very furious. He said I should cut the strings."

The strength of these ties or "strings" that bind Filipino gay men and their families are tested during times of crises such as financial, emotional, or physical misfortune. Many of my informants told me that they would first approach a family member for help during these situations. In chapter 6, I explore similar situations within the context of AIDS, illness, and death.

When I asked informants about approaching friends and lovers here in America, many of them said that even in the most intimate relationships, friends and lovers are still not as reliable as the family. Although several voiced the fact that their friends and boyfriends are important, it seemed to be the consensus that such ties are sometimes fleeting and weak. Arthur encapsulated this view when he said that it was really hard to run to friends for help in the United States.

While traditional social science literature on Filipino families stresses smooth and functional interpersonal relationships, the situation of Filipino gay immigrants reveals the formation of a multidimensional picture. For example, Roldan's breadwinner role created a kind of ambivalence. There were times when he bemoaned the fact that his family was overly dependent on him and other times when he suspected with feelings of guilt that he was only as good as his next remittance. For that matter, the all too familiar queries about being unmarried were glossed over by many informants as being an integral part of the usual family reunions during visits back to the Philippines. Indeed, family conflicts were almost always smoothed over in the life narratives. Conflicts were one of the more sensitive issues that were narrated to me after informants became very comfortable with the interview and lost their defensiveness. For example, Eric, who had been living away from his family for more than ten years, clearly harbored some ambivalent feelings when he confided that his family was beset with problems and drama that were more akin to soap operas. He said that one might think that "*Eight Is Enough* ang biyuti namin pero *Gulong ng Palad* talaga ang drama" [as if *Eight Is Enough* (American family comedy show in the 1970s and 1980s) is our biyuti but *The Wheel of Fate* (a Tagalog soap opera) is really our drama].[1]

Despite the conflicts and ambivalence informants may have had about their families, most of them viewed familial ties as enduring and persisting through the many changes that they as individuals undergo. Roldan said it best when he noted that, despite the distance and the effort to put family obligations behind, one could never escape them. While Roldan and many other informants recognize that "becoming American" and belonging in American society are popularly conceived in terms of autonomy, most Filipino gay men assert the abiding and constant image of the biological family as a source of support and identity on the one hand, and ambivalence and anxiety on the other.[2]

While many informants talked about the durability of the family, a significant number also emphasized the integral role of friends and lovers. Friendships, particularly those forged since childhood, were cherished and deeply regarded. Several immigrant informants talked about the network of Filipino friends they utilized when they first arrived in America. Rico told a typical story of his bakla friend, Vanessa.

> Nang dumating ako dito sa States, wa ako family. So nagstay ako sa isang kaibingang kong bading si Vanessa. Si Vanessa ay friend ko noon pang malalandi kaming coeds sa ( ). Ay naku, marami na kaming pinagdaanan ni Vanessa. Siya ang nagturo sa akin tungkol sa pagmumujer. Noong wala pa akong trabaho, pinahihiram niya ako ng pera at ilinibot ako kung saan-saan. Tatanga-tanga pa naman ako noon. Siya ang nagturo sa akin tungkol sa mga pasikut-sikut dito. Kung wala si Vanessa, siguro noong pa ako sumuko at umuwi sa atin.

> [When I arrived in the states, I did not have family here. I stayed with my bading friend, Vanessa. Vanessa has been my friend since we were still whorish coeds in (a private Catholic college for boys in Manila). Oh dear, Vanessa and I have been through a lot of things. He taught me how to cross-dress. When I did not have a job, he lent me money and he took me around everywhere. I used to be so naive.

He taught me about the intricacies of life here. Had Vanessa not been here, I would have surrendered long ago and gone back home.]

Friends are the repositories of secrets that many informants will not tell their families. Romy, for example, said that only his closest friends knew a lot of his never-to-be revealed secrets, such as the time when he was mugged. These secrets, he maintained, would never reach the ears of his mother. He said, "I only told my two good friends Edna and Biboy. These guys [one of them is a woman] have been the reason why I am still sane. You see, if I told my mother about that mugging, she would literally drag me back home — she is super-*nerbiyosa* [nervous]."

Friends are differentiated from lovers or boyfriends *(siyota)* and spouses *(asawa* or *jowa)* as people with whom one is emotionally but not physically or sexually intimate. Sexual intimacy is so taboo between friends that the tone of the discourse around such an occurrence borders on the catastrophic and abominable. Mel exemplified this view when he exclaimed, "Ano? Makikifag-seks ako sa aking mga amiga? Naku, baka magkabuhol-buhol ang aming mga tirintas at matabunan kami ng aming mga belo. Please lang, baka biglang lumindol at magunaw ang mundo." [What? I will have sex with my (gay) friends (in the feminine form)? Oh my, our braids might get entangled and we might be smothered by our veils. Oh please, an earthquake may occur and the world might end.]

Friends, in this instance, are gendered. Informants' gay friends, especially other Filipino friends, are feminized and therefore are not part of the pool of potential sexual partners. This is often seen by immigrant informants as an extension of the practice in the Philippines where other Filipino bakla friends are not only feminized but are seen as kin. Informants also reported the continuing use of kinship terms such as *tita* (auntie), *atche* or *ate* (older sister) for this group of friends. This practice creates a kind of incest taboo that can be articulated in different ways. For example, at the mere suggestion of having a couple of his close Filipino gay friends as his lovers, Oscar exclaimed, "Ano ako kanibal? Kakain ako ng aking ka-dugo?" [What am I, a cannibal? I will eat those of the same blood?] Another informant articulated this taboo in yet another fashion when he responded, "Ay naku, lesbiyanahan! Magkakapaan kaming magkakafatid! Que horror!" [Oh my, lesbianism! We co-siblings will grope each other! Horrors!]

In these situations, many Filipino gay men acknowledge the difficulty of having what the mainstream gay community members call "fuck buddies," or casual/occasional sexual partners who may also be friends. One Filipino informant talked about his confusion with this category, or practice, in terms of eating food that did not go together. He said, "Ano ba yang fuck buddy na yan — para kang kumakain ng karne at leche flan." [What is this fuck buddy business — it is like eating meat with sweet custard.][3]

Friends are also the source of intrigue *(intriga)* and gossip *(tsismis)*. Some informants actually pointed to other Filipino gay men as being more apt to be gossipy and bitchy. This perception more often than not extended to the general Filipino immigrant community where, according to informants, jealousy, bickering, and gossip prevail. However, this perception is intensified in relation to other Filipino gay men. Such perception is usually couched in terms of a competition. Lex echoed this idea when he said, "Ayaw kong makipagchicahan sa mga Pilipino, lalo na mga bakla. Que bakla, que diretso, maraming intriga. Pagtsitsimisan ka o kung hindi naman e inggitan naman." [I don't want to socialize with other Filipinos, especially other bakla. Whether bakla or straight, there are too many intrigues. They will gossip about you or else they will be envious of you.] In the same vein, Bert, another informant said,

> Mahirap makipagbarkada sa mga bading. Ang drama talaga 'y siraan. Kaya ako, puro mga puti ang mga friends ko. Hindi ako nakiki-join sa kanila. Mahirap na. Baka masangkot ka pa sa iskandalo. Alin? Maglakad ka diyan at if I know, ginegradan ka ng mga bading, parang beauty contest. Mamatahin ang suot mo, ang kilos, o pagjojongles.

> [It is difficult to be friends with badings. Their drama is really about dissing. That is why all of my friends are white. I don't consort with them (Filipinos). It's difficult, you might get involved in a scandal. What? You walk around and usually these bading(s) will judge you as if you are in a beauty contest. They will look down on your outfit, your manners, or your English-speaking ability.]

When I was interviewing Edsel, he mentioned that he got into an *intrigahan* (conflict) with his former *barkada* (peer group) of Filipino gay men. His story was as follows:

> Noon, about a year ago, may mga kaibigan ako sa Jersey City. Mag-kakasama ang tatlo sa amin — magroomate, tapos yung dalawa,

kapitbahay. Marami kaming pinagdaanan. Pero unti-unting dumating yong mga ingitan at awayan. Minsan tungkol sa renta. Minsan tungkol sa lalaki. Aba, yong si Fidel nagalit doon kay Berta e sinumbong kay Tita Imee. Si Berta e you know, TNT. Nagalit si Fidel dahil inaakit daw ni Berta ang kanyang jowa. Say naman ni Berta, sa biyuti daw niya hindi na niya kailangang magakit at ang jowa ni Fidel ang nagmamakaawa. To top it all, si Berta, nagmalaki at biglang siney niya kay Mama Fidela na naiinggit lang siya at pati yong napulot niya sa tabi-tabi e nabibighani sa biyuti niya. Ay naku marami pang sinabi si Berta so gumanti ang Mama. So where is Miss Berta now? Napa go-home bigla ang biyuti niya.

[Then, about a year go, I had these (four) friends in Jersey City. The three of us lived together as roommates, and the other two were our neighbors. We underwent many travails. But slowly, jealousy and quarrels erupted. Sometimes it was about the rent. Sometimes it was about men. Then Fidel got angry with Berta and he (Fidel) snitched to Tita Aimee (Immigration and Naturalization Service). You know, Berta was TNT (undocumented). Fidel was angry because Berta was supposedly stealing his boyfriend. Berta countered that with his biyuti he did not need to attract (other people's boyfriends) and that Fidel's boyfriend was the one begging (for his affections). To top it all, Berta was being arrogant and he told Mama Fidela that he (Fidel) was just jealous and that his boyfriend, whom he just picked up on some sidewalk, was enraptured by his (Berta's) biyuti. Well, Bert said a lot of things and Mama exacted his revenge. So where is Miss Berta now? His biyuti has been sent home (to the Philippines).]

The social institution of the *barkada*, or peer group, is decidedly inflected by class. Most informants would refer to this group often in terms of people who were former schoolmates. Having hailed from the same province or speaking the same language or dialect is another marker of group cohesiveness. However, despite all these connections, there were several reports like that of Edsel's above that point to the instability of such groups' cohesiveness. The barkada, according to many informants, may be a source of support but can also be the source of conflict.

Despite all of these rather convoluted webs of intrigue several informants mentioned the importance of having Filipino gay friends. Danny said, "Filipino badings know you better. I think there are some jokes that do not translate as well." He further said that these kinds of jokes were not as dry as American jokes. Furthermore, they were more physical and were based on the ironic juxtapositions of Tagalog and English words and situations.

The ultimate praise friends would have for each other is to consider them as kin. "Parang kafatid" [like a sibling] was often the phrase used to describe the closeness of the friendship. It is in these junctures in informants' narratives where friends acquired the kind of durability and persistence of familial influence. However, most informants agreed that despite these situations where friends play important roles in their lives, friends are, in the final analysis, not "real" family members.

While friends occupy a desexualized space for Filipino gay men, lovers and boyfriends are the exact opposite. Lovers are highly sexualized but only in the eyes of people who would recognize the sexual component in these relationships, such as other gay men. Most families who are tolerant about their gay family members usually cast the boyfriends as best friends. In most cases, lovers are seen by the families of Filipino gay men as surrogate caretakers or nurturers. However, in contrast to family and friends, lovers are seen as unstable and less permanent than friends and family. As one informant said, "With family, you always know where and who you are, but with lovers, magkawrinkle ka lang—leave ang biyuti niya" [you get wrinkles and his biyuti (the lover) leaves].

The possibility of acquiring a partner, or a jowa, away from the prying eyes of the family is one of the impetuses for moving away. Many of these men would not have thought of living and consorting with another man if they were still back in the Philippines. For most immigrant informants, moving in and sharing a household with somebody who is both a sexual partner as well as a source of emotional and sometimes financial support is one of the biggest changes in their sexual and social lives. These kinds of relationships were, according to informants, not widely practiced in the Philippines. Additionally, acquiring a lover is seen to be one way to assuage the fear of being alone in America.

Weston (1991), in her landmark study on gay/lesbian families, remarked on the inadequacy of the "looking glass" argument, or the stereotypical view that lesbians and gays are looking for mirror images or virtual likenesses of themselves. She further argued that this view fails to address the complexity in the dynamics of attraction and relationship building and maintenance among lesbians and gays. Nowhere is this truer than with my informants. Of the fifty men who participated in life-narrative interviews, twenty-eight reported having lovers. Of these men, two had Latino lovers, two had African American lovers, one had a Japanese American lover, and two had Filipino lovers, while the rest, a clear majority, reported having Caucasian lovers. Interracial gay relationships, which are the norm among my informants, provide clues to the dynamics between race and sexuality (discussed further in this chapter's subsection on Orientalism) but more importantly, shed light on the complex processes that occur in these relationships.

Such interracial relationships are seen as the logical extension of being in America and being away from the Philippines. An informant, Art, told me, "Bakit ka pa maglolonganisa at tapa, e dito frankfurter at filet mignon ang makukuha mo. Kailangan mo naman tikman ang kakaiba 'di va!" [Why would you have *longanisa* (native sausage) and *tapa* (cured beef) when you can have frankfurter and filet mignon here?] Sex taboos are couched in food terms and at the same time are inflected by race.

The racial constitution of the "lover" or "boyfriend" is especially pronounced in terms of their desirability. Several informants informed that they would never even think of having a particular group of men as sexual partners or lovers because of their race. Most of the time, this group was that of African Americans. Racialized and racist assumptions prevailed. One informant told me how his Filipino gay friend, who was fond of "coal," or *uling* (African Americans), was robbed and nearly stabbed by one of his African American lovers. A few informants also mentioned how, even if they did find an African American man attractive, they might attract the scorn or cruel jokes of other Filipinos if they were with this putative partner. Arthur aptly reported, "Believe me, dear, hindi ka i-ismolin ng mga Pinoy kung puti ang dala-dala mo, pero once mag-display ka ng jowing na jutam, ay for sure — pagtsitsimisan ka ng mga bading. Para bang, hanggang itim ka lang." [Believe me, dear, you won't be looked down upon by other Filipinos if you have a white man in tow, but once you display a black boyfriend, for sure the other badings will gossip about you. It's like you are only good for black men.]

Arthur points to a hierarchy of racialized desire among Filipinos with Caucasians as the most valued. In the past few years, there has been a heightened consciousness concerning this hierarchy. Many Filipino gay men have forged relationships with other racial and ethnic groups. In fact, during the late 1980s and early 1990s, many informants observed that Asian gay men's organizations were implicitly encouraging members to go into relationships with other Asians and Pacific Islanders, sometimes to the point of being perceived as "anti-white."

Mario, one of two informants who had another Filipino as a lover, said that he was lucky that he came to America with his jowa, Raymond. He said he was able to escape a lot of the pitfalls of gay life in America, including going to the bars and picking up men, which, in a way, prevented him from getting AIDS. When I asked him whether he and Raymond were in a monogamous relationship, he just smiled and said, "Well, we are pretty much faithful, but once in a blue moon, kailangan mo namang tumikim ng ibang putahe" [you need to taste other entrees]. One reason why he believed his relationship to be valuable was that he had escaped a lot of the heartaches that seemed to plague many of the interracial gay relationships that he knew about. For example, he said that he and his lover did not have cultural barriers, particularly around communication. He noted that there were problems in other relationships where a Filipino was not fluent in colloquial English or the partner did not understand the Filipino's unspoken messages. Then he observed some kind of inequality between Filipinos and their mostly white partners. He said that usually the white partner was more well off and more masculine. Here Mario was alluding to the popular belief that in such white-Filipino gay relationships, the white man, or afam, dominated the Filipino gay man in daily affairs.

I discuss the dynamics of such relationships in a later subsection in this chapter. Mario's statement is only partially true. For many Filipinos whose white lovers were more economically well off, this was seen as a major reversal to the situation in the Philippines where the bakla is seen to provide some kind of incentive (usually monetary) for the allegedly straight partner to stay with him. Consider Eric's exuberant observation when he proclaimed, "O, 'di va yan ang biyuti ng Amerika, ang bakla ang liniligawan ng mga men. Instead of na ang lalaki ang inaalagaan gaya sa atin, usually, ang vading ang imaalagaan, ay talagang type ko ang mga kadramahan dito." [That's the biyuti of America. The bakla is courted by men. Instead of the man being paid like back home (in the Philippines), it is usually the bakla or bading. I really love the drama here.] Here, Eric's words reveal one of the major reversals in the roles Filipino gay men play in the everyday drama of socializing with other men. The first point in Eric's statement is the process of gendering in the relationship. He echoes the bakla as a pseudo-female who is courted by men. Following popular discourses in the Philippines, the bakla is feminized. However, unlike these discourses, the bakla is the one pursued and desired. Most of the Filipinos in these interracial relationships reported that they perceived the mostly white men to be more masculine than they were. Whether this translated into actual domination or oppression, as many popular rhetorics in the gay community portray it, is discussed below.

Eric's statements may also help illuminate how a number of Filipino gay men who cross-dress have actually encountered and engaged with the reality of "sex work." Having sex for money is something that many of my informants reported to be an established practice in the drag-queen world. Oftentimes, many first encountered it as a pleasant surprise. One of my informants who was part of this world of Filipino gay men warned me that if any of my informants who went in drag and frequented particular bars ever told me they had never been paid or been offered money, they were in fact lying.

However, most of my informants in interracial relationships were neither involved in sex work nor cross-dressing. One such person in this kind of a relationship was Romuel, whose white lover was not only twenty years older than he was but was also a successful lawyer while Romuel worked several part-time jobs. Romuel's lover paid for most of their daily expenses. Romuel was very proud of this relationship and called it his "trust fund."

> Okey, I admit that ako ang dinadatungan. Granted that is true, okey, pero navavalidate nang husto ang biyuti ko. Hindi ako nagbubuy, ako ang binibigyan. Saan ka makakakita nang ganyan sa Pilipinas — ang bakla ang nasa pedestal. Pero, hindi naman call boy ang biyuti ko — ako — call boy — ay please! Para sa akin, kasama na yan sa pagmamahal. Si Tony, ang lover ko, nagbabayad nga siya ng kung anu-ano, pero kasama naman yan sa pagmamahalan — 'di va? Ako, I take care of his needs. Ako ang nag-gogrocery at nagluluto. Kung sana, pera lang ang habol ko sa kaniya. 'Day, ang bait na guwapo pa at napakadako! O sey ng iba bakit daw ako parang girl sa relasyon na ito. O e ano ngayon, pwede na rin akong girl [laughter].

[Okay, I admit that I get money (out of this relationship). Granted that this is true, okay, but my biyuti is validated. I am not the one buying, I am the one being given money. Where can you find something like this in the Philippines, where the bakla is placed on a pedestal? But my biyuti is not a call boy. Me — a call boy? Oh, please! Tony, my lover, pays for everything, but it (the money) is part of loving, isn't it? I am not in this relationship for the money, darling. He (Tony) is so kind and well hung! Other people say that I am the "girl" in this relationship (laughter), so what! I could be a girl (laughter).]

Here, Romuel makes a point about money as the nexus in what he considers love. He said that while he comes from a relatively well-off family and had a good education in the Philippines, he is still struggling to make it here in America. Tony, his partner, is helping him.

On the other side of the coin, there were a couple of Filipinos who told me that they paid for sex and that they financially supported their white boyfriends. Ronnie, who frequented a well-known hustler bar in Manhattan's East Side, said that there was an allure to having sex with men who ordinarily will not have sex with other men except in such situations. Ronnie said the financial component added to the men's machismo. When I interviewed him, Ronnie was living with a man named Kenny, an Irish American construction worker who was unemployed at that time. Ronnie admitted that while Kenny might have some sexual flings on the side, he knew that these were with women. When I asked him whether he knew that other people would take him for a fool, he replied that he had accepted the possibility that the relationship was not going to be forever and that his lover would leave him. When I asked him whether he thought he was still following the same kind of drama of the Filipino bakla in the Philippines, he reasoned:

Wala naman talagang masama diyan sa bayaran. Kung type mo ang biyuti ng kasama mo at hindi ka naman ganoon ka ganda, well mag-datung ka na. Ang advantage dito e in control ka. Alin, yan sinasabi nila true love, pinagdaanan ko na. Ang gabaldeng luha na linabas ko dahil sa mga true love na yan, walang katumbas sa pera. At saka, teka, kung wala kang datung di magtiis ka. Mas madaling malungkot ka na nag-iisa kesa sa para kang Perla Bautista na naghi-hinagpis sa asawa mo. Hindi na oy. [There is nothing wrong with paying (somebody). If you like the biyuti of your partner and you are not that pretty, then you should pay. The advantage here is that you are in control. What's with that "true love" thing that people talk about? I am over that! There is no comparison between the buckets of tears I have shed for these "true loves" with the money I pay. And by the way, if you don't have the money, tough luck. It is easier to be lonely being alone than being like Perla Bautista (Filipino film actress known for melodramatic tearjerkers) languishing because of your husband. No thanks.]

Both Romuel and Ronnie talked about the ambivalence of love and money in their relationships. While it may be easy to construct a simple equation between money and control, and between race and dominance, things are not that simple. The arrangements both men had created for themselves were fraught with the complexities of feelings and actual behavior as well as the articulation of a particular kind of idiom of *pag-aalaga* or nurturance. This idiom, which I observed among Filipino gays/bakla in the Philippines, extends the material power of money into the realm of love and nurturance, of pleasure and control.

The economic inequality between Filipino gay men and their mostly white lovers is superseded by the seeming awkwardness of the American discourse on class. This issue is further explained in the next section. This inequality is explained and euphemized by several Filipino informants in several ways. First, the financial situation can be explained away by the notion of *pag-aalaga*. Celso, who worked as a $30,000 administrative assistant in a Manhattan law firm, told me that his lover Shawn took care of all his expenses. This arrangement was desirable, according to Celso, because he was able to send more money to his family back in the Philippines. Celso added that he needed all the help he could get since he had only been in the United States for about six years. For some Filipinos, there was the allure of economic inequality, particularly if the Caucasian had the upper hand. The pleasure they derived when their lovers picked up the tab compensated for what other people perceived as shameful. Like Ronnie, several other Filipinos actually found pleasure in being on the receiving end. As one of them facetiously gushed, "Ganito pala ang America, ang biyuti ng bakla [So this is America, the biyuti of the bakla is] appreciated, adored, and . . . compensated!"

In sum, for Filipino gay men, lovers are sexualized individuals who are racialized, classed, and gendered in various situations. The racial component in these relationships complicates and troubles the supposedly level playing field in situations involving lovers in popular gay lore. These relationships are further elucidated by the following section, which deals with the intersection of sexual attraction and emotion with race, class, gender, and religion.

DE BUENA FAMILIA: THE BANALITY OF CLASS

In this section, I examine how class is transported and translated in the American setting within the context of everyday life. Among Filipino gay men, issues of class can be seen as interruptions into everyday life in seemingly egalitarian America.

For many of my Philippine-born informants, class was perhaps one of the more important markers of difference among Filipinos, overriding the so-called regional or ethnolinguistic affiliations. There was consensus among the informants that unlike in the Philippines where one's "place" in society was stable, in America status was mutable. This mutability was very evident in specific situations. For example, many immigrant informants said that in coming here to America they experienced an increase in their buying power. Consider one such conversation between Eric, an informant (B), and me (A):

A: Ano ang class background mo sa Pilipinas? [What was your class background in the Philippines?]

B: Middle class.

A: Bakit middle class? Ano ba ang middle class sa atin? [Why middle class? What is middle class back home?]

B: Well, hindi naman kami squatter. Maganda naman ang nirerentahan naming apartment sa Manila. Hindi kami nagugutom. Nakapagaral kaming lahat. Nakapagcollege. [We were not squatters. We had a nice rental apartment in Manila. We all were able to go to school. We all attended college.]

B: E ngayon, pagkarating mo dito sa Amerika, ano na ang class mo? [Here in America, what is your class?]

A: Well, mahirap sabihin. Ang mga kapitabahay ko dito sa Queens mga mukhang trabahador. Ako, living from paycheck to paycheck. Marami akong nabibili na hindi ko kaya noong nasa Pilipinas ako. Siguro medyo mababa ng kaunti sa middle class. [Well, it is hard to say. My neighbors in Queens look like laborers. Me, I live from paycheck to paycheck. I can buy a lot more things than when I was in the Philippines. Maybe a little lower than middle class.]

Here the informant reinforced the conflation of an upper-class status with increased consumption and buying power, but this was coupled with the contrary signs such as working-class neighbors and the struggle to survive financially. The translation of the term "middle class" for Eric had to do with a sense of comfort, but this sense of comfort experienced while growing up in the Philippines was not replicated here in America. The difficulty of finding one's class location in the United States is very evident.

For many Filipino immigrant men, perceived class status or class origins in the Philippines functioned as a semantic anchor in which to view social situations here. Class or elements of it, according to some informants, sometimes travel well. Language and nonverbal behavior were part of these elements. These formed part of specific scripts that spell the difference between those who have "good breeding" and those who do not. One informant said, "You can come here [to America], dress up like an East Side preppy, pero [but] once you open your mouth or start gesturing, say goodbye to the kiyeme [artfulness or dissimulation]." Class was also used as a vantage or lens through which other Filipinos were evaluated or "sized up." Rene, an informant, said:

Naku, dito sa Amerika, napapasama ka sa mga Pinoy na hindi mo makakasalimuha sa Pilipinas. Yun bang, mga baduy na if I know e taga Cainta o Bukawe. Alam mo na mga public school graduates. As you know, equal daw tayong lahat sa America. Etsing!"

[Oh, here in America, you are thrown into the company of Filipinos whom you would not hang out with back in the Philippines. The ones who are tacky or from Cainta or Bukawe (allegedly tacky areas in the Philippines). You know, public school graduates. As you know, we are supposedly equal in America. Not!]

Rene's statement about class in America is very instructive. On the one hand, it paints a picture of America where Filipinos from different classes are thrown together. On the other hand, while there is a conscious recognition that despite the popular belief that America is a great equalizer, this is only true to a point. Rene's statement suggests the kind of incongruous scenes that Filipinos find themselves in with other Filipinos who "are not of their kind."

Class, as many informants have experienced in America, is inflected in many ways in which race is the most important node of articulation. Following the mestizo complex in the Philippines, informants were explicit about the connections of upper-class status with whiteness and lower-class status with dark complexions. More often than not, this hierarchy was confounded by everyday situations. Gerry told me that he once chose a blond, blue-eyed man over a dark Middle Easterner. He later found out that the blond was unemployed while the Middle Easterner was a doctor. "Nagtititili ako" [I started screaming], he said.

Many believed that despite the inconsistency, America has leveled off some of these distinctions. As one informant said, "There are some Filipinos I would normally not have contact with back home in the Philippines, but here in America we are thrown together in the bars, in the streets, [and] some neighborhoods, you know." David's narrative is particularly instructive. A Filipino of aristocratic background, he found America to be very funny because he was able to maintain relationships with people who were not from his class. Coming from a landed family in the Philippines, he said that he tried to create some distance from people he perceived were not his equals. But this was not true in America. His white lover of several years was a telephone linesman with only a high school degree. He said there were times when the class disparity showed. For example, conflicts occurred in situations when their tastes for particular leisure activities were divided into, in his mind, the classy and the tasteless, such as a concert and bowling. David said, "Oh dear, if my friends in school [in Manila] ever heard that my boyfriend is a phone linesman, they would just scream! But then, they have not seen him. Sometimes I think like an American and put class aside, and yet there are times when my boyfriend acts like a total ass, when his working-class background shows. Ashamed bigla ang biyuti ko." [My biyuti is suddenly ashamed.]

David further reported that his first ten years of living in America were spent as an illegal alien. Despite having money and a good education, he started in menial jobs, such as being a janitor or a busboy, owing to lack of legal papers. He said, "I guess living during those years and doing those kinds of jobs were exciting in a way . . . a different way of experiencing America," he said. Indeed, David's own class-conscious ways have been tempered to a large extent by the immigration experience. In David's case, immigration status became a transformative catalyst in class position and attitudes. He is not alone.

Many Filipinos, including those who came to America from upper-class families, were aware of the difficulties of settling in especially if one did not have the right legal papers. Some arrived ready to "do anything in order to stay, including doing menial work." The experience of this "different America" was seen by many as a rite of passage!

Armand, who confessed to being an undocumented worker, reported that many of the so-called successful Filipinos he has met here were people who immigrated either as part of family reunification or by marriage. He told me of one interesting and quite disturbing experience meeting Marta, one of his family's former maids in the Philippines, who was now married to an American and living on Long Island.

> 'Day, nakakahiya. Si Marta sinundo ako sa aking dampa sa Queens. Then, dinala niya ako sa isang mansiyon sa Long Island. Medyo strombotic at gaudy ang decoration pero, darling, ang laki! To top it all pa, si Marta, may I senyorito pa ang call sa akin. Kahit na sinabi ko na, "Marta, dito sa Amerika, wag mo na akong tawagin niyan." Well, kahit na malaki ang agwat ng aming class, di pa rin maalis ang aming relationship sa Pilipinas. Alam mo ba, hindi sa pangiisnab ha . . . kahit na may mansiyon na siya, feeling ko pareho pa rin ang aming katayuan.

> [Girlfriend, it was so embarrassing. Marta (the former maid) picked me up in my little hovel in Queens. Then she took me to a mansion in Long Island. The decoration was kind of ostentatious and gaudy, but darling, it was huge. To top it all, Marta still called me señorito (master), even after I told her, "Marta, in America, don't call me that." Well, even if we have class differences, one cannot erase our relationship in the Philippines. Not to sound snobbish, but you know what, even with her mansion, our relationship has not really changed.]

These stories of the dissonance and almost carnivalesque types of situations where class origins are turned upside down are a major part of many informants' narratives. More than anything, these stories show both the continuities and discontinuities of class as it is transvaluated in the context of diasporic living. Class remains a strong force in delineating similarities and difference, affinities and distance in many Filipino gay men's lives. Class, despite its relative illegibility in

American popular mainstream and gay discourses, has a powerful presence in these men's everyday lives.

In 1993, I was invited by Gerardo to his apartment in Queens for a rosary session as part of block rosary activities in his home.[4] The Virgin Mary, or more specifically Our Lady of Perpetual Help, was to be delivered to his home, and several of his friends, most of whom were gay, would be there. When I got to Gerardo's apartment, the guests, including the one who was supposed to bring the statue, were still not there. Gerardo was fuming when he said, "Filipino time again. When will these people ever learn they are not in the Philippines anymore? You can't keep people waiting here, especially in New York. Time is precious." Then, when the rosary devotion started, Tonette, who was leading, started rushing through the prayers. Gerardo screamed, "Hoy, bakit ka nagmamadali? Ano ka Afam? Wala kang respeto!" [Hey, why are you in such a rush? What are you, an American? You have no respect.]

Religion, for many of my informants, stands in sharp opposition to secular America. For many of them, religious devotion is the mark of being Filipino. For most of my informants, going to mass in America allowed them to reexperience something from childhood. The comfort of this familiar activity stands in contrast to the fact that many of them have to attend mass alone and not in the company of the family. Many Filipino gay men found comfort in the familiarity of the surroundings and the people in the church. In one Catholic Church in Greenwich Village, which had a large Filipino congregation, Jose, an informant, was delighted to be invited to a social where all the refreshments were Filipino delicacies. He said that the mass and the social afterward brought to mind many pleasurable memories. The church, therefore, is a space for nostalgia, a place for remembering as well as a way of settling in. Feeling at home despite the realization that the Village was not part of the Philippines was important to Jose and to many informants. Like Alden's "Philippine corner," these moments and spaces are, in the words of one informant, "lifesavers." Sunday mass is then a moment when "home" is both mnemonically evoked and physically manifested by the rituals and structure of the church.

For most Filipinos, religion is usually circumscribed to Sunday within a routine week. However, several informants told me how religion pervaded their daily lives. Roldan's routine included the mass as a regular part of the weekly itinerary and was altered only during extreme situations such as illness.

A few informants reported the practices of morning and evening prayers. Religion, for these men, was a way to safeguard against the possible danger and unknown hazards of living in New York City. One informant in particular said, "Dito, you never know kung ano ang mangyayari—baka ma-mug ka o mahulog sa subway, mabuti na yon na parang may proteksiyon ka." [Here (in New York) you never know what will happen—you might get mugged or fall in the subway. It is better to have some protection.] For many others, a simple sign of the cross in front of their small altars was usually their daily encounter with religion.

As the religious ritual described in the next chapter shows, many Filipino informants admitted to having to make changes or accommodation in their religious beliefs. They believed they were now less susceptible to the kinds of narrow-minded moralizing that allegedly existed in the Philippines. A few informants reported having changed their religious beliefs into some form of informal atheism or agnosticism. The change was perceived to be in tandem with the realities afforded by their experiences in America. In addition, many of these men believed that the increasing secularization of their lives was reflected in their daily routines. Unlike Roldan's routine, they spent their Sundays trying to recover from Saturday nights out in bars or leisurely preparing for the onslaught of the working week.

In addition, their break from the Catholic Church was seen to parallel their own physical and sometimes emotional distancing from their families. Teddy, an informant who was born and raised in a heavily Filipino neighborhood in the San Francisco Bay Area, reported, "My weekends are less hectic than the ones of my childhood. During those times, it seemed like my weekends were orchestrated from morning 'til night by my parents . . . visiting relatives or going to church. Now I don't feel like I have to do anything. I am on my own. My weekends belong [now] to me."

Bert, an immigrant Filipino man in his thirties, recalled that the weekends of his childhood really meant family outings and activities. The church and Sunday mass were the high points of the weekend for many of these men when they were growing up. Mass was usually followed by lunch or dinner and other gatherings orchestrated by family members.

The changes in some of these men's religious beliefs were also based on particular negative experiences with the church and church authorities. Some recalled instances of religious training and rituals with either humor, nostalgia, or utter disgust. The "chore" or routine of Sunday mass was associated with some kind of stifling family influence many of these men have tried to escape. In addition, these men also recalled the kinds of oppressive and downright cruel experiences with religious personnel and practices. Weekends for many of these men are now more relaxed and are devoted to leisure activities. Some informants boasted that while many of their friends in the Philippines attended mass on Sundays, they, being Americanized, were fast asleep in their beds until noon.

A couple of informants complained about instances of discrepancies, ironies, and hypocrisies that enabled bakla Catholic devotees to participate actively in the church, which did not formally acknowledge their existence. The church denied homosexual behavior but not the body of the bakla or gay man. These two men reiterated the rhetoric of many gay and lesbian activists who railed against the church as being homophobic.

Some would say that they have lost the kind of "superstitious" or even "idolatrous" style of Catholic worship prevalent in the Philippines. Thus, the church and religion were seen as anachronous objects that needed to be discarded. As one informant aptly said, "When I entered America, I left a lot of things behind, including my religious beliefs." However, this shift to a more secular view by those who professed to agnostic or atheistic beliefs was tempered by specific situations where informants reported a kind of renewal or revivification of dormant beliefs in crucial moments such as crises and tragedies. In chapter 6, I describe one such situation involving the AIDS pandemic. Religious beliefs were also revivified at other times of hardship, including financial problems and other kinds of death. For example, Dodie, who said proudly that he did not go to church on Sundays, admitted that he frequented church more often when his mother died in the Philippines and when he was about to be interviewed for his green card.

Another example was Raul, whose mother died a few months before I interviewed him. He talked about "coming back" to the church. He said, "It used to be, wa ko type magsimba o magdasal pero after my mother died, I decided mabuti pa na magdasal uli kasi nanakaalis ng lungkot." [I used to dislike going to mass or praying, but after my mother died I decided it would be good to pray since it takes away the loneliness.] In both cases, life crises became a catalyst for these men to recall their initial distancing from the church and to return to practicing religion.

In sum, religion and religious practices are seen as distinctive markers of "Filipinoness." The dominant idea among many of my informants was that if you needed to look for any bakla, you could find them either in a drag beauty contest or in a church. Like the rosary ritual and as Gerardo's words would attest, religion is a central symbolic anchor for many Filipino gay men and an indelible part of their everyday lives.

Queer Habits and Queer Routes to Modernity

The two stories of Alden and Roldan and the stories of the other Filipino gay men affirm the view that immigrants, particularly those from the Third World, "always perceive themselves onstage, their lives resembling a mediocre fiction with occasional romantic outbursts and gray dailiness" (Boym 1998: 502). In other words, citizenship for queers of color and diasporic queers is neither a birthright nor is it about the romance of dissidence and resistance, but is about struggling to create scripts that will enable them to survive. Such queers are compelled to perform various kinds of negotiations, such as those made by Roldan, whose stunning self-reflexive statement about becoming bakla as part of immigration reflects the multiple routes available to queers in the diaspora as well as the Philippines.

In this chapter, informants constantly recognized the range of scripts and processes of scripting available to them in instances of quotidian articulations of class, family, religion, and race relationships, practices, and identities. The drama of everyday life for Filipino gay men involves complex maneuverings in relation to class, religion, family, and racial/ethnic differences. For example, Filipino gay men contest hegemonic practices such as racist and racialized Orientalist beliefs and behaviors by acknowledging the disjunction between images and ideas and the range of possible action in everyday life. A Filipino drag queen is not the unwitting dupe in a play of racist images but an active participant in the reformulation and deployment of such images in everyday life.

Moreover, Filipino gay men's sense of belonging, or cultural citizenship, is performed within competing scripts of self-formation. Becoming American, seen as a kind of autonomy from pressures of family, strict religious rules, and overt class and racial difference, is negotiated with persisting ties to the church, the biological family, and the social hierarchies that were part of growing up in the Philippines.

Filipino gay men also experience the displacement of diasporic life from the difficulties of living away from familiar systems of support to encountering new kinds of social ties such as "fuck buddies." However, these men also experience a kind of pleasure and a process of settling in from their sense of marvel at the kinds of things that are available to them. Far from being either completely forlorn and displaced or extremely assimilated and content, Filipino gay men encounter and engage varied and complicated conjunctions of Filipino and American social, cultural, and political practices and categories in multiple ways.

Indeed, everyday performance is suffused with the complexities of problems and issues and the range of possible dramaturgical styles of engagement. In other words, unlike a scripted ritual or a stage show, Filipino gay men's acts go beyond the strictures of textual genres and perform strategies in confronting differences such as class or race. The illuminating fact about everyday life, as the initial quote at the beginning of the chapter suggests, is that quotidian struggles are not complete theatrical works with beginnings and endings. Rather, as we have seen with the Philippine and American corners in Alden's studio apartment and with Roldan's routines, the drama of everyday life is about the continuities and discontinuities of negotiations and crossings between gay and bakla traditions, Filipino and American norms, and varied cultural practices and identities.

The space of the everyday as in Alden's apartment portrays an ironic kind of movement inherent in settling in. His narrative also portrays the possibility of performance in the global/local stage. That is, the story of his apartment narrates in spatial terms the constant engagements with experiences of emplacement and displacement. While physical distance from his family and the Philippines has allowed Alden to create his intimate, seemingly private local space, the routine intrusions and almost habitual hauntings of familial images, voices, and sentiments of both family and organized religion unravel the "locality" of his Village studio and showcase its transnational connections.

The Philippine corner and the American wall reconstruct national landscapes, but also are spatialized translations of desire and propriety. The grammars of desire and propriety are expressed in the kinds of situational and diachronic movement between guilt and pleasure, and between land of settlement and the homeland. It is perhaps no wonder that Alden, who has not been home, realizes a kind of homecoming when certain sentiments arise after sexual encounters or after missing his usual weekly overseas phone call to his family. The ambivalence and troubled relationship between "being at home" and "homecoming" beset queer immigrants like Alden.

Diasporic people today are confronted with the challenge of creating multistranded relationships with the homeland and their new land of settlement. No longer is assimilation the only fate for the present day immigrant. Immigrants are compelled and propelled by new developments in technology and by increasing mobility of capital to devise a flexible performative repertoire that increases their survival and success in an increasingly unequal yet global world. Familial ties for both Alden and Roldan, as well as for many of my informants, mark the continuity and discontinuity of the immigrant experience. Phone calls, monetary remittances, and regular trips back to the homeland rescue the queer immigrant from this assimilative fate.

Roldan's mental and physical reflections in front of his mirror on a workday reveal how the routine regimes of race and gender permeate if not infect daily assessment of situations involving confrontations, disputes, and obedience. Roldan's astute observation of the forms of racialization in America and its articulation with gender points to the power of his daily experiences and their impact on identity. Because of this situation, bakla as an identity becomes a possibility in the metropolis. While bakla is seen as rooted to the homeland, it becomes a tool to negotiate Roldan's cultural discomfort with mainstream gay public life. At the same time, Roldan's move is not a retreat from modernity; rather, it unwittingly destabilizes a monolithic gay identity. Roldan's recuperation of bakla, of alienation to both transgender and gay identity politic, are the result of the kinds of daily barrage of images, ideas, and bodies in the global city.

The intimate spaces and routines of the everyday may be seen by many as a kind of "retreat from wordliness" on the part of an individual or as a kind of warm refuge of authenticity bounded from the harsh realities of the public sphere (Boym 1998: 500), but as many of my informants have unwittingly performed, for immigrants and exiles the everyday is an incomplete if not imperfect colonization of the wildness and trauma of displacement (ibid.: 499–500). The everyday is an important arena open to manipulation and intrusions by the state. Roldan's fear of being caught by the INS or other authorities extends to his practice of cross-dressing and his cultural discomfort with gay mainstream practices. His routines are tracked by his own fear of being found out as an illegal alien while at the same time he consciously accepts his place in the queer cultural world in New York City. He realizes that the script, or more appropriately the drama of dissimulation, is crucial for his legal, cultural, and physical survival. His marginal status in relation to what is considered authentic forms of citizenship and belonging compels him to refigure his routines and recreate his biyuti in America.

Filipino gay men's actions and reactions to diasporic life refuse to cohere into one totalizing narrative. Despite the kind of gay lifestyle ascribed to men in the gay community, Filipino gay men's quotidian experiences reject the kind of homogenizing tendency of what is seen as a gay ghetto or "circuit" way of life. Filipino gay men are in fact continually positioning and repositioning their performances and themselves through varying modes of drama and biyuti depending on the kinds of exclusions and affinities they face in daily life. In the next chapter, I take these insights from Filipino gay men's everyday life and use them in a detailed discussion of a "staged" public performance.

Diasporic queers in particular refuse the assimilative framework not because they carry with them much of the baggage of tradition but that — to use the idioms of biyuti and drama — their sense of selfhood and belonging are framed in the process of cultural translation and transformation. Indeed, the concepts of biyuti and drama partake of this negotiated space between tradition and modernity. Their deployment by Filipino immigrant men living in New York City points to the kinds of negotiation that create an "imperfect aesthetics of survival" (Boym 1998: 524) as well as a counter-narrative to the prevailing view of the immigrant route as a movement away from tradition in the homeland and toward an assimilated modern life in the land of settlement. Moreover, these idioms constitute what can be considered as an alternative form of modernity (Gaonkar 1999). The bakla is neither a ludic nor anachronous figure, but a subject in constant mediation, whose modernity is not always dependent on Western mainstream queer culture. Therefore, the everyday struggles of queer subjects such as Filipino gay men form a strategic path leading not to a teleologically determined home but rather to other more exciting possibilities.

Five

"To Play with the World": The Pageantry of Identities

Ano ang diperensiya ng pagrarampa sa beauty pageant sa harap ng maraming utaw at pagrarampa sa kalye mo? Wala! Pareho pa rin ang dramang dinadala mo. Basta, hayaan mo ang biyuti mo.

[What is the difference between walking down a beauty pageant ramp in front of a lot of people and walking down the street in your neighborhood? None! You still carry the same drama. Just let your biyuti lead the way.] — LEILANI

Leilani's provocative observation breaks down the artificial demarcation between performance in everyday life and performance in a structured ritual such as a beauty pageant. As he suggests, the same kind of drama is in operation. The previous chapter revolved around the issues of quotidian struggles and identity expression. The inchoateness of everyday life masked important nodes of identity articulation such as the family, religion, class, and race. In this chapter, I utilize these nodes to analyze the public negotiations of Filipino gay men between the Filipino bakla tradition and American/Western practices and beliefs around gay identity. I focus on a detailed analysis of a public cultural event, a cross-dressing performance of a Catholic ritual, the Santacruzan by Kambal sa Lusog, a group of Filipino gay men and lesbians, to showcase the poetics of the Filipino gay diasporic experience. I conceptualize the ritual as a public arena in which individual and collective identities of Filipino gay immigrants are articulated and represented. In particular, I briefly demonstrate that identity formation among this group of diasporic men and women involves the incorporation and creative amalgamation of practices and ideas from different historical, cultural, religious, geographic, gender, racial, and class locations including colonialism and folk Catholicism.

With the historical shift from a gendered homosexuality to gay identity in Western societies, cross-dressing becomes a kind of borderland in which other such historical moments are replayed and refigured.[1] At the same time, cross-dressing has been disparaged as a premodern vestige of an archaic homosexuality that existed before Stonewall. Contrary to this view, I deploy cross-dressing in this chapter as a space or arena of contestation and rearticulation of identities and a strategic practice in refiguring difference and hierarchy. I position this argument in relation to the notion of the bakla as cross-dresser and how this is articulated with prevailing hypermasculine images and ideals in the mainstream gay community. Most importantly, I argue that cross-dressing practices and rituals are vehicles and spaces through which Filipino gay men in New York City create and promulgate their sense of belonging and citizenship amid competing images and practices of the "gay community" and the nation.

The Performance: A Cross-Dressing Santacruzan

In March 1991, Filipino queers in New York City established an organization called Kambal sa Lusog, which literally means "twins in health," but is interpreted as "comrades in the struggle." Kambal sa Lusog was unique among the city's Asian gay groups because it included gay men, lesbians, and bisexuals. The reasons given for creating the organization vary. Some members said that the group was formed in part owing to the controversy surrounding the production of the

Broadway show *Miss Saigon* and the decision by Lambda Legal Defense (a national gay and lesbian civil liberties group) not to cancel its benefit for the gala opening of the show. The broader context of the controversy, which I have discussed in an earlier work (Manalansan 1993), revolved around the alleged racist hiring practices and the Orientalist overtones of the play's libretto and narrative. The controversy within New York's gay and lesbian community left Filipino gay men in an awkward position. Many Filipino gay men were ambivalent about the controversy because Lea Salonga, a Filipina, was the star of the show. Filipino cross-dressers were known to appropriate images and songs from the show, but a few other Filipinos were steadfast in their opposition.

One of the founders of the group offered another explanation for its formation. He suggested that many Filipinos did not relate to other Asians or to an Asian identity. This belief was shared by other Filipino gay men. Many informants perceived the term *Asian* only in terms of geography and believed that significant differences existed between other Asians and themselves. They perceived *Asian* to mean East Asians—Japanese, Korean, and Chinese. A number of informants mentioned having more cultural affinity with Latinos. Thus, many felt that their interests as gay men were not being served by a group like GAPIMNY (Gay Asian Pacific Islander Men of New York), which was largely composed of East Asian men.

Kambal sa Lusog met as a group every month at the Lesbian and Gay Community Center in Manhattan and published a newsletter. They held fundraisers and other group activities such as socials, video/ film screenings, and discussion sessions. The Santacruzan, held in August 1992, was one of the group's fundraising activities that also attracted Filipino gay men and lesbians who were nonmembers. This traditional Filipino ritual evoked the kind of community and identity formation Filipino gay men in the area were struggling to achieve.

The Santacruzan is an important traditional Catholic celebration in the Philippines and began as a response to the radical changes caused by Spanish colonization, which started in 1521 and ended with the conclusion of the Spanish-American War in 1898. Celebrated every May, the Santacruzan has been appropriately called the "Queen of All Filipino Fiestas." The procession, which essentially begins and ends at a church, is a symbolic reenactment of the discovery of Christ's cross by Queen Helena, or Reyna Elena, the mother of Emperor Constantine of the Holy Roman Empire. The ritual enacts a pivotal event in Emperor Constantine's life. According to popular lore, Emperor Constantine, a non-Christian, had a dream that he would win a battle if his soldiers would mark their shields with the cross. When he did as his dream suggested, he won the battle. Grateful about the outcome, Constantine urged his mother to look for the cross. The procession builds on this basic story.

The ritual combines biblical myth with world history (from medieval times to the modern era). The procession includes a series of *sagalas* (muses). These sagalas are a constantly changing coterie of personages, which makes it possible to adapt the ritual to changing historical and cultural contexts. Because of this characteristic, the procession has become more than a religious procession of biblical figures. It has been transformed into a pageant of Philippine history. Although the main character in this ritual is always Reyna Elena, the creation of new muses or personages in each performance of the ritual is constrained only by the imagination of the people staging the procession.

In the Philippines, the important figures in the Santacruzan processions are usually portrayed by women with male escorts. Apart from the bishop of Jerusalem (who is not portrayed frequently), Constantino is the only named male figure who is usually played by a child (either male or female). In typical performances of the ritual, young women from a particular town or city district are chosen to participate. To be chosen is perceived to be a singular honor for both the woman and her family. Like some kind of postcolonial potlatch, the procession is constructed as a showcase of family pride and honor, not simply for the women's family but also for the families who sponsor a feast and, in some cases, underwrite the expenses of putting up the Santacruzan. Sponsoring a Santacruzan means that a family or household must spend a lot of money on food and decoration, and sometimes on the gowns of the Santacruzan queens. Failure to do so would bring shame to the families concerned. In addition to individual families' honor, at stake are the town or district's collective pride and solidarity. Comparisons between the scale of different towns' Santacruzans become part of the rivalries and lore between neighboring districts.

Many Filipinos regard the Santacruzan as the quintessential Filipino ritual despite its foreign roots. Travel posters, school textbooks, and tourism advertisements usually include an image of this ritual. Nowhere else is the Filipino's appreciation for spectacles such as beauty contests given free rein and imbued with theological relevance. There have been cases when cross-dressed men have participated in these processions. In fact, one of these "infamous" Santacruzans is held in Pasay City (one of the cities in the metropolitan Manila area). Informants who had participated in cross-dressing Santacruzan processions in the Philippines reported that the content and symbols of these performances were no different from the traditional women-lead processions. The procession was still a kind of popularity contest in which each queen's popularity was gauged by the number of people (especially young men) who followed her. After the cross-dressing procession and feast, the cross-dressers reported gathering together their choices of men and slipping away to secluded areas to have sex while still in their gowns.

These cross-dressing processions are possible because of a long tradition of male cross-dressers in other spectacular venues such as the *karnabal* or *perya* (carnival or fair). As I mentioned in chapter 3, the bakla is popularly seen as the ultimate mimic or expert in physical transformation (Cannell 1991). Stereotypically, the bakla is viewed as an artisan in crafts that involve mimicry and transformation such as lip-synching, cosmetology, and female impersonation. The cross-dressing Santacruzan is merely the logical extension of such views and ideas into the realm of practice.

The lineup of personages in the New York City reenactment of the Santacruzan included a combination of reconfigured traditional figures and newly created characters. Significantly, unlike the usual Santacruzan in which interpretation of a sagala or personage is more collectively controlled, each sagala was individually reconfigured by each performer. Each performer was assigned a character but was left to craft and create his or her own persona and costume whether or not it conformed to the scripted roles of the queens. Some individuals actually made up "new" sagalas that went beyond the religious and mythical components of the Santacruzan. Unlike the typical Santacruzan, this particular Manhattan performance of the Santacruzan was not presented as a procession, but as a fashion show. The focal point of the show was the stage and runway. At center stage, before the runway began, was a floral arch reminiscent of the mobile arches of flowers that are carried through the streets for each mythical or historical personage in the usual procession.

The audience also responded differently. During the usual Santacruzan processions, the people who line the streets or take part in the procession usually carry candles, sing religious hymns, and/or pray. However, in this gay rendition, the audience hollered and screamed phrases of encouragement that come right out of vogueing, or house culture, phrases like "work it girl." In the typical Santacruzan, the popularity of specific queens was seen in terms of the number of people who lighted her way through the procession and formed part of her entourage; in this case, audience applause and comments became the barometer of popularity. In a double departure from the traditional procession in which Emperor Constantine is usually portrayed by a male or female child, this version featured a man clad in Speedos. In the usual procession, Constantino would move along the route to act as Reyna Elena's escort. In the Manhattan performance, he remained on stage during the whole time to escort each queen from the side of the stage to the runway. He resembled the macho or exotic dancers/strippers who performed in many gay bars in the Philippines and New York.

The other traditional muses were also reinterpreted in complex and hilarious ways. Reyna Banderada, or the Queen of the Flag, who usually carried the Philippine flag, incorporated the symbols of the flag in a slinky outfit. In this deconstruction of the Philippine flag, the three stars were strategically placed, one over each nipple and a third over the crotch. A mask of the sun was carried by this new version of the motherland, who eschewed the prescribed demure walk for a prancing display of seductive and slutty poses. Reyna de la Libertad, or the Queen of Liberty, was dressed as a dominatrix complete with a whip. Her costume was composed of straps and pieces of black leather that strategically left parts of her body—notably the derriere—teasingly exposed. During the performance, Reyna de la Libertad pranced menacingly at the audience and before stepping down from the stage he simulated whipping the behind of Constantino. Rosa Mistica, or Mystical Rose, a theological emblem for the Virgin Mary and not an actual person, was wearing a multicolored, sequined cocktail dress. Many people in the audience started snickering when someone said "Fourteenth Street Special," meaning that the dress was bought in a bargain store. Both Rosa Mistica's interpretation and the audience response suggested the mutual recognition not only of the theatrical or comedic form of drag but also of the way the drag persona fulfilled the demands of "femme realness."

A new kind of queen was created for this presentation in the person of Reyna Chismosa, or the Queen of Gossip. Clad in a tacky dressing gown and hair curlers, Reyna Chismosa screamed on a cordless phone, then walked up and down the stage teasing people from the audience while they egged him on. He also worked the audience to a teetering frenzy by screaming bitchy comments like "Your mother said that you should go home" to individuals he singled out in the crowd.

The three Virtues were the only figures portrayed by lesbians. Two wore denim shorts, combat boots, and *barong tagalog* (the traditional Filipino male formal attire) while the third wore a cocktail dress. The "femme" or feminine lesbian was the only Virtue to walk the runway. Like Constantino, the other two remained on the side and acted as escorts.

Reyna Sentenciada, or the Queen of Justice, usually portrayed carrying scales of justice or blindfolded with her hands tied in front of her, was again dressed in leather sadomasochistic dominatrix garb and dark sunglasses. His hands were tied by a black leather strap as he took to the runway, and he untied himself at the center of the stage. Before he left the stage, Reyna Sentenciada lifted his wig to reveal his bald head.

Another muse was the Infanta Judith, or Judith of Bethulia, who saved her people from the domination of the Assyrians under the leadership of a man named Holofernes. In the biblical account, Judith seduced Holofernes and beheaded him. In this performance, which was held during the 1992 presidential election campaigns, Judith came out as a Greek goddess dressed in flowing robes; instead of the head of Holofernes, the gay Judith revealed the head of George Bush.

However, the finale of the show returned to tradition as Reyna Elena and Emperatriz (the empress) came out dressed in traditional gowns and tiaras. Reyna Elena carried flowers and an antique cross as all Reyna Elenas have done in the past. There was no attempt at camp; rather, there was an insistence on, to use a word from vogueing, or house culture, "femme realness" in deference to tradition. Or more appropriately, there was a return to the kind of mimicry or imitation that was valorized in the Philippines.

Walking through the Runway of Difference

The Santacruzan as a ritual provides a heuristic dimension that furthers the understanding of its performers. Clifford Geertz (1986: 373), paraphrasing Victor Turner, writes:

It is with expressions — representations, objectifications, discourses, performances, whatever — we traffic: a carnival, a mural, a curing rite, a revitalization movement, a clay figurine, an account of a stay in the woods. Whatever sense we have of how things stand with someone else's [or some other group's] inner life, we gain it through their expressions, not through some magical intrusion into their consciousness. It's all a matter of scratching surfaces.

Rituals are important social practices because they present a metacommentary on the world (Bruner 1986: 26). For an immigrant or exilic group, "rituals provide the terrain in which the consciousness of communal boundaries is heightened, thereby confirming and strengthening individual location and positionality as well as social identity" (Naficy 1991: 295).

In a world where identity is not rooted or territorialized within a specific place, rituals become the signs at the crossroads. Rituals, which are public arenas of liminality, provide the most appropriate points of departure in trying to apprehend the lives of a group of diasporic gay men of color since as James Clifford has noted, "Diasporic histories may not be necessary conditions for developing performative visions of gender, sexuality, race and ethnicity, but their liminal spaces, displaced encounters and tactical affiliations provide apt settings for such visions" (1994: 331). The queer performance of the Santacruzan creates a vital liminal site in which the conjunctions of identities, cultures, histories, and geographies are played out and performed.

The combination of secular, profane, and religious imagery as well as the combination of Filipino and American gay/mainstream icons provided an arena where symbols from the two countries were contested, dismantled, and reassembled in a dazzling series of cross-contestatory statements. I consider this ritual as a perverse, dissident, or transgressive performance of identities. Not only did the elements of the ritual deviate from the dominant regimes of meaning, they did so through inversion, subversion, and reversal of dominant symbols (Dollimore 1991). This particular perverse performance was structured according to the following multiple hierarchical, or power, arrangements, which are mutually reinforcing:

God — Men
Sacred — Profane

Men — Women
White — Nonwhite
Colonizer — Colonized
Adopted Land — Homeland

These hierarchies reflect both the colonial and postcolonial experiences of Filipinos with Spain and the United States. The images and practices in the ritual were in part due to what a popular Filipino cliché explains as "more than three hundred years in the convent [with Spain] and thirty years of Hollywood [with the United States]."

The partial secularization of the ritual allowed a wider range of social commentary. First, the head of George Bush enabled the group to make a political statement during the 1992 presidential election. It localized this transnational performance by an allusion to this important American political event. Furthermore, it pointed to the putative citizenship status of the performers by providing a space for a momentary critique of the then ruling regime. These men were able to make some provisional statements regarding their need to address questions about sexual freedom. As we have seen in performers' translation and reinterpretation of Liberty, these statements involved articulations of Filipino gay men's emancipation from the inabilities of Philippine and U.S. governments and established religion to deal with issues of homosexuality. Moreover, this ritual's concession to American colonial rule became a complex icon of American imperial expansion, Filipinos' postcolonial reconfiguration, and gay immigrants' idealization of homophilic spaces of New York. Reyna Libertad did not symbolize the promise of economic prosperity for immigrants. Rather, her persona enacted the breaking of the chains of sexual puritanism and the conquest of new frontiers.

The characters of Reyna Banderada and Reyna Chismosa represented a kind of oscillation between idioms of vulgar sexuality and comedic domesticity. The spectacular Reyna Banderada, flimsily garbed in the diaphanous colors of the Philippine flag, reconceptualizes *Inang Bayan*, or the motherland, by wresting it away from its virginal and maternal tropes. Together with the half-naked figure of Constantino, Reyna Banderada invoked, defied, and hyper-performed the stringent national rules regarding the representation and handling of the Philippine flag. These rules, learned by all Filipino schoolchildren and by men in compulsory military training, were not really about the proper handling of the flag but about acceptable display of patriotism. Therefore, Reyna Banderada is an embodiment of the transgression of "love of country."

Reyna Chismosa is an anomalous addition to the usual coterie of mythical and biblical characters. The persona combined the stereotypic dichotomy of housewife and whore prevalent in many cross-dressing events. However, the character was not just any housewife, but rather a Western or Westernized one who had the economic means to stay at home and gossip on the phone. Such a domestic persona was in sharp contrast to the glamorous figures of the other queens. He subverted the "proper" notion of the Santacruzan sagala, or muse, and provided an ironic figure that questioned the regal-religious status of the whole ritual. Signifying the liminal space of the domestic/private sphere, Reyna Chismosa confronted the forbidding image of the public arena (church and state) and parodied the notion of a sagala, or muse, which were usually figures from historico-mythical realms. The phone, in part, symbolizes one of the main connections of diasporic Filipinos to their homeland. More importantly, Reyna Chismosa provides an apt analogue to both church and government as instruments of surveillance. But gossip is perhaps one of the integral strategies of resistance of oppressed people against hegemonic structures and agents. The process of gossip, which according to my informants is a regular activity of Filipinos both gay and straight, provides one possible way of communication among equals in defiance of a superordinate arrangement.

The juxtaposition of religious elements with secularized, profane, and sexualized images not only allowed a wider range of social commentary (e.g., George Bush's head) but also enabled the men to construct shifting notions of here and there. The sexualized images relocated the ritual from a religious domain to a gay terrain, thereby mimicking the movements and tensions between the nation of birth and the nation of settlement. Such shifts unravel the instability of the notion of "home."

Such a tropic play emphasized the shifting nature of locations and spaces. Implicit in the structure of this ritual performance were the mercurial notions of here and there. The sexualized images relocate the rituals from the religious domain to a gay terrain. The remapping achieved in this ritual establishes the tension between the nation of birth and the nation of settlement, thereby unraveling the exigencies of home. While a literal reading of the ritual may see it as an echo of the secularization process that supposedly happens to Filipinos in the diaspora, I suggest otherwise. My discussion in the previous chapter and the finale in the performance with Reyna Elena in the proper religious and cultural attire manage to "bring it all home" and create an underlying religious aesthetic that permeates not only the spectacular sites but also the quotidian spaces of Filipino gay men in the diaspora.

Invisible Baggage, Drag Persona, and Nostalgia

Apart from marking difference, nostalgia was an important element in the Santacruzan pageant. The pageant was a way of "resurrecting time and place" (Stewart 1992: 252) for the largely immigrant group of Filipinos present that evening, as well as a way of revivifying memory and feelings of reterritorialization. As one informant said, "It made me feel like I was in Manila again." Cross-dressing, therefore, was a vehicle for nostalgia. It accomplished this by shattering "the surface of an atemporal order" (ibid.). While this production may have had its distinctive elements, it nevertheless enabled them to think of other Santacruzan productions in the cities and towns of their childhoods. To some extent, the Santacruzan is part of the invisible baggage that they brought with them from their childhoods and that propelled them to travel back through their memories of "being there." Even those who were born and raised in California talked about how the Santacruzan was a major event in their childhoods, and one of the few times they felt they were "Filipinos."

The shock of the familiar, particularly in the finale with Reyna Elena, had a tremendous impact on many of the Filipino gay men present. Nostalgia revivified the image and memory of the Filipino homeland while at the same time acknowledging their settlement in a new home here in the United States. Paradoxically, it not only created an invigorating energy in which to imagine a "parallel comradeship" among these men, but also established a defiant marker of difference from the rest of America. As one informant noted, "Iba talaga tayong mga Pilipinong bakla. [We Filipino bakla are really different.] When we get together we are able to express something that goes beyond the usual petty quarrels, gossips, and jealousies."

The links between nostalgia and cross-dressing were further exemplified by a Filipino cross-dresser whose drag names included Miss

Saudi, as he had worked in the Middle East before coming to the States, and Sarsi Emmanuel, the name of a B-movie starlet in Manila during the 1980s. I met him at the New Manila, a restaurant owned and operated by Filipinos in Queens, the site of a big Filipino enclave. On this night (already discussed a bit in chapter 3) the usual karaoke segment was the first in a series of performances that highlighted sentimental folksy tunes such as Simon and Garfunkel's "Homeward Bound" and the ballads of Barbra Streisand. Afterward, while tables filled with regular customers, families with children eating Filipino food, a special event took place, a talent and beauty contest involving cross-dressing Filipino gay men. I was able to interview Sarsi, who organized the contest, and the two contestants, who discussed their chosen drag names and personas. Sarsi commented on the evening's events:

> Hindi ba tayo kakaiba? Ang galing nating mangaya? Nakita mo ba yung mamang kumakanta ng Frank Sinatra? Sugro kahit na walang blue eye, magaling talaga—no? Noong kumakanta siya parang na-isip ko yung mga English songs napinapatugtog sa radio station sa Maynila. Ano nga ba yon? Ay, nahohomesick na ako. Well, sa tingin ko mas magaling tayong mga bakla. Tingnan mo 'ko at ang name ko. O 'di va? Di' mo ba hinahanap ang mga Tagalog movies? Hindi ko lang nireremind ang mga Pinoy dito tungkol sa Pilipinas. Ako mismo ang laman ng mga memories nila. Kamukha ko siya, 'di va?

> [Aren't we Filipinos unique? We are so good at imitating. Did you see that man sing Frank Sinatra? . . . I guess despite the lack of blue eyes, he was really great, don't you think? He was singing that song that reminded me of the other popular English songs played on Manila radio stations . . . what was it? . . . I was getting homesick. Well, I think we bakla are even better. Take a look at me and my name . . . O 'di va? (Isn't it?) Don't you feel nostalgic about Tagalog films? I don't remind Filipinos here about the Philippines—I embody those memories—I look like her (like Sarsi), don't I?]

Memories of the homeland and the issue of postcolonial cultural and psychic displacement persist in many Filipino gay immigrant lives. Sarsi's image of his drag persona as memory invoking was similar to the power of the Santacruzan. It belied not only nostalgia but the very construction of the Santacruzan as multiply transplanted from Spain, then the Philippines, and now America. More importantly, it called to mind the mimicry that was seen as the natural fate of Philippine and other postcolonial cultures and peoples. Sarsi's ironic and defiant statement, however, recognizes mimicry's potential for engaging with inherently unequal relationships, such as the relationship between hegemonic Hollywood icons and non-Western performers (Cannell 1999).

Sarsi's symptomatic, succinct, and brilliant statement of embodying memory or provoking homesickness is not an altogether isolated case. Other drag names and personas of Filipino gay men that I have encountered in different situations were again those of starlets or big Tagalog movie stars, as well as the names of specific places in the Philippines: Maria Christina Falls, Anna de Manila, Cory Antipolo, Lily Ermita, and the like. With the exception of Manila, only the well-traveled or geographically well-informed non-Filipino would be able to decipher these names.

For these Filipino gay men names are like coded messages, which on the one hand locate them temporally and spatially, while on the other hand provide them with mnemonic fuses. Through the process of imitating familiar gestures — acting demure or bitchy, holding the butterfly sleeve of the *terno* (the female native costume) — or familiar physical characteristics (e.g., a mole or long hair in a bouffant), these men are able to evoke memories of people and events from another time and space.

Far from being just a remnant or a vestige of homosexual traditions from the homeland, cross-dressing has become a space for articulating and marking difference and a particular kind of modernity. For many of my informants, cross-dressing was an attempt to mimic real women. In contrast, they saw another kind of cross-dressing popular among Caucasians that revolved around parody. According to my informants, Caucasians used drag as a way to reveal the very constructiveness of the mimicry, that is, to parody the real. The pageant oscillated between this theatrical or comedic form of drag to a kind of "femme realness" cross-dressing. Filipino informants have made a point about how their cross-dressing style differed from that of Caucasian Americans.

The comedic figure of Reyna Sentenciada pulling off his wig to reveal a bald head was set against the demure, femme real Reyna Elena. One Filipino gay man who was a member of the audience said that Reyna Sentenciada's shocking act of pulling off the wig was not seen favorably by other Filipino gay men. While it was funny, he believed that showing the incongruity between dress and persona destroyed the entire purpose of cross-dressing. As he said, "The illusion died." The tension between these forms of drag was evident in the New York City Santacruzan. Shifts occurred between a kind of drag that most Filipino cross-dressers described as their own and in opposition to the parodic, scandalous, and comedic form of cross-dressing that they saw as a white or Western practice.

To understand this idea of cross-dressing properly,[2] it is necessary to locate the practice within a larger Filipino cultural context. The performative dynamics of Filipino cross-dressing practices have connections with the kinds of transformations and mimicry valued in healing, Catholic religious processions, and beauty pageants. As I have mentioned earlier in this book, mimicry plays a major part in Filipino Catholic culture. This is evident not only in the valued practice of imitating the lives of Jesus, the Virgin Mary, and the saints, but also in the performance of the Santacruzan and other religious processions and pageants. One unique form of supreme imitation and transformation is in the Penitensiya. During Holy Week, adult males in different parts of the Philippines reenact the sufferings of Jesus Christ from the flogging and scourging to the crucifixion. Such reenactment involves "real" whips and in some cases actual nailing to the cross. This kind of imitation of Christ's suffering is perceived to be a kind of penance for the forgiveness of sins, and as such is a way of negotiating with the Supreme Other.

Such transformations are part of postcolonial culture and are symptomatic of the "damage" (to use a word from minority discourse) wrought by political, economic, and cultural imperialism (Lloyd 1996). Cannell (1991, 1999) suggested that imitation in lowland Filipino Catholic culture is a way of negotiating and engaging with various real and imagined others. In many of the beauty pageants (both gay and straight) and singing contests in the Bicol town where she conducted ethnographic fieldwork, the appreciation and valorization of any performance are not merely about taking on the dress of another gender or singing a popular English song, but putting on the trappings of another place, an Other culture—the America of Filipinos dreams. For the Filipino bakla who has indeed crossed the borders, living in New York City—the iconic place for America—mimicry is transformed from a longing for an America whose physical space he now occupies into a struggle for a symbolic place in the U.S. social imaginary.

Mimicry, in the context of the Santacruzan, fully exposes the ambivalence on which it is founded. Cross-dressing for these Filipinos, as exemplified by the Manhattan Santacruzan, articulated an aesthetics that engaged other forms of "distance" with the white hegemonic world and realigned their relationships to other groups such as the home country and Latino and black gay men. Unlike "femme realness," which does not take into consideration the subjectivity and historicity of the performer, Filipino gay performers, while adhering to ideal "realness," also possess the baggage of history and culture. That is, they hail from the only former U.S. colony and the only predominantly Catholic country in Asia.

Such "baggage" as exemplified in the Santacruzan performance produces the excess that transforms mimicry from mere simulacrum to a strategy that questions colonial and postcolonial power. The idiom of "playing with the world," usually uttered by Filipino cross-dressers, wrests the feminine ideal as object of scrutiny and spectacle into a vital medium in negotiating the interplay of difference, borders, and hierarchies. Though not an annual event, the 1992 Santacruzan should not be seen as an idiosyncratic act, nor merely as an amusing entertainment fortuitously stumbled upon by an eager ethnographer. Rather, the ritual performance was a complex bundle of meanings, a "moment" of critical conjunctions that suggested the critical dimensions of the Filipino gay diasporic experience.

Wearing Your Body: The Spectacle of Orientalism

This pageant, this reprocessed procession, provided the space in which differences were confronted, refigured, and juxtaposed. Many of the Filipino gay men present were able to recognize the division or borders between these two kinds of cross-dressing practices. It raised the very notion of racialized spaces in the gay community in New York City, as I have described in chapter 2. This ritual provided Filipino gay men symbolic access to spaces where they were not visible or even allowed to enter. This was made more explicit by the use of icons from different American gay traditions: the muscular Constantino as a paean to white mainstream gay culture's hypermasculine images; the paraphernalia of the gay leather set; the use of linguistic devices and cross-dressing practices from black and Latino voguers; and the use of shocking acts such as pulling off the wig from American camp modes.

The Santacruzan ritual performance mirrored the experience of displacement, dislocation, and discrimination felt by some Filipino gay informants. As I have described in the previous chapters, these informants are silenced by oppressive regimes and practices expressed in Orientalist terms even within the gay community. Informants have reported being seen as passive, exotic, and/or sexless creatures by other gay men. Many informants told me that they felt awkward or uncomfortable in gay sites and occasions that celebrate muscular bodies or traditions such as the leather culture. In many gay bars in New York City, race and ethnicity are clearly demarcated. As one informant said, "You just can't go anywhere. You have to know whether you will be the odd man out in bars. You have to know your place."

In the one-man show *Cinema Verite,* the Filipino gay performance artist Ralph Peña (n.d.: 16–17) played the lead character, Gerry. As he traipsed along the stage he mouthed these words: "Now, do I look Filipino to you? Do I? I mean, most times, I'm taken for any nationality but 'Filipine,' as some of them say. I myself am not sure if I am. I used to be. Oh I admit, I tried to hide my roots — literally. I dyed my hair red. I was going for pale blond, but with blue contact lenses I looked like a Siamese cat." These same words evoke memories of similar experiences among Filipino gay men. "How does one look?" The question highlights the corporeal aspect of race discourse. Many informants offered their own experiences regarding the way they "wore" their bodies. In other words, far from recognizing the immutability of their physical characteristics, Filipino gay men knew that an invasive surgical procedure is the not the only means by which to alter, revise, and configure their bodies. As one informant said, "You can live with what you've got. You just need to know how to project it to your admiring viewers."

Filipino gay men's corporeal strategies are shaped by many tensions, including prevailing Orientalist notions. Some instances of racialized and racist encounters such as those below may be perceived as merely irritating and vexing. Many informants would say either you learn to forget them, deal with them, or go crazy. However, there were many instances when some informants thought that particular encounters went beyond the benign and the irritating.

One informant who immigrated to the United States five years ago told me about the disquieting remarks made by some of his coworkers (a mixture of Caucasians, Latinos, and African Americans), all of whom were gay. He related how many of them would make fun of his accent and his unfamiliarity with particular idioms and icons. When several of them were talking about their childhood idols, one of them mentioned the name Bette Davis. He asked who that was, and they all looked at him. One African American said, "And what part of the jungle did you come from, East Mars? Darling, are you gay or are you E. T. Junior?"

Another informant told me how no one would talk to him in gay bars in upstate New York. He related how the gay cliques that formed in Albany never opened up to accept him, much less include him in any informal conversation. Rene, another informant who grew up in New York, talked about the time when a gang of young guys in Minnesota, where he lived for ten years before migrating to New York, just picked on him. I asked him whether he thought it was because he was gay or because he was Asian. He answered, "What's the difference?"

All of my informants were aware of the Oriental stereotype, but some did not think it a major problem. They felt that the Oriental stereotype fit their physical image, but they were insistent on not being passive or subordinate in their relationships and encounters with Caucasians. The kind of "native" body valorized by many Caucasian gay men who desire Asian men is characterized by having a short stature, dark complexion (light/yellow skin for those who have East Asian/Japanese/Chinese features), and a slim build. One informant called these highly desired features "the rice queen's delight." Interestingly, this valorization contrasts sharply with prevailing notions of skin color hierarchy in the Philippines. In the Philippines, the mestizo, or the white hybrid, is the valorized body. For many informants, this is not the case, at least in the interracial gay scene in New York City. Mario, a self-professed mestizo, or *tisoy,* bemoaned his predicament in a racially as well as class-laden monologue:

> Ay mama, hindi ako mabili sa mga rice bars. Hindi nila type ang pagka-tisay ko. Type nila ang mga mukhang native. Iniisnab ang biyuti ko dahil matangkad ako. Ang gusto nila mga DNG — you know, bansot! Excuse me, yung isa bakla na kamukha ng aming boy, mukhang nagtitinda ng diyaryo sa Manila, nakabingwit ng blondina. Nakakalukris talaga ang standards nila dito.

> [Oh mother, I am not marketable in the rice bars. They (Caucasians) don't prefer my mestizaness. They like those who look native.

They overlook my biyuti because I am tall. They like the DNG (did not grow) — you know the short ones. Excuse me, this one bakla (the previous night in a rice bar) who looked like our houseboy, he looked like he sold newspapers in Manila, he hooked a blond guy. Their (American gay men) standards are so crazy here.]

In the performance piece *Cinema Verite*, corporeal images were used by Gerry, the protagonist, to illustrate how race and desire construct the body within the space of the rice bar. "I go to this Asian bar in the Village, appropriately called: the paddy. Not to drink really. I'm not much for alcohol, you know, the svelte, starving, Third World look. Sometimes I meet some very interesting men here. I remember this guy coming up to me and asking me where I was from. 'The Philippines,' I said. He went on to ask, why is it that Asians all look alike?" (Peña n.d.: 10).

To designate a bar as a rice bar, as with dinge bars for black gay men or cha-cha bars for Latinos, reifies and fetishizes the corporeality of Asian men. The question, "Why is it that Asians look alike?" logically follows the structures of racist sentiments and attitudes that have given rise to such an institution. This is made more dramatic by the fact that Gerry is a gay man who immigrated to America only to find these effacing institutions, persons, and practices. Indeed, Gerry's question, "Do I look Filipino?" is a product of the erosion that has plagued him since he started imagining and desiring America.

In the late 1980s and early 1990s, Asian gay men were becoming politicized, particularly around racial politics in the gay community. There were strong separatist sentiments then around interracial gay relationships and cross-dressing. One of the popular beliefs at this time was the ideal of dating other Asian men only. This of course has been dealt with in the previous chapter, but apart from the metaphor of incest, there were a lot of anxieties among Filipino men who were active in Asian queer organizations. Another belief was not to cross-dress so as not to validate Orientalist ideas about Asian gay men. However, Filipino gay men have formed varied strategies in addressing and confronting Orientalist sentiments, ideas, and images in various ways in daily life. For example, Miss Java (the alias of a Filipino drag queen) may seem at first glance to be the quintessential Oriental "male." Miss Java (he has a long list of "exotic" names) came to the United States from the Philippines ten years ago. He is now thirty-five.

He lives with his lover, a Caucasian male of thirty-eight. Miss Java always used the feminine form when he talked about himself. "Well, my husband always wanted a very good geisha . . . well, he thought he got one . . . was he surprised!"

Miss Java and her lover played up the dichotomy mentioned in the various discursive forms (i.e., they went out as male and female even to straight public places; Miss Java was the wife and was called Nancy in their house; their conversations always pointed to the imagined gender difference between the two of them). Miss Java, however, provided a counterpoint to the beliefs about stereotypical Oriental queens. While he reveled in the physical difference between him and his tall (6′4″) lover, he emphasized that the roles and the physical disparity hid the total reversal of roles possible in particular instances. He said that while he played the bottom or passive partner in the sexual act, he was not the passive or demure partner in everyday life. In fact, he said, when he and his lover got into fights, his big lover was usually the one in tears afterward. He said that even though he cross-dressed, acted in an effeminate manner, and even seemed to be the "gorgeous housewife," he could still "kick ass." Miss Java reveals that the iconic or the visual image that he presents does not always directly index the complexity of the roles he and his partner take on in everyday life. He emphasizes the fact that this external hell is of his own choosing and completely volitional. Miss Java perceived his cross-dressing as a way of manipulating the world, of making himself desirable and making the world desire him. He used the words "to play with the world" *(paglaruan ang mundo),* to describe his drag persona, which in various contexts is meant to confuse, distract, and fool the public. The "deal" for Miss Java meant the struggle of everyday life. It was in this space where the oftentimes unnoticed and unwitting acts of resistance occurred.

Other informants who were not cross-dressers like Miss Java utilized other strategies such as bodybuilding. Unlike the stereotype, many of my informants participated in what is seen to be the typical gay pastime, going to the gym. Art, a gay Filipino in his thirties, emphasized the fact that he was "different from other Filipinos and other Asians" because he "looks" different. His body is bigger than that of other Asians. He said, "I go to the gym because I try not to look like the other Asian queens." Art thought that most Asian and Asian American gay men were very effeminate or were perceived as such. He said his activities such as joining sports organizations in the gay community were evidence of his struggle against being seen as the "typical Orien-tal." Moreover, he felt very strongly against cross-dressing, which he thought to be too demeaning and low class. In his relationships with other men, Art maintained that there were no gender-marked roles. He said that he had no "illusions" about being a woman trapped inside a man's body. He felt that his lifestyle was just like that of any straight guy except for the sexual part. Despite Art's view about the bakla, he still considered it an important image that continually influenced his view of himself.

Most Filipino gay men are neither cross-dressers nor body builders. However, all of them know about and acknowledge such Orientalized images and some even use them in maintaining some fantasy. Ricardo, a Filipino informant, observed, "Sometimes, a white guy comes over and he thinks I am fresh off the boat and in need of all the assistance he can provide. He will then buy me drinks, tell me how beautiful I am, and ask me out. Well, do I do it? Of course. I play the little innocent. So maybe I get dinner and some other perks — it is not so bad."

Race and racial difference, which are not popular discourses in the Philippines, acquire important dimensions for many of my informants. While only a few of them reported direct racial discrimination, they recognized that not all gay spaces were open to them. Some informants have told me of how they were ostracized by several gay establish-ments that catered to particular racial and class groupings. One infor-mant said, "I may be a doctor and wear expensive clothes, but when I go to [a predominantly white upper-class bar in the Upper East Side of Manhattan], I feel left out. Like I do not belong." Some have reported being hounded out of predominantly white or black gay bars. Others have complained about how the gay media does not consistently have many images of "people who look like them." The crucial markers of difference among bakla in the Philippines do not readily cross the borders to the United States.

Amid the realization of racial tensions and differences, there have been attempts by Filipino gay men to create ties and establish affinities with other groups of gay men. While racial stereotypes about the Chi-nese and Japanese and some aversion to being called "Asian" still exist among a few Filipino gay men, the situation in the gay community that lumps them into "Orientals" and ghettoizes them into rice bars has encouraged the creation of Asian gay men only groups. Hector, an-other informant, said:

I know we are very different from the other APIs [Asian and Pacific Islanders], but we're always placed in situations where we are together, and in fact whether we like it or not are oppressed together. Remember we are the gooks, chinks, and brown-skinned fags — even other fags can't seem to stand us. So, I think that if we are to survive in the gay world, we need to connect with other Asians. I used to think, what for? Now, I realize there are a lot of things we can do if we band together.

In many of these political activities and despite the initial political imbroglio about its political incorrectness, cross-dressing has provided a kind of anchor for the creation of affinities with other Asian men, Latinos, and African Americans. One informant suggested that cross-dressing among minorities or people of color contrasts sharply with white notions of drag. Vogueing or culture houses, as discussed in chapter 2, which are composed predominantly of Latino and African American gays and lesbians and are notorious for excluding or being particularly unfriendly toward Caucasians, have in many cases, been welcoming of Asians, specifically Filipinos. I witnessed a ball, or competition, where a Caucasian was dissed and booed while he was on the runway, while in the same category, a Filipino gay man who was a member of a house was wildly applauded. This Filipino voguer, or house member, rationalized the disparate reactions in this way:

> We know all too well that there are very few places where people like us can really feel at home. I know that some of my Filipino friends think that associating with Latinos and African Americans is kind of tacky, but tell me where can you find better cross-dressers than these guys? And where else can our skills as bakla be better appreciated than in those fabulous balls? White men are not really skilled. They are too big and too "unreal."

Orientalized stereotypes have the semblance of fixity. They exist in "eternal time" and are composed of essential elements that are seemingly unchanging (Bhabha 1992: 316). However, the image of the Orientalized male is not a monolithic and stable construction (Kondo 1990). Most importantly, Lisa Lowe (1991: x), in her theoretical exposition of Orientalism in French and British literature, notes that while Orientalism presents its objects as fixed, the contradictions and disjunctures within Orientalist discursive situations actually reveal the instability of this system of practices. Cross-dressing practices among Asian American queers are not always and already Orientalized. Filipino gay men's rituals, images, and everyday practices of cross-dressing, such as the Santacruzan, reveal the instability of Orientalist practices and demonstrate how these racist practices are less totalizing than what most activists' polemics assert. The situations revealed by many of the informants exemplify such moments of instability that allow for these Filipinos' particular dramas of engaging and contesting these practices in everyday life.

A Performer's Point of View: R. E. and Immigrant Imaginings

To understand further the dynamics of the Santacruzan event, it is beneficial to understand the ritual from the point of view of the performers. The following is a fragment of an interview with one of the ritual's performers. This fragment aims to provide biographical and personal anchors to the abstract analysis of the ritual that follows this section.

R. E. was twenty-three years old when I interviewed him in 1991. He was a student in an art school in Manhattan. The youngest in a large family of ten siblings, he came to the United States when he was eighteen. He was very excited to participate in the Santacruzan, particularly as he had been designated as the Reyna Elena, the central figure in the ritual. To be chosen as the Reyna Elena was an honor for anyone (man or woman). He said that as a child he used to watch annual Santacruzan pageants in his hometown in the southern Philippines, and that one of his dreams, apart from eventually living in America, was to be Reyna Elena. He said, "Ever since I was a small kid, I used to watch those spectacular parades and all I always dreamed was that one day I would be wearing a spectacular gown. Not just any ordinary sagala, for I wanted to be the center of attention — be the most stunning Reyna Elena of all time. When I came to the United States, I thought I would never be able to fulfill that dream. I thought that I would need to visit the Philippines to realize this dream."

R. E. had a dressmaker in the Philippines make a *maria clara*, a traditional Filipino costume, and borrowed his family's antique cross for the Santacruzan procession in Manhattan. These were then flown to New York a month before the event. After the Santacruzan at the Gay and Lesbian Community Center, I asked him whether he thought that it could have been different had his dream been fulfilled in the Philippines. He replied: "It would have been very traditional and not a lot of campy behavior in the parade. You know, we take the Santacruzan seriously in the Philippines, especially in our hometowns. As you saw, there were some of us [in the gay Santacruzan] who wanted to carry on with the tradition. I carried flowers and a cross."

However, he further remarked that despite the difference in the performance of the Manhattan pageant, it would not have been possible for him to participate in a similar one in the Philippines. "My family would not have approved. We are one of the more prominent families in the province. They may know that I am bakla, but it would have been shameful. You see unlike the straight Santacruzan where it is an honor to be a participant, the drag Santacruzan is more like a sideshow albeit with a religious element. I guess the distance between my family and me has allowed me the freedom to do this."

I asked him how he felt when he was on stage in costume. He confessed: "I knew I was in Manhattan, in Greenwich Village, on stage at the Community Center, but in my mind I was back in the Philippines, in my hometown, walking through the streets where I used to play as a child. People I know and whom I grew up with were singing hymns and lighting my way. I felt like I was back home." For R. E., the culmination of childhood dreams in America came as a delightful surprise. He saw these dreams as both continuous and discontinuous with his original ideals.

> I know I would never have the same opportunity in the Philippines, but then again, even if I were able to join the drag Santacruzan in Manila, it would not be the same thing. We are in America, darling, we have to make do. When I came here, I had to adjust to conditions like having no maids, living alone, and going to gay bars without hustlers. It is the same thing with my dreams. I needed to be a little flexible. If not, I will not survive . . . I will be one lonely queen.

Flexibility was R. E.'s diplomatic way of talking about the kinds of hierarchies and dislocations he has confronted while living in the United States. He continued:

> It is amazing what I have put up with, and what I have to fight here. Things I would never even dream of encountering back home. I had to get some part-time work — washing dishes in some restaurant.

Que horror! [How horrible!] We have maids for these kinds of things in the Philippines. And to top it all, I have been called a chink in, of all places, a dance club in Manhattan. But anyway, I guess it is the price one has to pay to live here.

R. E.'s narrative may seem to be a distinct one, yet his views and dreams parallel other Filipino gay men's experiences. The tensions between memories of the Philippines and the realities of living in the United States underscore R. E.'s narrative and, to a large extent, the narratives of other Filipino gay men living in the diaspora. The disjuncture between notions of home and nation, particularly between the land of birth and the land of settlement, forms part of the diasporic rhetoric. The practice of drag, or cross-dressing, specifically in the ritual of Santacruzan, is a crucial point for reviewing and critically analyzing both R. E.'s story and many Filipino diasporic gay men's lives.

Rosemary George has suggested that it is the "search for a location where one can feel at home, in spite of the obvious foreignness of the space, that propels the discourses engendered by the experience of immigration" (George 1992: 79). R. E.'s words, his life trajectories, and his dreams present a rich source of insights on specific issues of immigration, specifically on the notion of home. The seemingly ironic juxtaposition of dreams and home in R. E.'s words marks the contingency of these concepts' provenance and existence. Using the invisible baggage or gunnysack of dreams and cultural practices, R. E. and other immigrants refigure their lives and selves within existing constraints.

R. E. points out that it is possible for a dream first hatched amid the restrictions of a Philippine town and the (dis)comforts of family life to be realized in a foreign space. The realization of R. E.'s dream in America, the land of dreams for many Filipinos, unwittingly exposes the complexity of "the process of making oneself at home" (ibid.). This process continues in several successive generations as part of the struggle to create some coherence among spaces, dreams, and bodies. Yet such a coherence will never be complete. R. E.'s flight from the potential shame and loss of family honor through cross-dressing back in the Philippines to freedom in America is tempered by the secularization of the ritual in New York City's gay mecca and the difficulties of living in a foreign land. As R. E. pointed out, one must "make do." I construe his words not as a kind of defeatism, but rather as an exhortation to engage with the contradictions of his transnational existence. Indeed, despite the physical absence of his townspeople and other familiar scenes of his childhood, R. E. gracefully traipsed down the runway in his gown in a rundown former school building in Manhattan and felt at home.

The Pageant of the Nation and the Performance of Diaspora

The significance of this particular performance speaks to the larger issues of immigration and queer diaspora as well as the cultural struggle of the formerly colonized. In addition, it unwittingly disrupts various national narratives. The performance also demonstrates how immigrants negotiate between the hegemonic imperative of assimilation and the subaltern option of total defiance.

In this ritual, American and Filipino social idioms, icons, and symbols fuse in order to provide a structure to an implicit narrative of a gay diasporic community. Performers in the Santacruzan, and R. E. specifically, are actively fabricating selves from strands of competing national traditions. In a sense, this "syncretic dynamic" appropriates elements from hegemonic cultural forms and in the process "creolizes" them by "disarticulating given signs and re-articulating their symbolic meaning" (Mercer 1988: 57). By fusing and infusing ritual religious components with the mundane and the taboo, Filipino gay men are in a sense "translating" their dreams, visions, and practices in creating and representing their lives in their land of settlement. Stuart Hall (1990: 235) notes that experiences in the diaspora are neither essential nor pure but heterogeneous and diverse. He argues further that identity within the diasporic context is marked by its transformative nature and emphasis on difference.

Nowhere are Stuart Hall's ideas more profoundly evident than in the words of R. E., who with a pragmatic tone narrated how his own dreams were transported and configured according to the exigencies of immigration. In many ways the elements involved in the fruition of his dreams have changed them. The transportation technology that allowed his costume to be flown from the Philippines and the existing racial and sexual politics in the gay community are but a few of the transformative elements that reconfigured his dream. Furthermore, the simultaneous presence/absence of people, places, and events in his memories and dreams paradoxically enabled R. E. to feel at home in the enactment of the ritual.

Individual identities are not the only ones implicated in this process. The rescripted Santacruzan can be seen as "a style of imagining" a community. In other words, the performance can be seen as an attempt by Filipino gay men to negotiate and represent their collectivity to themselves and to (sometimes more powerful) others. Such a ritual showcases the complex alliances as well as the fluid and multiple fields of social relations and identities of this group of gay immigrants. In particular, the ritual coalesces the agency of this group of men as they reinvent, resist, and refigure hierarchies and hegemonic ideas and practices in various locations (Glick Schiller, Basch, and Blanc-Szanton 1992: 11).

Immigration, George argues, "unwrites the nation and national projects because it flagrantly displays a rejection of one national space for another more desirable location, albeit with some luggage carried over" (George 1992: 83). In this ritual, transplanted individuals reinvented meanings that interrogate the divergences and continuity of experiences and images between the nation of origin and the nation of settlement. As such, it is important to note that in the performance, the very idea of the nation is brought into question. Indeed, as the ritual and its performers, like Reyna Banderada, have unwittingly asked: Which nation? Whose nation?

This ritual space enabled Filipino gay men to "return the gaze," that is, to reinvent themselves according to their own terms. Cross-dressing is a cultural practice that is both tolerated and ridiculed in the Philippines and the United States. This ambivalence is manifested in New York City's mainstream gay community's belated avowal of cross-dressing gay men not as anachronistic relics of the past, but as vibrant and significant members of that community. Deterritorialized moments and sites such as the Santacruzan (an ancient rite handed by Spain to the colonies and now re-presented in metropolitan America) allow us to derive insights into how Filipino gay men and other diasporic deviants author themselves, make sense of their immigrant experiences, and indeed, "play with the world."

Six

**Tita Aida:
Intimate
Geographies
of Suffering**

In 1991, I had worked and lived for two years in what is touted to be the epicenter of the epicenter of the AIDS pandemic, the Chelsea district of Manhattan. I was working at the Gay Men's Health Crisis (an AIDS service organization), a few blocks from my basement studio apartment. A thought crossed my mind one day as I walked back from work to my apartment. By then, I had witnessed a friend and several acquaintances die of the disease. Because my neighborhood is basically considered to be the city's gay ghetto, images of AIDS proliferated on the walls of many buildings, restaurants, shops, bars, and business establishments in the neighborhood. On the walls of buildings, on storefronts, even on mailboxes, the red ribbon, the words "Safer Sex" and of course, "AIDS" were plastered all over. AIDS at least in my immediate surroundings was never more than a few feet away.

It suddenly occurred to me that the terror of living in the pandemic had dissipated into a routinized banality. More often than not, I walk away from any discussion about AIDS at parties and social gatherings. One of my office mates said huffily that if Michael Callen, an AIDS activist and performer, sang his signature song, "Love Don't Need a Reason" one more time, he would leave the room. The song was supposed to be the anthem of AIDS awareness, yet after more than a decade into the pandemic, the cultural practices and icons that have emerged from it have become boringly ordinary for many people.

I heard very black and cruel humor about the disease, some coming from AIDS sufferers themselves. I once heard a story of a guy who had AIDS and had a yeast infection. His doctor forbade him to eat cheese, which he loved. At a party, he couldn't resist the urge so he took a slice of havarti and said, "I have to feed my yeast." I know of one gay man who had three remaining T-cells and had given them pet names.

All these scenes made me think back to years ago when I was living in the Philippines under martial law and the Marcos dictatorship. At that time, despite the numerous repressive measures that left thousands of Filipinos dead or in dire poverty, there was a fatalism that found its voice in humor, gossip, and satire. I left in 1984, two years before the Marcos era came to an end. I know that living under a dictatorship and living under a pandemic have important differences. However, as in the Philippines of my memory, the horror of the disease has in some ways become a commonplace part of everyday life. Terror becomes muted. Yet one feels that underneath all these placid surfaces there are rumblings, explosions of anger, and silent acts of defiance.

This chapter presents how AIDS has affected Filipino gay men's lives and the kinds of practices, experiences, and beliefs these men have faced and created for themselves. The first part of this chapter presents a discussion of the epidemiological facts about AIDS among Filipinos in the United States and in the Philippines. In this section, I argue that the AIDS pandemic should be seen within a transnational framework. I utilize this perspective in the succeeding sections of this chapter, particularly in the sections on immigration, mourning, and the oral histories of AIDS among Filipino gay men. To illustrate the points made in this first section of the chapter, I present several life histories. In all these sections, I describe and analyze the influence of friendship and familial/kin networks in various junctures of the pandemic. The second part of this chapter is a presentation and analysis of the idiom of

Tita Aida, the name Filipino gay men have coined for AIDS. I connect this idiom with swardspeak and the epidemiology and history of the pandemic. In this section, I include a life history of a Filipino who has AIDS and examples of the use of the idiom in AIDS prevention efforts in California. I argue that AIDS provides a space in which the celebratory tone of postmodern travel and play confronts its limits and alternative possibilities. In other words, I submit that AIDS not only provides ways for Filipino gay men to construct cultural citizenship but also poses the irony and pain behind the endeavor.

AIDS, Identity, and Immigration: Some Vignettes

When I was growing up [in the Philippines] there was this huge bridge that connected my town, which was on an island, with the mainland. When I came back
[from America] after being away for more than a dozen years, I realized that it was
not as big as I remembered it to be. Actually, it was very small. — JOJO

These words of a gay Filipino informant who immigrated to America best symbolize most of the underlying issues I will explore in this section. I locate the interconnections between subjectivities or identities in conducting an ethnography of AIDS among Filipino gay immigrants with the larger framework of anthropological practice and transna-tional social, economic, and political processes. I argue that issues of self and other in this particular fieldwork situation illustrate the ambiv-alent, contingent, and shifting character of subjectivities in an increas-ingly migrant world. I discuss how immigration affects specific identi-ties, such as being gay and being Filipino amid the AIDS pandemic, and how these, in turn, affect the position of a "native" anthropologist like myself in conducting research among his own people.

I have decided against focusing on reflexivity as an exclusively phe-nomenological or autobiographical experience, because I believe that the historical moment we live in today should shape the way we as anthropologists reexamine or revise our identities and experiences in the pandemic in particular and in the study of human societies in general. Amid a burgeoning global cultural and economic system where people, ideas, machines, and diseases cross terrains and borders, the need to connect seemingly individual/personal and local experi-ences of various life trajectories with a systemic and structural frame-work is more compelling than ever. Immigration, as Homi Bhabha

(1992) has noted, brings to light the ambivalent, hybrid, and dissembling character of life away from the homeland. What this means is that difference, be it racial, ethnic, cultural, sexual, or economic, becomes central to the identification process of migrants and their engagement with the pandemic. However, this kind of difference is neither fixed nor clearly bounded by a specific territory. Moreover, the intrusions of spaces and memory brought about by immigration become part of the engagement.

I argue that these spaces and memories bring forth what can be called an intimate geography of suffering. By this I mean the various ways in which suffering under the pandemic is structured and constituted not just by the here and now, but by remembered spaces and time fragments of one's biography and history. Suffering in the case of Filipino gay men in the diaspora is experienced and understood through and refracted by the exigencies of home and the problems of displacement and settlement. Suffering is not a process imbued only with forlornness but rather is a purposive series of acts that build and create spaces for negotiating location and positionality. The spatial aspects of AIDS and Filipino gay men can be properly understood by other studies on AIDS. Cindy Patton (2002), for example, explores the creation of "official maps" that seek to contain and naturalize the pandemic in strictly geographic terms. Additionally, Paul Farmer's (1992) study of AIDS in Haiti critically examines what he calls the "geography of blame" that morally inscribes the spread and provenance of the disease in Haitian bodies and social landscapes. Building on these examples, I aim to create an alternative mapping of AIDS in Filipino gay men's lives that brings together public and official discourses with private and intimate ones.

What follows below is not a sorrowful portrait of these men. Rather, suffering is rendered, appropriated, and performed in ambivalent and complicated ways but always in relation to the operations of power (Kleinman, Das, and Lock 1997). Pleasure, humor, and gossip intersect with mourning and abjection as part of the attempt of Filipino gay men to wrestle with, understand, and survive the onslaught of the disease.

It is often assumed that Filipinos will readily and easily assimilate into American culture since they have had some kind of cultural head start from their colonial and postcolonial relationships with America. There is nothing further from the truth, as my years of fieldwork in

New York City have shown. The shifts in the way Filipino gay men represent themselves, particularly in the idioms they use to construct a sense of being during this pandemic, illustrate, if not evoke, displacement or dislocation as well as the ambivalent qualities that are constitutive of the immigration experience.

I would like to present four stories, vignettes if you will, of gay Filipinos living in New York to explain this assertion. These four stories provide a way to view the multilocality and transcultural sources of identity formation of Filipino gay informants from the vantage points of class, race, homosexuality, and AIDS. In turn, the shifts in identities in the following stories explode the myth of a monolithic Other perpetuated not only by scholars but more importantly by health and AIDS experts.

The first two stories are about the lives of Eric and Leila. These two gay Filipinos extend what are seemingly traditional Filipino homosexual practices such as cross-dressing into an encounter with American gay lifestyles. In addition, they appropriate the racial exoticism accorded to Asians by dominant Western discourses either to obfuscate their "real" identities as Filipino or as men, or to rationalize their roles and ideas about the AIDS pandemic.

Eric, who was in his thirties, recounted his experiences as a migrant worker in Saudi Arabia, where he said that underneath the strict Islamic rules against homosexuality there were several venues for same-sex encounters. This was the milieu in which he came out. As long as things were kept under wraps from the conservative American multinational corporation for which he worked and the Saudi theocracy, which kept watch over all activities, he had what he called a "paradise" for his desires and practices, including having a Miss Gay Philippines-Saudi Arabia drag contest.

Interestingly, when he came to America, Eric was shocked at the rather open way gay men went about their business. He was disappointed, however, that these gay men were too open, too vulgar. There was no "mystery," he said, no excitement of doing things secretly. It was also about the time he came to America that AIDS started to unleash its devastating effects on the gay community. He started noticing other gay Filipinos coming down with the disease in 1986. Soon, his own friends started getting sick and dying. He was appalled to hear that Filipinos have the highest number of cases of AIDS among Asians and Pacific Islanders. He said, "As usual, Filipinos top the list again . . .

especially when it comes to 'bad lists' like the number of illegal immigrants or high school dropout rates." This was one of the reasons why he told people that he was Samoan or Guamanian or the ubiquitous "Hawaiian"; there was less stigma attached to these identities than being Filipino, and more importantly, these identities sounded more exotic.

Leila was the drag name of Mando, who was in his late thirties. For Leila cross-dressing was a way of getting men. Like Eric, he liked assuming more exotic identities and aliases such as Suzie Wong or Nancy Kwan. In the Philippines, he said, he was able to get men for sex, but he had to pay them. In America, he said, there was a market for his cross-dressing talent and exotic beauty, although he could not compete in the hypermasculine, gym-oriented world of mainstream gay life in New York. "With my slight build, who would even give me a second look if I were wearing a T-shirt?" he said. However, there were men, particularly those who were not gay-identified, who were attracted to beautiful Oriental cross-dressers. Here in America, Leila did not have to pay the man to have sex with him. Rather, it was the other way around. "Sometimes, I feel so cheap," he said. "The man will insist on paying for everything, including the pleasure of having sex with you. It's like everything goes on an opposite current here in America. I like it."

Because of the epidemic, Leila said that the contents of his purse now included a condom, which was meant for the use of the Caucasian partner. Being the "lady" in the encounters or relationships meant that he had to be like the "typical woman" and carry the burden of making sure that the sex was safe. Furthermore, he said, "The whites [Caucasians] are less concerned about safety . . . they are not concerned about their family, so why would they be concerned with other people's lives, much less their own?"

The last two life vignettes are those of David and Raul. Both are HIV seropositive, and this situation creates, to use a term by Deleuze and Guattari (1987), a deterritorializing effect in the way they locate themselves in America and in the AIDS crisis. The intersections of class as consciousness and class as access to resources intersect with the process of immigration.

David, whose narrative I have cited in chapter 4, was very proud of his aristocratic background in the Philippines. He found America to be funny because he was able to maintain relationships with people who were not of his class. David was in a hospital when I met him. After being undocumented for nearly ten years, he became a legal resident and was diagnosed with AIDS three years later. Already in the terminal stages of AIDS, he rationalized his AIDS diagnosis in terms of taking the bad with the good. He succeeded in his professional life after years of hardship living as an illegal alien. He said, "I have seen America. America has been kind to me, but I am ready to go home [to the Philippines]."

Raul, the fourth informant, was quite different from David. He did not want to go back to the Philippines. In fact, he was on his way to legalizing his stay in America when he discovered that he was positive in a mandatory HIV test for potential immigrants. He found out that he will never be granted the green card and attain the American citizenship he has dreamed of. Ironically, it was his condition too that allowed him to stay in America for humanitarian and medical reasons. One of his worries was that while he could stay in America, he could never acquire the full rights of being an American permanent resident or citizen. He could not go out of the country. He could not visit the Philippines. Not that he had any desire to go back. There were no treatment facilities or medical trials there during the late 1980s and early 1990s. The dilemma worsened when he heard that the Philippine government had discriminated against and even deported Filipinos who had AIDS who were now citizens of other countries. He heard a story about the body of a Filipino who had died of AIDS abroad. Philippine authorities refused entry of the remains to the Philippines unless the remains were cremated. "I don't want to be cremated," Raul said, "so that takes care of ever going back to the Philippines."

These short vignettes illustrate how AIDS and immigration emphasize the unboundedness of culture, people, and identities. In doing an ethnography of AIDS among immigrant gay populations, one comes across the appropriation and reconfiguration of identities, both mainstream and marginal. In the vignettes, the representations of self and others are seen from different angles or vantage points: class in the case of David, gay identities in the case of Eric and Leila, and legal/political identities in the case of Raul. Therefore, the demarcations between self and other are constantly being redrawn: Filipino and non-Filipino, "gay-identified men" and practitioners of same-sex encounters, white and nonwhite, legal residents/immigrants and illegal aliens, upper class and lower class.

The informants' experiences have brought me a keener sense of awareness of the paradoxical nature of identities, locales, and relationships present in the various individual and collective struggles in the pandemic. More importantly, this awareness has created a stronger conviction that despite all pronouncements of the exhilarating feelings of movement and travel, AIDS has ironically brought back the notions of "boundedness and fixity" and made more dramatic the experience of "in-betweenness" (Behar 1996) that exists in diasporic life. By in-betweenness, I mean the kind of spatial, emotional, and cultural displacements between homeland and new home.

Legal, political, economic, physical, and moral realities during this pandemic have rendered the celebratory image of the cosmopolitan immigrant into, at certain points and spaces, that of a war casualty or a political prisoner. However, under the shackles of disease and stigma there are moments of disruptions and interventions both in the realm of the everyday and in landmark events of illness, death, and mourning. The following sections are elaborations on these views and ideas. They are tentative forays into the different moments and domains that show how Filipino gay men's drama in the pandemic is different from that of other gay men.

AIDS as History, AIDS as Space

For many Filipino gay men, AIDS was a marker for significant times and places in their lives and in their own understanding of transnational history. For many of those who were here in the 1980s, there was a time before AIDS and after AIDS. Before AIDS meant that life was carefree. One informant said, "The only thing you had to worry about were those STDs [sexually transmitted diseases] like gonorrhea or getting crabs. You know the STD clinic was like a social club then, since almost everyone had or thought he had one of those diseases and was very nonchalant about it."

Gay social life then had no bounds. Ricardo, another informant, described the scene with this anecdote:

Day, alam mo naman, noong 1970s makakabingwit ka dyiyan sa tabi-tabi. You know, sex was free and the men were wild, and you just had to — grab it! Well, yoong dalawang kaibigang kong afam — parehong puti, ininvite nila ang biyuti ko for dinner. So bago kami kumain—steak ang ulam, sabi ni Shawn na wala daw A-1 steak sauce. So itong si Mike e pumunta sa deli. Aba, inamag na ang steak at inagiw na kami—isang oras at kalahati na e wala pa ang malanding pinabili ng patis. Well dumating din, kumain kami at umiskapu na ang biyuti ko dahil knows ko na magaaaway na ang mag-asawa. Nagkita kami ni Mike a week later at may-I-say niya na may na-meet daw siyang hunk on the way to the deli, nagkatiningnan lang ang dalawa, pumunta sila sa apartment ng lalaki at ayun, nagdotsingan sila. Ay talagang kakaiba noon. The 1970s were wild—hindi na siguro babalik ang panahon na yon.

[Girl, as you may know, during the 1970s you could hook anyone just about anywhere. You know sex was free and the men were wild and you just had to—grab it! Well, I had these American (white) friends who were a couple who invited my biyuti to dinner. So before we ate—steak was the main fare—Shawn said that we did not have any A-1 sauce so Mike went to the deli. Well, the steak had started to rot and we had started getting cobwebs around us and the whore we sent to get *patis* (fish sauce) was still not there. Well, he came, we ate, and my biyuti left quickly since I knew the two would start fighting. Mike and I saw each other again the next week. He confessed to meeting this hunk on the way to the deli, they eyed each other, and they went to the guy's apartment and they did each other. Oh, it was really different then. Those times will never come back.]

Filipino gay informants in New York reported being aware of the epidemic as early as 1981, not only because they were here when the first cases were being reported but, most importantly, they were among the first to witness or know other Filipinos who came down with the illness. In fact, the first documented case in the Philippines was from a Filipino who had been a guest worker abroad. Most of the AIDS cases among Filipino gay men in the United States were usually regarded as statistically insignificant until 1987, when a dramatic increase in cases was seen among Asian and Pacific Islanders. Filipinos have one of the highest number of AIDS cases among Asian Americans (Woo et al. 1988). Until 1988, AIDS was a real drama among Filipinos in the United States, but only among Filipino gay men. These realities have created a unique gay Filipino discourse about AIDS in America.

I remember that around 1986, I began to hear about some Filipino bakla dying of AIDS on the West Coast. Then soon after that I heard about a Filipino who died here [in New York City]. Then, I heard about this famous Filipino hairdresser who died. Afterward, the first of my friends came down with pneumonia. Then, he was followed by another. *Parang* [like] domino effect. It was of course, Tita Aida. She struck again and again.

Ricky's reminiscences above point to 1986 as a critical year. It was around the period from 1986 to 1988 when the rise of AIDS cases among Asians in San Francisco was first documented. It was the same period of time when many of my informants started to become aware of the devastation of the disease. Most of them thought that the disease only affected white men. One informant said, "I thought that only white men, *yung mga biyuti* [the beautiful ones] who were having sex constantly, were the only ones getting it." As late as 1989, most Philippine newspapers were either silent about the epidemic or were publishing articles about the genetic immunity of Filipinos to the disease. Some articles talked about the diet (such as eating *bagoong* or salted shrimp paste) as the reason why there were no Filipinos with AIDS.

This was soon dispelled by the sudden onslaught of Filipino cases. An informant remembered how he took care of five friends.

Ang hirap . . . manash. [It was hard . . . sister.] I had to massage, clean, shop, and do so many things. It was a horror watching them die slowly and painfully. And when they died . . . my friends and I realized that there was no money for a burial or to send the bodies back to the Philippines. That was when we had some fundraising dinners. We just had dinner, not the *siyam-siyam* [traditional Filipino prayer ritual held several days after a burial], just a simple get-together at somebody's place and a hat was passed to get some money to defray some expenses.

For Filipinos who have been diagnosed with AIDS, the disease marked a turning point in their lives. An AIDS diagnosis meant different things to Filipino gay men depending on their life trajectories. Jake, a Filipino gay man who immigrated in the late 1970s, saw his diagnosis as an amplification of the solitary nature of immigrant life in this country.

Dumating ako dito, wala akong masyadong dala. Wala akong mga kamag-anak. Ngayon may isa akong pinsan sa Ohio. Pero nagpursigi ako. Sinubsob ko ang aking sarili sa trabaho. Gumanda naman ang buhay ko. Nakapagpadala sa atin. Hindi naman ako nagkasuwerte sa lalaki. So nang malaman kong meron akong AIDS bigla kong nakita na nagiisa ako. May mga kaibigan nga ako pero ako talaga ang mag-isang magkikipagbunuan—tulad ng dati, ako lang.

[When I came here, I didn't have too much luggage. I didn't have any relatives. Now, I have a cousin in Ohio. But I really persevered. I pushed myself and worked hard. My life prospered. I was able to send money back home. I was not lucky with men. So when I learned I had AIDS I suddenly realized that I was alone. I have some friends, but I am alone in facing this—as always, just me.]

Brian, a Filipino born in California, saw it differently. When he was diagnosed with AIDS, he saw it as a way to straighten out his life and have some kind of impact on other people.

I was not exactly living a virtuous life before I came down with AIDS. I was involved in drugs, really all the sex you can imagine. But more than that, I really wasn't doing anything with my life. I had friends who would fuck and drink their brains out and the next day they would go to their offices as stockbrokers or would start writing plays or design clothes. Me? I was just a zombie the next day. AIDS was a kind of slap on the face to get my life in order. After the initial shock I started thinking of a career. Isn't that ironic? I was thinking of the future when there might not be a whole lot of it before me. Shit, at least I won't go out leaving a trail of coke or angel dust.

AIDS seems to loom over the mundane drone of day-to-day living. A popular conception is that AIDS, except for those who have contracted it, can be completely separated from the struggle of daily life. However, the next section debunks this perception as AIDS decidedly transforms the seemingly placid and predictable tone of the everyday.

AIDS and the Everyday

Bago ako pumunta sa ospital, kala ko, eto na nga—tigbak na ang biyuti ko. Kaya tinapon ko lahat ng mga bills kong 'di ko nababayaran. Sinigurado kong malinis ang apartment ko at nilinis ko ang mga maruruming pinggan sa sink. Nakakahiya kasi baka pagnamatay ako e may makakita na ang sink ko may kaning napanis.

[Before going to the hospital, I thought, that was it — my biyuti was dead. I tossed all my unpaid bills in the garbage. I made sure I cleaned the apartment and washed all the dirty dishes in the sink. It would be embarrassing if I died and somebody would see the sink filled with rotting rice.] — DIDA/DODI

For many people, AIDS was something they saw mentioned on public service billboards in the subway or heard about on TV news. For most of my informants, AIDS was something that they tried to keep at bay, but which nevertheless reared its ugly head too many times. The calm of the everyday sometimes masked the feelings and images of those who live in the pandemic's epicenter. Filipino gay men I interviewed talked about how in seemingly innocent situations the tranquility was destroyed when connections were made between banal phenomena and the dreaded disease. Ernie, an informant in his forties who has lived through the 1970s and 1980s, said:

> Sometimes, I am sitting with my friends and the talk turns to physical appearance — alam mo na — puro mukha, katawan, and biyuti ang dinadaldal ng mga bading [you know, all the bading talk about is face, body, and biyuti]. Then, somebody mentions a guy we know who seems to be losing weight. Tilian bigla. Ay naku ha, di namin gusto yan. [We suddenly start screaming. Oh my, we don't like that.] Or at a party, the usual catching up with friends we have not seen for a while — biglang o ano na yan? [Suddenly, what is happening?] I have not seen her for a long time . . . may sakit ba? [Is he/she sick?]

Other informants told me how a blemish, a bruise, a lump, or even a cold become sources of anxiety. For those who were not infected or who did not know if they were infected, mundane activities sometimes took unexpected significance. Rene, an informant said, "Every time I shower, I give myself a physical. I look in the mirror for signs. You can't be too careful."

Religion and religious activities are also spaces for articulating anxiety and reactions to AIDS. Another informant, Arthur, mentioned how going to Sunday mass was also an event of thanksgiving for being alive and being HIV-negative. As mentioned earlier, Our Lady of Pompeii in Greenwich Village in lower Manhattan had a strong Filipino congregation that met weekly for devotions to the Infant Jesus (Santo Niño de Cebu) and Our Lady of Perpetual Help. During Wednesday novenas, petitions or wishes that people had written on slips of paper were read publicly before beginning the prayers. In many cases, the petitions mirrored the aspirations of the largely immigrant population. For example, some asked the Infant Jesus or the Virgin Mary to grant them permanent residency, or to allow them to pass certain exams, or to take care of family back in the Philippines. But others were about finding a cure for AIDS or receiving a negative HIV antibody test result.

Gossip, the quintessential mundane activity that is seen as the downfall of both the Filipino mainstream and gay communities, becomes the arena for AIDS and its concomitant scenarios. Filipinos, especially Filipino gay men, are seen to be proverbial gossips. It is perhaps the most quotidian if not stereotypic activity of Filipinos. As such, AIDS is grist for the rumor mills and betrays the intricate network of Filipinos both gay and straight. In June 1993, Bong, a Filipino man who had been diagnosed with AIDS, told me that he was entering the hospital for more tests. The next morning Bong checked into a Lower East Side hospital. Within an hour, a friend of his who knew a Filipino gay lab technician in a hospital across town was calling him in his hospital room. Bong's friend was told that a Filipino had checked into the wing and had Bong's surname.

Humor is also a venue in which AIDS becomes articulated. Another stereotype is that a Filipino can go through a lot of suffering and oppression but he or she will never lose his or her sense of humor. As a matter of fact, during times of extreme economic and political repression such as the Marcos era, the Filipino's gift for the facetious becomes very evident. Macabre as it may be, AIDS is another source for jokes and puns. A popular set of jokes at parties and gatherings includes the Filipino versions of the acronyms, HIV and AIDS. HIV is spelled out as "hair is vanishing" while AIDS now means "*anit* [scalp] is definitely showing." The ridiculousness of growing bald provides the laughable image that deflects the shock when somebody jokingly proclaims "So-and-so has HIV." When the usual reaction of shock is met by laughter, the process of converting the fearful into the banal is completed. This strategy is very evident in the section on the discourse on Tita Aida below.

For those who are infected, there are other ordinary activities that attain particular meanings and become ways to subvert the burgeoning weight of living with AIDS. Eating, for some informants who have AIDS, acquires the rarefied air of a survival struggle. Rene pondered on how eating has become an integral part of the battle against AIDS.

> Noong unang nagkasakit ako. Nawala ang aking panlasa. Lahat ng matikman ko parang gamot o lasang ewan. Hindi ako makakain pero sabi ko sa sarili ko, kailangan kong kalabanin ito. Kaya kahit na pag minsan wala talaga akong gana. Subo lang ako nang subo.

> [When I got sick, I lost my sense of taste. Everything I ate tasted like medicine or like leather. I could not eat but I told myself, I need to fight this. So even when I don't have any appetite, I keep on feeding myself.]

Eating is also a kind of path that leads to both the memory of home and the dream of an eventual survival and cure. One informant talked about how he thought *kangkong,* a kind of watercress popular in the Philippines, may be one reason why he has not been sick for a long time. It may be, he said, an answer to the search for an AIDS cure. He talked further about how Filipinos who have AIDS may be more hardy than Americans since they eat a lot of vegetables and have been exposed to more bacteria.

Cleaning up one's apartment is also an activity that transcends the semantics of the everyday. For Dodi, it was one way to avoid being shamed after he died. For another informant, cleaning was a metaphor for control over one's life as well as a cathartic activity. Ray looked at cleaning in this way:

> Kapag naglilinis ako, gumagaan ang pakiramdam ko. At least, alam ko may kahihinatnan ang pagvavacuum at pagpupunas. Gaganda ang studio ko. Para bang, eto ang isa sa mga nalalabi kong maga-gawa since wala na akong trabaho—may inaatupag ako. 'Di ba, para may relevance naman ako araw-araw.

> [When I clean (my apartment), I feel less burdened. At least I know there is a goal to all the vacuuming and dusting. My studio looks nicer. It's like this is one of the few things I can do since I don't have a job. I have something to keep myself busy. Isn't it? So I can have "relevance" everyday.]

In this section, I have described how routine is reconfigured and transformed into a kind of disruptive rhythm. In the next section, the stark moments of death and mourning provide a glimpse into the different ways meanings and relationships are produced and reproduced in the pandemic.

Death, Mourning and the Family

The typical response and buffer to illness and death is to turn to the family. For Filipinos, being surrounded with family and friends during times of crises is an indicator of being able to live through them, if not being able to make the best of them. As such, a person's life is not the only basis by which other people morally assess an individual. The strength of one's family ties plays an important role in the way people perceive the life one lives or has lived, and, in this case, the death one dies.

When I talked to Filipinos, both gay and straight, the concerns about those who were ill were articulated in terms of family members who were available to take care of them. In America, particularly in the gay communities, the "families we choose" or the network of friends that go beyond biological ties are the important caretakers of people when they become ill. However, Filipinos did not find these caretakers to be the appropriate people to handle the situation. As many of them would say, "Iba talaga ang pamilya, iba ang aruga ng di mo ka anu-ano." [Family is different, different from those with whom you do not share blood ties.]

Informants found it doubly tragic to become ill and have no family there to help. Many of the Filipino gay men I interviewed reminisced that hospitals in the Philippines allowed families to camp out in their loved ones' rooms and that wakes and burials were communal activities. A statement of a Filipino gay man encapsulated many of these attitudes: "Nang mamatay si ( ). Naku wala man lang kasamang kamaganak. Magisang namatay sa [hospital]. Kaya kung titignan mo ang mukha niya sa burol. Parang hindi masaya." [When ( ) died, oh, he did not have family with him. He died alone in (name of hospital). So if you looked at his face during the wake, he did not look happy.]

The stigma of AIDS and the exigencies of immigrant life prevented many Filipino gay men from attaining the ideal situation of having the family nearby during the times they were ill and/or dying. However, some families took these ailing relatives back; others refused to acknowledge both these men's disease and their sexual orientation.

In some cases, the stigma of homosexuality became enmeshed with the stigma of the disease. This situation created different scenarios. An informant told me about another Filipino gay man whose family kept telling people that he had AIDS because he was a drug addict. Another story that went around the gossip circuit concerned a Filipino gay man whose mother allegedly kept insisting that her son had a case of severe diarrhea. Despite the fact that the family knew about his lover, she was shocked when the doctor said that her son had AIDS. The mother responded, "But doctor, my son is not a drug user."

However, there were also a number of families who accepted them, their gay friends, and lovers. A mother I interviewed was emphatic about how the idiom of the family is stronger than any stigma and danger of the disease. She was seventy years old when her youngest son became ill in 1987. At that time, many people, including doctors, were emphasizing strict rules when coming into contact with people with AIDS. She said:

> Ano naman ang ikakatakot ko? Matanda na ako. Anak ko naman siya. Wala silang masasabing kahit ano. Hindi ko pwedeng iwanan ang anak ko o kaya e hawakan siya may gloves at mask. Bakit ako mandidiri? Anak ko yan — kahit ano ang mangyari.

> [Why should I be afraid? I am old. He is my son. There was nothing they could say. I cannot leave my son or touch him wearing gloves and a mask. Why will I be grossed out? He's my son — no matter what.]

When he died, she said, "Akala ko hindi ko makakaya. Alam mo, hindi dapat mauna ang anak sa ina. Nagkasama naman kami. Sa tingin ko tahimik siya nang iwan niya kami." [I thought I would not survive it. You know, a child should not go before his mother. But I think that he was at peace when he left us.] Her statement points to the core of contentions in Filipino conceptions of death. There are good deaths and there are bad ones. The "goodness" comes, on the one hand, from the way the person lived his life. In most cases, this predicts the way the person will die. For example, criminals often meet tragic or violent deaths. Virtuous people, it is believed, die in more peaceful conditions. The face of the dead person is usually evaluated during wakes for signs of peacefulness or turbulence.

In cases where there was a lover (usually Caucasian), it was he who oftentimes took care of the ailing Filipino. Colleagues in AIDS service organizations for Asian Americans have told me how, in most cases, the family was not informed of the situation, and so it was left to the lover to be the primary care partner.

William, a forty-five-year-old Jewish man, talked about the travails of being an "AIDS widower" and being a member of an interracial couple. William talked about how AIDS transformed their relationship.

Jesse [his lover] was always the dominant one in the relationship. Ours was the opposite of the stereotypical view of a masculine Caucasian master and an effeminate submissive Asian man. Jesse earned more money, was physically bigger, took care of all decisions, and actually steered the whole relationship. When he became ill, it was a big turnaround for both of us. All of a sudden, I had to take on his former duties. I had to take care of him when he used to take care of me.

In cases when the Filipino was alone, going back home to the Philippines was not a viable option. First, there were no adequate medical facilities that could take care of a patient with AIDS. Second, there were horror stories during the late 1980s and early 1990s about how some Filipinos with AIDS who carried American passports were deported from the Philippines after authorities found out about their HIV status. Third, coming down with the disease was seen by some in terms of failing to attain the American dream.

AIDS has created a common experience from which gay Filipinos in New York build and create new discourses and practices particularly around burials and wakes. *Abuloy,* or alms for the dead, have acquired a new dimension. Gay Filipinos put on fashion shows and drag parties to help defray the burial or medical expenses of gay Filipino friends. These collective efforts of networking among Filipino gay men have become a regular occurrence. One Filipino drag queen narrated a particular event.

Maraming nagastos sa pagkakasakit ni Raymond, so naisip namin na para makatulong naman sa pamilya e magkaroon ng isang salu-salo. Tapos — may we pass the hat. Pero medyo kakaiba ito. Naka mujer kaming lahat. Para bang in tribute to Mona este Raymond.

[There was lot of money that was spent on Raymond's illness. So we decided to help out the family (after he died). We decided to have a little get-together. Then we passed the hat. But it was different. We were all in drag. It was like a tribute to Mona, I mean Raymond.]

One American ritual that Filipino gay men have learned quickly is the memorial. Many have told me that they felt awkward during the whole affair because people stood up and talked about the dead person. In one burial mass, a Caucasian man who had taken care of a Filipino gay man who had died read from the Bible and then started to talk about the deceased, to the chagrin of the family and other Filipino friends. One informant said, "Sobrang drama yan ha. Ano pa ang hinahalungkat nila e patay na ang tao." [That is too much drama. What more do they have to unearth about the person? He's already dead.] Another Filipino gay man who died of AIDS was memorialized at the Gay and Lesbian Community Center complete with all the public testimonies. An informant rationalized this situation in this way, "Well, he had a lot of American friends — that's why."

Other collective efforts by Filipinos include symposiums about AIDS in the Filipino community in New York. A group of Filipino men and women was formed to institutionalize efforts to help Filipinos with AIDS. There are still problems. Some Filipino gay men with AIDS are wary of being helped by other Filipino gay men because of the interlocking network of gay Filipinos and the proverbial rumor mill. There is a real possibility of coming into contact with other Filipinos whom one knows or friends of Filipino friends. Gossip about one's HIV status may spread. Other problems include Filipinos' inadequate access to services owing to fear and lack of information.

The Discourse of Tita Aida

Informants who were born and raised in the Philippines and who migrated as adults to America before the 1980s have various theories on how Filipinos started talking about AIDS. Among my informants in New York City, most agree that it was after the change from GRID (Gay Related Immune Deficiency) to AIDS that there was a noticeable change in talking about the disease among Filipino gay men. It was during this time that many Filipino gay men in both countries were using tita as an endearment for other gay friends. Tita is the Tagalog word for aunt or auntie, and this kinship term is extended not only to gay friends and hangers-on but also to inanimate objects and social institutions.

Many informants said that the logical step in talking about something as frightening and mysterious as AIDS was to give it a female name and the kinship term *tita*. For example, names of Filipino beauty queens (*Nelia Sancho* for effeminate or "nelly" men) are used instead of English words. However, the name Aida, which is a play on the acronym for the disease, has a more intricate and confusing lore. One informant who immigrated in 1979 said that the name Aida is from Aida Atutalum, a woman who was raped in the 1960s. Another informant, whose life narrative follows, said it was from a movie star. The exact place of origin of the name Tita Aida may never be known. However, it is among the Filipino gay men in the United States where awareness of the disease is paramount and where a unique structure of meanings surrounding the illness is continually being deployed and reworked.

The unique situation of AIDS among Filipino gay men has produced a rich discourse. Lexical items are continually being reconfigured to represent various experiences during this epidemic. For instance, there is a practice of cremating the body of a Filipino who has died of AIDS outside the Philippines and who will be buried there because of specific Philippine quarantine laws. Cremation has become an ordinary practice that is part of the gay Filipino discourse on AIDS. Consider the text of this conversation between two bakla informants.

A: Nadinig mo na ba? Si ( ) ay nasa ( ). Na-Aida. Sinampal ni Tita! [Have you heard? (Name of a person) is in (name of a hospital). He has AIDS. (Here the speaker is using the prefix *na* to convert Aida into a verb.) Auntie (Aida) slapped him!]

B: O kailan siya lalabas ng ospital? [When is he coming out of the hospital?]

A: Wiz na siya lalabas. Malapit na raw siyang matigbak. Pagkatapos ay polvoron na ang biyuti niya. [He is not coming out (alive) (*wiz* is swardspeak for "nothing" or "not.") He is near death. Then, he will become *polvoron* (a Filipino confection made out of flour, butter, and powdered milk and is used to symbolize cremation in this context.)]

Conversations and interactions such as this conversation show that AIDS has become not only an intrinsic part of the gay argot among gay Filipinos in America but also a catalyst for the creation of more elaborate linguistic and social practices. Conversations at Filipino gay parties and other social activities are usually punctuated by gossip around the disease. Among Filipino gay men, Tita Aida has become an ordinary figure in their encounters with each other.

To illustrate this point, I will present two case studies. The first is a life narrative of a Filipino who has been diagnosed with AIDS. The second is a description and analysis of AIDS prevention texts in California directed to Filipino and Filipino American gay men.

RENE/AMALIA: A LIFE

I met Rene in mid-1991 at a Lower East Side hospital in Manhattan. He had undergone a surgical procedure on his lungs two days previously and suffered a high fever the night before. On that day, he seemed ebullient and talkative. I explained my mission. He readily accepted, and before I could ask him what day would be good to conduct the interview, he started talking about his life. Since we both knew each other as bakla and Filipino, we code-switched using English, Tagalog, and swardspeak. He first described himself in this way:

> Ang mga bading ang tawag sa akin Amalia, alam mo na . . . Amalia Fuentes. Alam mo kung bakit? Kasi, unang-una, maganda siya and maganda rin ako [laughter]. Pangalawa, pareho kaming butangera at matapang. Mga kaibigan ko sa Manila, masasabi nila na mahilig akong maghanap ng away at saka noon ako pa ang naghahabol ng aming mga kasera sa apartment naming na palaging huli sa renta, at kapag nakikita nila ako, sabi nila, "Ayan na si Amalia." Kahit na ang mga kaibigan ko sa California tawag nila sa akin yan kapag nagku-krusing kami sa mga park. May ka-do ako at madidinig ko silang tumatawa na, "Amalia, Amalia, malanding puta, nasaan ka?"

> [My (bakla) friends call me Amalia . . . you know . . . Amalia Fuentes (a Filipino movie actress). Do you know why? First of all, she is pretty and so am I (laughter). Secondly, she and I are both street smart and brave. My friends back home (in Manila) will tell you how I used to pick fights and how I ran after tenants in our apartment who were delinquent with their rent. So when the bakla are hanging out and they see me approaching, they say, "Here comes Amalia." Even my friends in California will call me that when we go cruising in those parks. I will be with someone (having sex) and I will hear them call, "Amalia, Amalia, you loose bitch, where are you?"]

He was thirty-four years old and had been born in Manila. He grew up in a lower-class neighborhood with his mother, sister, and a maternal aunt. His father abandoned his family when Rene was about two years old. In fact, he and his sister took their mother's maiden name. During the early 1970s, his mother married an American citizen and left for the United States, while he and his sister stayed with their aunt. Through their mother's sponsorship, he and his sister were able to immigrate to America in 1980. They settled with their mother in California where a number of their relatives lived. He did a lot of part-time work. During his first year in America, he met a Caucasian who was thirty years older than he was and only two years younger than his mother. They eventually became lovers. Rene's lover was a teacher who encouraged him to finish college. With his lover's support he went back to school and finished an accounting degree. They broke up in 1988 after his lover found a younger man.

Rene intermittently visited the Philippines, sometimes staying for as long as three or four months. He focused the discussion on conditions in the Philippines by asking if I had gone "home" recently. After I said no, he proceeded to discuss political corruption and how bad things were the last time he was in Manila. He compared conditions between the Philippines and the United States, and he realized that he was in a relatively more comfortable condition than most Filipinos.

Naalala ko nasa may downtown ako sa Maynila at nakita ko itong batang lalaki na nagtitinda ng sigarilyo sa matrafik na kalye. Bata ito ha. Ang galing niyang mangilag ng kotse pero nahuli siya ng pulis. Binigyan ng bata ng beinte pesos ang pulis. Alam mo ba yon, hindi na makukuha noong bata ang perang yon. Noon, nagcocomplain ako dahil poor ako dito sa Amerika pero alam mo, hindi ako ganoon kahirap. Hindi ako poor.

[I remember being in downtown Manila and I saw this boy vending cigarettes on the busy streets. A young kid. He was skillfully avoiding cars when a policeman accosted him. The boy gave him twenty pesos and the policeman let him go. Can you believe that? That kid will never recoup the money. I used to complain about being poor, but I realized that being here (in America), I don't have it so bad. I am not poor.]

AIDS for Rene and his Filipino bakla friends was always couched in feminine terms. He said that they called it Tita Aida, Aida, or Aida Roxas. According to Rene, Aida Roxas was a Filipino B-movie actress who became a nun. He used the term in this way:

Sabi ko dati sa mga kaibigan ko, kapag naglalamiyerda sila — na magingat kasi naghihintay si Tita Aida diyan sa kanto. Alam mo kapag hindi ka careful, makikipagaway sa iyo si Tita Aida. Mahirap siyang kalabanin. Well, may mga nagkokoka sa mga kaibigan ko, careless sila, pero sinasabihan ko na sa kakadrugs nila e baka sunduin sila nin Tita Aida. At alam mo kung saan ka niya dadalhin.

[I used to tell my friends every time they went out to party to be careful because Tita Aida might be lurking in the corner. You know, sometimes if you are not careful, Tita Aida might pick a fight with you. She (Tagalog does not have gender-specific indexicals) is a formidable foe. Well, some of my friends used cocaine . . . some of them are so careless, I still keep telling them if they persist on taking drugs, Tita Aida might come to fetch them. And you know where she may lead you.]

Religion played an important role in Rene's life both in the Philippines and in America. Rene said that his religiosity could be traced back both to his mother and his aunt and that it has been an essential part of his experience with AIDS.

Hindi naman nagbago ang buhay ko nang kinalabit ako ni Tita Aida. Relihiyosa ako. Pero mas madalas akong magdasal ngayon at puro novena to Our Lady of Perpetual Help . . . alam mo, sa Our Lady of Pompeii sa Village. Ginagawa ko 'yan. Pinalaki ako na relihiyosa sa bahay. Ang nanay ko at auntie ko. Ang auntie ko nagsisimba kami araw-araw. Oo, araw araw. Ang nanay ko nag-born-again noong dumating siya dito.

[My life did not really change when Tita Aida touched me. I have always been religious . . . although I say more prayers now and I do novenas to Our Lady of Perpetual Help . . . you know, at Our Lady of Pompeii Church in the (Greenwich) Village. I do that. I was brought up in a very religious household. My mom and my aunt . . . oh, those women should have been nuns. My aunt would take us to mass every day . . . yes, every day. My mother became a born-again Christian when she came here (to America).]

Rene tested positive for the HIV antibody in 1989. He had bouts of sudden weakness and unexplained fatigue. He came down with pneumonia a month later. He described his initial reaction to these developments in this way:

Yung unang reaction ko sa sakit ko e parang parusa ng Diyos sa pagiging bakla ko. Pero inisip ko nang husto at na-realize ko na hindi naman niya ako pinarurusahan sa pagiging bakla kung hindi sa mga ginawa ko. Napakataratitat ko pa naman lalo na kapag wala ang asawa ko. Nagpapaka-wild ako at namimik-up ako ng mga min. Ngayon, sa tingin ko pinarurusahan ako sa aking pagka-unfaithful at pagiging malandi.

[My first reaction was that my infection and illness were a punishment from God. He was punishing me for being bakla. However, I thought it over and I realized that he is not punishing me for who I am but for what I have done. I was so promiscuous especially when my spouse was away; I would just go wild and pick up men. So I now believe that God is punishing me for my unfaithfulness and rather loose ways.]

Rene was able to tell his sister and other members of his family right away, but he found it extremely difficult to tell his mother that he was bakla and had AIDS because she was old and was a born-again Christian. He was afraid of how his mother would react. He finally told his mother when they went to view the AIDS quilt when it came to California in 1990. He came out to her about his sexuality and diagnosis at the same time.

Naglalakad kami, titingin-tingin sa mga panel. Pero may nakita kaming panel na yung min kabirthday ko. Parehong day, month and year. Nasabi ko sa nanay ko at tumango siya. Sabi ko sa kaniya, gusto ko siya ang gagawa ng panel ko at gusto kong makita bago ako mamatay. Bigla siyang nagiiyak. Tinulungan kami ng mga volunteer doon. Nagka-usap naman kami. Very supportive siya ngayon.

[We were walking around looking at the different panels. We came upon one panel where the man had the same birth date as I did . . . same day, month, and year. I pointed it out to my mother and she agreed. Then I said that I wanted her to make my panel and I wanted to see it before I died. She broke down crying. Volunteers in the area helped us. We finally came to terms with it. She is very supportive right now.]

In August 1990, Jimmy, a bakla childhood friend of Rene who was living in New York, invited him to move east. Jimmy was called Pilar, after Pilar Pilapil, another Filipino actress. They had a happy reunion in the city. After a few weeks, they both confided to each other their AIDS diagnosis. Jimmy/Pilar became sick a few months after Rene's arrival. Rene remembered the ordeal.

> Inalagaan ko siya. Lumubha si Pilar. Para kaming magkapatid. Ang ganda naming dalawa. Sabi nga ng mga bading, "Ayan na si Amalia at Pilar." Naalala mo ba si Amalia Fuentes and Pilar Pilapil nasa isang magazine article years ago? Noong 1970s yata. Well, napaka-ganda nila. Gaya ko at ni Jimmy. Napakahirap noong panahong yon. Nakita ko siyang nanghina. Sabi ko, kailangan kalabanin ko ito. Si Pilar . . . namatay si Jimmy noong March.

> [I took care of him. Pilar just got sicker and sicker. We were like siblings. He and I were such a beautiful pair. Our bakla friends would say, "There goes Amalia and Pilar." Do you remember when both Amalia Fuentes and Pilar Pilapil were in a magazine article years ago? In the 1970s I think. Well, they were so beautiful, like Jimmy and I. We were really close. It was a very difficult time for me. I saw his slow deterioration. Somehow I knew I must fight this. Pilar . . . Jimmy died in March.]

A few months later, in July, Rene became sick again. He entered the hospital with respiratory problems in August. He felt that the opportunistic infection was more virulent than his initial bout in 1989. He noted that he was having more physical difficulties and he said, "When I came to the hospital a few days ago, I felt that this was it. I prayed, 'Lord, if it is my time, I am ready.'"

Rene died two months after I interviewed him. He first lost his voice and then eventually other infections set in. The hospital volunteer who introduced us said that Rene was very happy about my sessions with him. There was a moment during the interview when Rene's eyes welled up with tears. I felt a lump in my throat, and yet I cleared it and made a point to pause for a few seconds. When I saw that his emotion had subsided, I continued the interview. Meeting Rene affected me so much that I vowed not to do any more hospital interviews. After being trained at my work at Gay Men's Health Crisis to do epidemiological and behavioral survey interviews in the pandemic where the interviewer had to be more or less stoic, I realized I had became too skilled at it for my own good. There was also a moment when I even questioned telling his story, but he was adamant at the beginning that his story be told. As he said jokingly, "Para naman maging celebrity ako." [So I can at least become a celebrity.]

AIDS prevention experts in California have used the idiom of Tita Aida in several pamphlets and brochures targeting Filipino gay and bisexual men. They have appropriated the symbolics of Tita Aida and taken the personification process further. In two major pamphlets, "Hoy Loka — Importante Ito!" (Hey Crazy Woman — This Is Important!) and "Dear Tita Aida," AIDS as the image of the wise aunt takes over the image of the dangerous woman. Both of these brochures use some form of swardspeak.

In "Dear Tita Aida," AIDS acquires a Dear Abby persona. The disease becomes the benevolent wise and caring aunt who provides advice to people about safer sex and sexual identity. On the initial page, Tita Aida says: "Hoy my informants tell me *na hanggang ngayon* [even now], many still engage in risky behaviors, primarily by not using condominiums [condoms]. Again, take it from someone who deeply cares about the beauty of my nieces and nephews: don't take any unnecessary risk." In the succeeding pages, problems about safer sex, sexual identity, and AIDS are answered by Tita Aida. Paradoxically, she becomes an authority on relevant problems during the pandemic as well as becoming the focus of a discourse that aims to eliminate her.

In "Hoy Loka," swardspeak is used to convey basic AIDS information. Tita Aida is inscribed as a wise old woman mouthing Philippine proverbs and sayings *(salawikain)*. In the brochure, Tita Aida said, "Will you rush into the rain without a raincoat?" [Lulusong ka ba sa ulan ng walang kapote?] in allusion to the need to use condoms to avoid bodily fluids such as blood, semen, and vaginal secretions. In this phrase, raincoat is the metaphor for condom. Another section has Tita Aida saying "AIDS is not like steaming rice that you can easily spit out once you have placed it into your mouth." [Ang AIDS ay di parang kaning mainit na kapag isinubo ay madaling iluwa.] In the last paragraph, however, there is a warning that says, "Remember that anyone can be fetched by Tita Aida." The notion of "fetch" is an allusion to death, which when personified is usually described as a figure coming for his victims. In these two brochures, Tita Aida is constructed in a dual manner. The first facet of this construction is that of a wise and friendly family member who is ready to dispense advice while the other is a menacing if not ominous sign of "feminized" death. The dual nature of this construction led to some problems when a Filipino AIDS prevention group in California attempted to have a fundraising activity utilizing a standby in bakla tradition, the beauty contest. This contest was called the "Miss Tita Aida Contest." Trouble ensued because nobody wanted to enter the contest. Many gay Filipinos were afraid that if they participated and won the title, people might think that they had the disease.

I interviewed Mickey, a Filipino gay man in his twenties who goes around San Francisco's gay bars calling himself Tita Aida. He performs as Tita Aida as part of an AIDS prevention safer sex presentation by the Asian AIDS Project. He started doing this because no one wanted to join the Miss Tita Aida beauty contest I described above. He said there was a need to perform as Tita Aida on stage: "Filipinos would not usually ask questions in most public events — especially about sex and AIDS. It's taboo. So they need somebody who looks familiar. A friendly figure as well as a person they could look up to." I then asked him about his inspiration or model for the character. He said:

> When I started doing the act, you wouldn't believe it, I weighed two hundred and fifty pounds. So I looked for somebody Filipino gay men could easily identify and which I could easily imitate. So I decided on Donya Buding. Do you remember Nanette Inventor [a Filipino stand up comedian who gained fame doing a solo club act utilizing a fat social climbing rich woman]? I chose her because if you're Filipino, you have to be funny to be accepted by the people. You can't be all serious. Pero ako [but me], I may be funny but when it comes to giving information I have an aura of authority parang [like] a business executive style, a financial district approach, yung bang [it is like] the "I know this" look a la Cory Aquino. I put on that "Alam ko ang sinasabi ko" [I know what I am saying] image complete with coiffure and glasses.

Mickey settled in the United States in 1989. He reminisced about his childhood and how it related to his present preoccupation: "Well, when I was growing up, I used to dream of acting. I'm a frustrated actor. I could make people laugh. I got an offer from Regal Film [a Filipino film company], but my father said 'Hindi' [No]. My father thought it was nakakahiya [shameful]. So when I came to the States, I knew I just had to express what was inside me." I asked him what people thought of him going around as Tita Aida. "I think they could relate to someone who is funny. They could see that I am approachable parang [like] Dear Abby or Tiya Dely [Filipino radio personality who dramatized other people's problems and offered counsel]. They might think I am HIV positive. I am not. But the point is not if I am or if I am not — ano ang magagawa nila?" [What can they do?]

Mickey took his character very seriously, particularly the image he presented on stage. "Image, I'm always concerned about image when I go out on stage. I really get dressed. I want to make a sosyal hindi [tasteful and not] cheap presentation. But I also want to make it creative like my idol Nora Aunor [a Filipina actress who rose to fame from humble origins]. She is my idol — an idol because she made something out of nothing." Mickey felt that in his own way, he was doing exactly that — breathing into life out of nothing the character of Tita Aida. He talks about it using the metaphors of a fairy tale. "Doing what I do is very important," he said. "Especially if Filipinos are too shy to ask questions and access information. You have to do it creatively though. You can't force it. It has to be parang [like] Sleeping Beauty."

Tita Aida: Beyond Intimacy and Suffering

In the performance piece *Cinema Verite*, written by Ralph Peña, the question of identity and the body is complicated and troubled by the specter of AIDS. Toward the end of the play, Gerry, the protagonist, reveals that he has tested positive for the HIV antibody. His lover dies of AIDS and he himself attempts suicide but botches it. Then he calls his estranged parents in the Philippines, who tell him to come home. He agrees with them. The disease brings him back to his family and potentially repatriates and reterritorializes him.

However, Gerry is unable to "come home" to either the Philippines or the United States. He declares that because of U.S. and Philippine immigration and quarantine laws he is without a country. AIDS reterritorializes the corpus, but the legalities and policies of AIDS deterritorialize him again. At the end of the play, the character distributes a flyer that starts with "I am Gerry de la Cruz, I am a Filipino, and I am HIV positive." The juxtaposition of identity and disease is telling. In some way, it answers many of Gerry's rhetorical questions about being (or looking) Filipino. The exigencies of the disease have forced him to look into the possibility of repatriation, but they have also confronted him with a blatant and literal kind of "homelessness" that mirrors his own cultural homelessness as a gay immigrant.

AIDS becomes the body and the individual becomes the disease. Gerry embodies AIDS in several ways. AIDS perhaps is the best allegory of the gay immigrant experience. The pandemic is a transnational occurrence that traverses borders and at the same time demarcates borders (between gay and straight, between foreigner and native). It performs within multiple levels of marginality that make up the complex grid of race, nationality, sexuality, and class that gay postcolonials face. The dilemma of AIDS contains the necessary conditions of the gay immigrant body as it exists within the interstices of various discourses in the First and Third Worlds, and in gay and heterosexual communities. Gerry physically and symbolically carries the trappings of the so-called scourge of the twentieth century as he stands on the edges of medical quarantine and cultural and political exclusion.

The cases presented in this chapter illustrate the different ways the idiom Tita Aida has constructed constellations of meanings in numerous gay Filipino cultural and linguistic practices. These have enabled gay Filipinos to talk about the disease within their own terms. Tita Aida, like all other AIDS discourse, is not neutral (Leap 1990). To better understand this term it is important to unpack the layers of meaning behind the idiom.

As I mentioned in chapter 1, the notions of gender hierarchy in the Philippines have inscribed suffering within the social script of the woman and, by default, the bakla. The Roman Catholic Church, with its coterie of female saints, martyrs, and most importantly the Virgin Mary, has provided the models par excellence of suffering. In the *sinakulo* and *pasyon*, two of the most important Catholic rituals in the Philippines, which chronicle the suffering and death of Jesus Christ, the Virgin Mary is an integral character and Jesus Christ is described in many instances using feminine adjectives (Ileto 1979: 17). Philippine society's conflation of the feminine with suffering is given religious dimension.

In Philippine popular culture, movies and television dramas often portray women as sufferers. In many of the interviews I conducted there was a tendency, even with those who contended that they were happy, to acknowledge the existence of a "cross" they had to bear for being who they are. In some cases, these bakla(s) referred to the Tagalog melodramas in television and movies and saw themselves as the tragic heroines.

The intersection of suffering with sexuality, religion, and gender can be better understood with Philippine cultural conceptions of illness and disease in general and venereal diseases in particular. The Tagalog word for illness and disease is *sakit,* which can also mean pain. The same word but with a stress on the first syllable means suffering. Venereal diseases are euphemistically called *sakit ng babae,* or illnesses of women. In swardspeak, the names of Filipino beauty queens such as Vida Doria sometimes are used for these diseases. This gendered notion of venereal diseases is not unique to the Philippines (see Gilman 1988: 248–57), but it ties in with other Philippine notions of suffering.

This is the cultural tableau that informed, in part, Rene's experiences with AIDS. First, his sense of self/self-definition has been effeminate/feminine and the persona he presented was that of a "woman." His role model, Amalia Fuentes, was a Philippine actress. Second, the major figures in his life, his mother, sister, and aunt, were female. Third, his religious training and devotion, particularly to Our Lady of Perpetual Help, shaped his perception of AIDS as suffering inflicted by God.

Rene was able to accommodate his effeminate/feminine persona by utilizing the idiom of Tita Aida. By gendering AIDS, Rene and other Filipino homosexuals are able to talk about AIDS without creating a discursive upheaval or without reconfiguring the notion of bakla. By utilizing *tita,* which is both a kinship term and a camp term of endearment, Rene symbolically included AIDS in his own circle of friends and kin. Since other bakla are not potential sexual partners, the term *tita* as a camp endearment in Tita Aida enabled Rene to skirt the tricky issue of sexuality and sexual desire within the AIDS problematic.

The idiom also accommodates Rene's fascination with glamour, Tagalog movies, and Filipino actresses by exchanging Tita Aida with Aida Roxas, a Filipino actress turned nun. Here, both religious and cinematic images and symbols merge to form a kind of spectacle of the feminine, suffering, and AIDS. These kinds of intersections amplify what I have been arguing all along in this book, the idea of creating modern queer subjects not out of the "new" but in complex engagements with temporalities and spaces in the diaspora.

The use of Tita Aida in AIDS prevention literature utilizes the ambivalence inherent in the idiom. The brochures directed at Filipino gay men in California allow public health officials to tap into a discourse that constructs the disease with the use of inclusive and friendly tropes. Tita Aida as an idiom permits the use of humorous and effective channeling of information without becoming preachy or too ominous. Thus, as a common discursive system and practice, the idiom provides Filipino gay men a cultural space in which their sense of belonging or their citizenship is highlighted and articulated.

Despite the use of the kinship term *tita*, the idiom has another side, which is the image of death. Rene's warning about Tita Aida lurking in some corner or coming to fetch the careless bakla equated AIDS with death and personified AIDS as a feminized grim reaper. The failed beauty contest "Miss Tita Aida" is another example of how the stark biological realities trespass the otherwise friendly borders of the Tita Aida discourse.

Tita Aida could be seen as an anomalous category that is positioned between what Gilman (1988: 6) suggests as the two basic reactions individuals have to images of illness: denial or affirmation. Tita Aida oscillates between these extremes, between being the kind, wise kin to the dark, ominous figure of death. The ambivalence of the idiom parallels the position of the disease in the lives of gay Filipino immigrants such as Rene. Many who have come in search of a better life in America consider AIDS as a punishment. However, set within the contours of a gay transnational life like Rene's, the disease may sometimes be located within a bifocal vision, or "in-betweenness," that of America and of the homeland. Rene's anecdote of the small boy selling cigarettes matches other narratives from Filipinos who have AIDS. To them, the disease becomes another part of the balancing scales of life. For gay immigrants, this vision is a necessary component of seeing most life events. Such statements as, "Had I stayed in the Philippines . . ." or "I don't have it so bad . . ." may be to some just frantic attempts at justifying their predicaments, but in the context of the reality of a globalizing world, these are logical extensions of a framework in which to situate diasporic lives.

Studies of immigrant and exilic populations have often focused on the assimilation or violent resistance of groups. The creative responses of the groups utilizing resources from both countries are dealt with less often. Tita Aida is one such creative response. AIDS and a gay diasporic vernacular such as swardspeak have created this cultural amalgamation that has been effectively deployed in numerous communication arenas.

However, despite this seemingly heroic and valiant discourse of Tita Aida, I cannot help but think that the pandemic is a sobering experience and it presents, in the most brutal terms, the limits of play and transgression, as discussed in the previous chapter. But at the same time, the small triumphs and stories of Filipinos infected and/or affected by the pandemic that I have encountered suggest some kind of survival beyond the pandemic. The discourses around Tita Aida create "spaces of hope" (Harvey 2000) that are not naive celebratory moments, but rather are moments that open up dialogue while recognizing the constraints of being a marginal subject in a globalizing world.

The Tale of Two Viruses: An Ironic Postscript to the Pandemic?

While revising this chapter in early 2002, I realized that the volatile period of the late 1980s and early 1990s, when I was deeply involved in AIDS prevention and research, were the crucial years of political and ideological battles particularly in communities of color.[1] However, Americans tended to distance themselves from the pandemic starting in the mid-1990s. It seemed that after the so-called medical discoveries, AIDS was now considered as just another chronic disease and that people who die from it are those in the Third World who cannot afford the medications. This distancing of the popular imagination from the horrors of the disease, at least in the Filipino community in New York, is exemplified by the story of two viruses — HIV and the other, a computer virus called "I Love You."

In early May 2000, newspapers announced the spread of a sinister computer virus that was spreading via e-mail throughout the world. Usually the e-mail that contained the virus had the subject heading of "I love you." But once opened, this message of intimacy destroyed files and crashed computer systems. Spreading like wildfire through corporate and private computers in Europe, Asia, and the Americas, this virus precipitated a transnational manhunt for the responsible culprits. After a few weeks, the FBI announced that a male computer science student in the Philippines was the prime suspect. This piece of news was received by Filipinos in the Philippines and in the diaspora in a rather mixed and puzzling manner. There were the requisite angry outcries at the suspect for shaming the Philippines and for potentially harming the country by making Filipino computer programmers (who were in high demand in Western countries at the end of the millennium to mitigate the Y2K disaster) less desirable export commodities. Surprisingly, there was also an overwhelming sense of jubilation, especially among the people I talked to during this time, about how a Filipino was able to, as one informant quipped, "bring the world to its knees."

These events were happening at a time when AIDS agencies, particularly those who provided services to communities of color, were struggling to survive. It also occurred to me that Filipinos' ambivalent reactions to the "I Love You" virus stand in opposition to the earlier reactions to the AIDS pandemic in Filipino communities, which I have described in this chapter. And yet, I cannot but notice the stunning yet ironic analogy. I do not mean to imply that these two viruses are extremely similar, but at the same time, I am fully aware of the discrepant meanings behind each of the viruses and how these meanings demonstrate that Filipinos at "home" and abroad are linked—for better or worse, by e-mail and other intimate encounters—to each other and to the world.

Conclusion

Locating
the Diasporic
Deviant/
Diva

I leave one place for the other, welcomed and embraced by the family I have left —
fathers and brothers and cousins and uncles and aunts. Childhood sweethearts,
now with their own children. I am unable to stay. I make excuses, adhere to tight
schedules, I return only to depart. I am the other, the exile within afflicted with
permanent nostalgia for the mud. I return only to depart: Manila, New York, San
Francisco, Manila, Honolulu, Detroit, Manila, Guam, Hong Kong, Zamboanga,
Manila, New York, San Francisco, Tokyo, Manila again, Manila again, Manila
again. — JESSICA HAGEDORN, "Homesick"

As the Filipino American novelist Jessica Hagedorn poignantly suggests above, the seemingly mantra-like incantations of points of departure merging into destinations or periods of arrival are part and parcel
of immigrant, diasporic, and/or exilic lives. This work is constituted by

such lives and, therefore, it is only fitting that the journey that was embarked upon in this intellectual sojourn be also a space for a performance of the inevitable dialectic of departures and arrivals. Indeed, we always return to the point of departure.

In the introduction, the vignette in a New York City gay bar between Arturo, Exotica, and me encapsulates and embodies the idioms of biyuti and drama, and the varied experiences and engagements of Filipino gay men that I have described and analyzed in the previous chapters. Here, Arturo's final flourish unwittingly summarizes the continuities and discontinuities of Filipino men who identify as gay and yet find themselves in between competing traditions. The three-way conversation is in fact an attempt to locate and position selves, particularly Arturo's, within the quintessential space of gay identity — the gay bar.

Arturo and many of my informants find themselves willingly or unwillingly placed or positioned within such overt public spaces where actual physical presence stereotypically renders the individual as gay. Yet, Arturo's discomfort and uneasiness with the "gay arrangement of things" attest to more complex engagements with meanings, symbols, and images of gay culture(s) and identity. This work has attempted to delineate these various engagements as a way to show how Filipino gay men live "with and through difference" (Hall 1990: 235) and how they, as rightful cultural citizens, participate in the struggle for meaning and identity in the so-called gay community while maintaining their difference.

Most of my informants may indeed identify as gay and yet, in specific moments, whether in the mundane site of a Greenwich Village apartment or in a grand drag Santacruzan, find themselves in a liminal or marginal position in relation to mainstream white gay identity. Arturo and other informants exemplify such predicaments. Arturo's drama, part of his socialization in bakla culture, like that of many other informants, is indeed a different kind of drama that recalls other places, other images, and other practices. While some Filipinos, including Exotica, may apprehend this drama as anachronous or as remnants of a past that has been forgotten, Arturo's attitude and the strength of memories actualized in instances such as the Santacruzan or in everyday situations involving families and lovers present more complex articulations and negotiations.

As immigrant gay persons, Filipino informants' narratives betray the kinds of scripts that translate struggles in various quotidian and spectacular arenas. Religious, familial, racial, and class ties are refashioned and recast into new challenging roles and in the face of the difficulties of encountering dramas of modernity. These seemingly unfamiliar dramas or public and private practices of identity articulation recall the dissonance and incommensurability of *bakla* and *gay*. These situations also make apparent the ways in which bakla is not a prior condition before assimilating into gay identity. Rather, bakla is equally a modern sense of self that inhabits or dwells in the queer sites of the global city. Filipino gay men recuperate the bakla ideology as a way to survive and even flourish within the racial, ethnic, class, and gendered spaces of America.

Bakla, as I have argued, invokes particular kinds of scripts that point to notions of a self embedded in social relations. I suggest that the bakla is continually performing according to changing stages or performative spaces and conditions. Bakla linguistic practice, or swardspeak, exemplifies the kinds of shifting strategies that deal with various social hierarchies and dilemmas. Therefore, bakla is not an identity that is assumed by particular men but more accurately is a slippery condition, a performative event or series of events of self-formation.

However, the dissonance between gay and bakla traditions does not easily translate into estrangement or complete isolation. Filipino informants manipulate symbols and meanings, contest received notions of identity and selfhood, and create in the Santacruzan and in the codes of swardspeak scripts by which they can make sense of their worlds of perils and pleasures.

The struggles of Filipino informants are perhaps better understood in the continually shifting stages of the here and there. Home, as elaborated in much scholarship on diaspora and immigration, is popularly conceived as a quintessential place of either celebration or extreme despair. Filipino gay men's experiences contradict this simplistic belief. Filipino gay men see neither the heroics nor the hopelessness of homemaking or making oneself at home complicated by quotidian struggles. In the previous chapters, I have demonstrated how home and nation, particularly as they are embodied by the biological family, occupy a persistent yet vexed place in the lives of these men. In trying to create a life in pursuit of modern individualism, where one's independence and distance from familial constraints is a mark of Americanness, Filipino gay men concede that physical distance alone afforded by immigration does not render familial ties less influential.

Ang pamilya ay forever 'di va?

The family is forever isn't it?

Family occupies, if not haunts, the quotidian and spectacular lives of Filipino gay men. It pervades and influences how Filipino gay men assess other kinds of relationships such as those with friends and lovers. Family can also be seen as a haven in times of crises, such as situations involving AIDS. At the same time, family is also a source of anxieties that propel a need to escape or flee and to try new experiences. Alden's apartment is a stark and vivid example of how physical space and emotional/cultural space as they relate to family are complex and fluid. For Alden and many other informants, living alone marks the kind of disruption of the seemingly claustrophobic atmosphere of living with family in the Philippines and, at the same time, evokes a gap or void that is left unfilled. Many other informants have their own "Philippine corner," or moments and spaces when the familial domain troubles and intrudes into familiar everyday routines. Despite physically leaving the family, Filipino gay men agree that one never actually departs from it. In sum, for these men, family marks both the continuities and discontinuities of diasporic living.

Orientalia daw tayo. Well, ipakita nga natin kung ano ang ibig sabihin ng maging isang devastating biyuti from the beautiful country of the Philippines.

We are supposedly Orientals. Well, let us show them what it means to be a devastating biyuti from the beautiful country of the Philippines.

Racialized by both mainstream and gay communities, Filipino gay men discover that race not only incorporates skin color and/or cultural practices into its formation, but more importantly integrates these practices in intricate ways with class, gender, and sexuality. Filipino gay men are gendered as feminine because of their race. Prevailing racist assumptions about Asian men and women relegate them to passive, asexual, feminine, exotic, or oversexed individuals. Recognizing the parameters by which these Orientalist assumptions operate, Filipino gay men create strategies by which these very boundaries are transgressed, if not reconfigured. From cross-dressing to bodybuilding, informants report varied responses and engagements that establish not only their biyuti, but more importantly, their ability to act upon social worlds that may exclude them.

> *Class. May class pa ba dito? Di ba sa Pilipinas lang yan. Pantay-pantay daw tayong lahat dito — etsing!*

> Class. Does class exist here [in America]? Doesn't that only exist in the Philippines.
> We are all supposedly equal here — not!

Filipino gay men see class through many lenses. Belonging to a particular class becomes enmeshed with consumerist spending and racial and racist images. "Making it" in America, for many informants, was about buying cars, houses, and other consumerist symbols of success. Being able to send significant amounts of money back home was another marker. However, these markers may coexist with working-class status or being seen as a racial and ethnic "other." Economically successful informants reported instances or situations when the color of their skin and racist practices obscured or overpowered their material status and class mobility.

Some informants believed in America's equalizing tendency and the rootedness of unequal class structure in the Philippines. However, most recognized that despite the rhetoric to the contrary, America is suffused with implicit notions and strong undercurrents of class. Filipino gay men engaged heightened moments of class in terms of the travails of immigration. Some informants interpreted instances of class transvaluation as the logical extension of "being in America." An informant, who met a former servant who was now a rich woman in the suburbs while he himself lived the pitiful life of the undocumented, presented unique border crossings of class. Both the informant and his former employee still recognized the hierarchical relationships that existed between the two of them in the Philippines. Indeed, most informants agreed that notions and attitudes toward class might persist despite all these material changes.

> *Kahit nasaan ka, kahit ano pa ang drama ang gusto mong gawin, kailangang magdasal ka.*

> Wherever you are, whatever drama you might want to do, you need to pray.

Religion occupies a central place in what most people construe as a secular new home in America. Its persistence in the lives of these men is testimony to the glaring importance of this institution in Filipino and Filipino American societies. Moreover, religion provides a pool of overpowering symbols that are reconfigured in both spectacular and quotidian arenas and functions. They are less a lingering vestige of traditional culture and more of a pool of meanings that enable an aesthetic of survival. Folk Catholic beliefs around suffering and imitation are utilized not only to demarcate difference between Filipino gay men and other queers, but also to appropriate practices, images, and spaces from which Filipinos are excluded. Throughout this work, I have vigorously described how religion is continuously repositioned in the drag Santacruzan, in everyday routines, and in health crises such as AIDS.

Pag minsan, kahit na palagi kang nakikisama sa mga gay dito, kailangan mo rin ipakita na iba ka. Iba ang drama mo.

Sometimes, even after trying to fit in with other gays here, you need to show that you are different. One has a different drama.

Religion, class, family, and race are sites where Filipino gay men's articulations of belonging and being are performed. Such performances speak to and invoke the kinds of borders and cleavages that exist for and are confronted by Filipino gay men. In these sites and performances, Filipino gay men contest and reformulate hegemonic symbols into creolized ones. In the Santacruzan, described in detail in chapter 5, cross-dressing and the translation of important cultural symbols are both strategies by which Filipino gay men "play with the world" and iconic struggles with difference and power inequalities.

However, as the discussion on AIDS in the previous chapter suggests, the limits of play and contestation are also part of what Filipino gay men encounter in both everyday life and spectacular events. As one informant blurted out after an hour of the life-narrative interview, "I wish there were no need for visas. I wish I were a citizen of the world." He then informed me that he was an undocumented person. His statement is a crucial instance of how borders pervade the lives of Filipino gay men. Such a dilemma, in addition to other forms of racial, class, sexual, and gender exclusions, speaks to the irony of "traveling cultures" where transgressions or unbounding of borders run concomitantly with their fixing or reconstitution.

To go back to the initial question posed in the introduction: Are there no borders? The elision or denial of cleavages in the "gay community" and the idealization of a globalizing gay culture deny the ways difference actually operates in gay men's lives, particularly the lives of immigrants. Borders, as I have argued, are part of the realities of survival among Filipino gay men. This work speaks to the danger of focusing on a global or monolithic gay culture. As I have shown above, the articulations of *bakla* and *gay* involve diverse engagements from different locations. The local and national are inflected and implicated in manifold ways with each other and with the international/transnational on the level of everyday life. Conversations about globalizing tendencies in gay identity, politics, and culture are accompanied by disruptive local dialogues from people who speak from the margins. Such eruptions, such as those of my informants, need to be heard. In particular, Ted Nierras (1994), a young Filipino gay man educated in the United States, articulates a strategy for Philippine gay politics that I believe is also quite relevant to Filipino gay men in the diaspora:

> Thus, our perspectives are always partial, always interested. When we say to straight people or more rarely, to Western gay people, "we are like you," we must also remember to add "only different." When we say "we are different," we must remember that only our difference at the margin creates their sameness, already bifurcated into a violently oppressive hierarchy of gender at the straight Western center and replicated and transformed into another oppressive hierarchy of gender here. . . . We need yet to listen more carefully and more seriously to narratives of global and interconnected sexual and racial dominance and subordination, to narratives of our poor and unjustly inequitable national social reality, to narratives of the women in our society, whether they attempt to destroy or to affirm our "humanity." We need yet to speak our different desires, we need to speak our name. (1994: 199)

In this work, I have argued that Filipino gay men living in New York City contend with the displacing processes of immigration, racism, class elitism, and cultural dissonance. As such, these men struggle for survival, attempt to wrest control over meanings, and at the same time, create a sense of citizenship or belonging within a complex "stage." Performance within such locations or positions highlights structural and spatial arrangements of history and culture.

The Filipino gay immigrant is in fact multiply positioned between bakla and gay traditions, between notions of Filipinoness and Americanness, between memories of homeland and the glaring realities of living in another country. Thus, the lives of Filipino gay men are not merely about various modes of sexual behaviors or social participation in the "gay lifestyle," but rather are about struggles that go beyond the strictures of a white gay mode of living and are always mediated by experiences of travels, border crossings, and the translations of class, race, gender, and sexuality. Filipino gay men, such as Arturo and many others in the diaspora, continuously recreate their biyuti in the face of conflicting and converging dramas.

Notes

Preface

1   The names of informants have been changed to protect their anonymity. I mostly use "Filipino" instead of "Pilipino" to mean those who are citizens of the Philippines and Filipino immigrants living in the United States regardless of legal status. My use of the word Filipino with an "F" and not a "P" conforms with most, if not all, of my informants' usage. The debate regarding the use of "P" is rooted in what many Filipino American activists and scholars in the Asian American ethnic studies movement have considered to be an important symbolic act of ethnic nationalism. For this group of people, the use of "P" is based in a more "native" orthography. More importantly, my use of the word "Filipino" acknowledges that this book deals not only with people, practices, and ideas in America but also in the Philippines, where the dominant English spelling, "Filipino," connotes citizenship, culture, or people, while "Pilipino" refers to the national language. Sometimes informants use the words *Pinoy* or *Pinay,* which are diminutives for Filipino or Filipina. These words have resonance, albeit in different ways, for Filipinos in the Philippines and those in the United States.

2   Although cross-dressing is an important complex of practices among a signifi-
    cant number of informants, transgender was not a term they typically used.
    For an excellent study of this complicated intersection of gay and transgender
    among queer communities of color, see Valentine (2000).
3   I continued to meet with several informants through 2001.
4   For extended discussions of life narratives and their uses in anthropology, see
    Personal Narratives Group (1989), Watson and Watson-Franke (1985), Lang-
    ness and Frank (1981), and Kleinman (1988).
5   Taglish is code-switching between English and Tagalog. Tagalog is one of the
    main languages in the Philippines and is spoken mainly on the island of Luzon,
    where the national capital, Manila, is located. It also functions as a lingua
    franca in various parts of the country and in the Filipino diaspora. Pilipino, the
    official national language, is based on Tagalog. See Bonus (2000: 5–6) and
    Rafael (1995) for critical analyses of Taglish.
6   Interviews lasted between one and one-half hours to eight hours (staggered at
    different time intervals). These interviews were conducted mostly in people's
    homes; a few were conducted in my office, restaurants, and in the Lesbian and
    Gay community center. More than two-thirds of the interviews were taped.
7   In my original group of informants for my dissertation, eight were American
    born or second generation Americans and forty-two were immigrants. For this
    book, I have added eight more immigrant informants; the immigrant group is
    the main basis for the book. I am using the views of the American-born infor-
    mants as illustrative contrasts to the main group. Of the fifty immigrant men,
    forty-five arrived in America when they were eighteen years of age or older. Five
    of the fifty are "one point fivers" (1.5) since they came to America as young
    children or teenagers. At least thirty of the informants reported working in
    white-collar jobs such as nurse, computer programmer, chef, bank executive,
    and doctor. The rest reported being unemployed, or working as store clerks and
    busboys, with the exception of three, who reported doing "sex work." All fifty
    informants reported coming from middle to upper middle-class backgrounds
    from the Philippines. The difficulty of ascertaining class among the informants
    and the complexities of class status and identity are discussed in the succeeding
    chapters.
8   See Mahler (1998), Guarnizo and Smith (1998), and Schein (1998) for discus-
    sions of transnationalism "from below."

Introduction

1   Here, I am referring to Altman (1996) and Adam, Duyvendak, and Krouwel
    (1999). While I would agree that their works have enhanced the discussion on
    the global and the transnational, I believe we need a more dynamic view of the
    local that engages with the state and established social movements in more
    nuanced ways.
2   See Appadurai (2000) for a critical formulation of "optics."
3   The new queer studies include such works as Aguilar-San Juan (1998), Amory
    (1998), Gopinath (1996, 1998, n.d.), Eng (1997), Eng and Hom (1998), Fer-
    guson (2003), Larvie (1999), Luibheid (1996, 1998, 2002), Muñoz (1999),

Murray (2000), Reddy (1998), Reid-Pharr (2001), Shah (1993), Somerville (2000), and Wat (2002).

4 This includes Norma Alarcón (1990), Lata Mani and Ruth Frankenberg (1985), and Audre Lorde (1984).

5 Louisa Schein (1998) provides an ethnographic example of the Hmong/Miao, who traverse borders with what she calls an "oppositional cosmopolitanism." See Abelmann and Lie's (1995) productive formulation of mobility and modernity as the dual pivot of Korean migration to the United States. See also my critique of movement in multi-sited ethnography and in the study of Asian American communities (Manalansan 2000: 5–6) where movement can be perceived in terms of "how people navigate their marginal status not only across but also within such spaces."

6 Among these kinds of words are Appadurai (1988, 1990, 1991, 1996), Hardt and Negri (2000), Giddens (2000), and Sassen (1998).

7 I would like to thank Margot Gallardo for permission to reprint the song.

8 See Jane Margold's (1995) study of masculinity and Filipino migrant laborers to the Middle East.

9 According to Census 2000, Filipinos in the United States are the second biggest Asian American group after the Chinese, with 1.9 million residents. Filipinos in New York City number around 95,000. See Okamura (1998), San Juan (1994, 1998), Bonus (2000), and Tyner (1994, 2000) for studies on the Filipino global diaspora.

10 See Constable (1997) and Parreñas (2001) for studies of Filipina domestics in such places as Hong Kong, Los Angeles, and Rome.

11 See Campomanes (1992, 1995) for a persuasive and trenchant analysis of how American colonization and postcolonial presence in the Philippines have created a unique sociocultural and politico-economic context that differs not only from other Asian immigrants to the United States but also from other immigrants in general. Filipinos' postcolonial predicament is a compelling example of what David Lloyd (1996) has termed as "damage."

12 I am grateful to Dara Goldman for this felicitous definition of palimpsest.

13 See Ong (1999), Chakrabarty (2000), Ong and Nonini (1997), and Gaonkar (1999) for more extensive analyses of "alternative modernity."

14 Numerous studies on the cultures and histories of Filipinos in America include Ngai (1998), Campomanes (1992, 1995), Cariño (1987), Cordova (1974), and Bulosan (1973). For other works that set Filipinos in the United States within the broader context of Asian Americans, see Chan (1992), Paisano (1993), and Takaki (1989).

15 For extended analyses of globalization, see Sassen (1994, 1998), Gibson-Graham (1996), and Giddens (2000). For critical works on diaspora, see Clifford (1992, 1994), Brah (1996), Lavie and Swedenburg (1996).

16 See Bell and Binnie (2000) for a review of various theories of queer citizenship.

17 See also Case (1990) and Case, Brett, and Foster (1995) for further discussions of performance and performativity.

18 Performance has been an important element in studies of power and gender in Island Southeast Asia, which includes among others, the Philippines, Indonesia, and Malaysia. Anderson (1972) suggests that power, or rather potency,

unlike its Western equivalent, is more fluid and is subject to constant transformation. This idea of potency is relevant in Cannell's (1999) formulation of beauty as a constitutive element of a fluid self in contemporary Philippines. See also Errington (1990), Peacock (1968), Oetomo (1996), and Wikan (1990).

1. The Borders between *Bakla* and *Gay*

1 See Duberman's (1994) historical study of this event.
2 See the important corpus of scholarship by Stephen Murray (1979, 1987, 1992a, 1992b, 1992c, 1996) for an analysis of various categories of homosexualities.
3 See Kulick (1997, 1998) for an incisive look at the boyfriends of Brazilian *travestis*. While there are obvious differences between the travestis and the Filipino gay men I interviewed, the gender and sexual configurations have stunning parallels between the two groups.
4 For various ethnic and historical inflections of coming out in America, see the following: Berube (1990), Brown (2000), Browning (1993), Chiang (1998), and Herdt (1992). For a different cartography of gayness, see Almaguer (1991).

2. Speaking in Transit

1 See Kulick (1999) for a review of queer languages and transnationalism. See also Leap (1990) for a pioneering study of "gay language." See also Linmark's (1995) novel, which focuses on the confrontation of Filipino gay men with Hawaiian pidgin as a literary example of other kinds of linguistic situations these men confront.
2 I use code and language alternately and in the place of argot. I also use swardspeaker as a word to denote someone who uses the code.
3 Cebuano is one of the major languages of the Philippines and is typically spoken in the Visayan region.
4 See Niranjana (1994) for an excellent discussion of the politics of translation in relation to colonialism.
5 Vicente Rafael's (1988, 1995) important works, including his book on translation and Spanish colonialism in the Philippines and an essay on Taglish, represent an important corpus that is relevant to my discussion and formulation of swardspeak.
6 See Bergmann and Smith (1995) for a discussion of "Entiendes?" or "Do you understand?" which is really a way of asking, "Are you queer?"
7 See Gladys Nubla's (2002) work on the politics of language and diaspora.
8 Livia and Hall (1997) theorize the importance of performativity to queer languages.
9 See Wong and Zhang (2001) for a case study of language and *tongzhi* (Chinese queer) community building.

3. "Out There"

1 See Weston (1995) for a nuanced and important essay on queer migration to the cities. Reyes (1993) is a fascinating and pioneering study of queers of color

spaces in Los Angeles. For more general studies of gay men, modernity, and the city, consult Bech (1997), Knopp (1995, 1998), and Bleys (1995). For a more general study of gay New York, see Kaiser (1997). See also Kenney (2001), Cooper (1994), and Bailey (1999) for more general studies of queer politics and the city. The discussion of this chapter can be seen in contrast to and in conjunction with the ideas set out in Auge (1995).

2 See Hennessy (2000) for cogent ideas about gay identity and consumer culture.

3 See Wat (2002) for an excellent oral history of Asian gay men in Los Angeles before the AIDS pandemic.

4. The Biyuti and Drama of Everyday Life

1 Eric's statement implies that the family in *Eight Is Enough* is seen to be less wracked with domestic upheavals than the family in the Filipino series *Gulong ng Palad*.

2 See Bernstein and Reimann (2001) for recent studies on queer families.

3 See Leach (1961) and Douglas (1966) for discussions of the relationship between sex and food.

4 Block rosaries are community religious practices where a religious image moves from house to house in a specific neighborhood and becomes the center of worship for groups of people.

5. "To Play with the World"

1 See Stephen Murray (1992a, 1992b, 1992c) for a cultural history of homosexualities.

2 See Sarah Murray (1994) and Halberstam (1998).

6. Tita Aida

1 See Herdt and Lindenbaum (1992) and the National Research Council (1990) for chronicles of the second decade of the pandemic.

An
Elusive
Glossary

This is an anomalous section of the book. While this list is an attempt to codify and transcribe what is essentially a verbal language or communication style, it is nevertheless doomed to failure. As discussed in chapter 2, swardspeak is always on the move: that is, its lexical and syntactic rules and items are always shifting and changing. This is not a comprehensive listing but a partial collection of words in use during the time of fieldwork. These words were elicited from 1991 to 1998, and many of the words will be considered obsolete. Many of these words may not be in use anymore but serve to mark conversations and other performances temporally. I used the English alphabet in the sequential ordering of these words instead of the Tagalog alphabet.

There may be contentious orthographic renderings of specific loan words that have c or z letters but are not part of the Tagalog alphabet. In words that are related to English or Spanish words, I have attempted to render an additional orthographic representation that best approximates the Filipino gay men's pronunciation. More importantly, Filipino gay men's play on the pronunciation (e.g., stressing specific vowels or replacing consonants) is part of the performance.

afam: white American; any white foreigner. Acronym for "a foreigner [in] Manila"

apir: to appear, to show up

asiatika, asyana: Asian (feminine form)

ate, atche: an endearment for a peer (*lit.* kinship term for older sister)

baccarat: bakla, bading (*lit.* a brand of crystal)

bading, badash, badaf, vading, vadaf, jokla, jokling: less offensive versions of bakla

bagets, bagetsing: young person

bakla: homosexual, effeminate person, hermaphrodite

barkada: peer group, gang

bayo: to masturbate

bigas: Asian (*lit.* Tagalog word for rice)

biyuti, BY, BYU, biyu: physical biyuti, health, personhood, social being, fate

bruha, bru: witch, feminine endearment

bumbayic: South Asian Indian (from *Bombay*)

charing, charot: artfulness, to fool, to joke around, to dissimulate (connotes the negative and/or ironic when used after making a statement or assertion)

chica, chika, tsika: to gossip, to socialize, to mingle

chicahan, chikahan, tsikahan: *see* chica

chinois, shinwa: Chinese (from the French word)

dako, Dakota, Dakota Harrison, dakila, dakis, dakish: big penis

datung: money

datungera: rich woman

dead hungry: greedy (playful literal translation of Tagalog idiom *patay gutom*)

deadma, dedma: feigning ignorance (literal translation of Tagalog idiom *patay malisya*)

diego: tomboy, lesbian

diyutay, dyutay, duty free: short penis

DKNY: "I didn't know that" (playful use of designer label as acronym for *di ko know yan*)

drama: personal problem, schemes, plans, mundane tasks, sexuality, occupation, one's business

drogas: drugs

ebak: to defecate (play on the English *evacuate*)

eclipse, eklips, eklip: to sleep; a total eclipse of the heart (after the title of an American pop song) is a deep sleep

ek, ekyem, ek-ek, eks, ka-ekan: *see* charing

Emma, Emma Thompson: to go barefoot (British actress Emma Thompson reportedly went barefoot in one period film)

er: blue-collar worker (e.g., construction worker, carpenter)

esdu: ejaculate, semen, come

etchos, etching: *see* charing

fa, fi, flung/plung: "Isn't it?" (used instead of the Tagalog preposition *pa*; note the use of "f" instead of "p")

fadir: father

feel, pil, feeling: to like, to want, to desire, as in "Feel mo?" (So you like/want/desire?)

getch, getsing: to have somebody, to have sex, to possess

girl, gel, mugel, girlie, Girlie Miranda: effeminate; also an endearment for friends

gurang, (w)rangler: old person

hala: trick, sexual partner

halahan: tricking, having sex

idiom, idiyom, idioma, idiyoma: black or African American (a play on *itim*, the Tagalog word for black)

im, imbiyerna: irritated, annoyed, angry

imbiyernadora: diva, bitch, annoying person

inday, 'day: term of endearment, female friend

intriga, intrigahan: intrigue, gossip, quarrel, conflict

irilim dirilim: black or African American

jo-a, joastra, diyo-a: foot

jowa, diyowa: spouse, boyfriend/girlfriend

julakis, julakish: man (a play on the Tagalog word *lalaki*, or man)

Julie Andrews, Julianne Forth, julian: to hurry up (a play on the Tagalog *dalian*)

jurang, jurangelya: old person (*see* gurang)

jurassic: old person (a play on *gurang* and *jurang*)

jutim, jutam, diyutim, diyutam: black or African American (a play on *itim*, the Tagalog word for black)

kagang: police

keber, kebs, queber: "I don't care"

keps: vagina

kimbo: to have sex

kiyeme, quieme: *see* charing or etchos

kufing, kufling, kuping, kofas: to have oral sex, to suck

lalique: man (a play on a brand of crystal and *lalaki*, the Tagalog word for man)

Lucita Soriano: to lose (a play on the English *lose* and the name of a Tagalog movie actress)

Lucretia, lukring, Lucretia Kalaw: crazy (a play on the Spanish word *loca* and the Tagalog word *loka*; the last term is the name of a prominent Filipino socialite)

Luz, Luz Valdez: to lose (the name of a Tagalog film actress)

madir: mother

manay, manash: feminine term of address for peer

merese: "Who cares?"

minus: used as a way of disapproving or pointing to the error of somebody's ways as if in a beauty pageant or contest where points are deducted

moroccan: lesbian (playful use of what is believed to be a Moroccan female greeting where a wail is inflected by vibrating the tongue against one's lips)

mujer, mujerista, nagmumu, mu, moojer: woman, drag queen, cross-dresser, cross-dressing

m.u.: make-up, cosmetics

natsapter: thwarted, defeated; *see* tsapter

nota, notes: penis

orly, orloc: crazy person

pa: prefix used to connote the acting of particular roles as in pa-girl (being girlish, feminine, effeminate, or trying to act like a girl) and pa-min, paminta (being masculine, trying to act masculine)

patutsada: rationalizations

plung: *see* fa

portugesa: lesbian (a play on *Lisbon*, the capital of Portugal)

purita, Purita Kalaw Ledesma: poor, penniless (the name of a prominent Filipino female socialite)

rampa: to walk around, to prance, to cruise (from the English word *ramp* as in a fashion show)

sey, sey mo: "What do you say?"

sight, sayt: to see

silahis, silahista, silaham: bisexual

slash: boring (as in slashing one's wrist owing to boredom and therefore needing to keep oneself awake); an extreme form of boredom would be to slash with a butter knife

slight lang: a little bit

smellanie: to smell

stop-pey: to stop

suso: to suck, perform fellatio

taray, tarayera, T, T factor, silent T: feisty, diva-like

Tiboli, T'boli, T-bird: lesbian (from *tomboy*)

tig, tigbak, tigbakera: death, to die, to insult, to beat up

tita: auntie

Tita Aida: AIDS

Tita Imee: the Immigration and Naturalization Service (INS) (a play on the name of former Philippine President Ferdinand Marcos's eldest daughter, Imee)

tsaka, chaka: ugly (from the name of African American female pop singer Chaka Kahn)

tsapter, chapter, chaptir, chap: ugly, failure; *see* natsapter

tsism, chism: short for *chismis,* or gossip

tsisims: gossip (from the Tagalog word *tsismis*)

tsug: to die, to kill, or to get killed (mimics the sound of a body falling to the ground)

tsurot, churot: boyfriend or lover

type, tayp: to like, to desire

ukray, okray, uk, ok: ugly

umebs, umebak: to defecate

uring, oros: anal intercourse

urulum burulum: South Asian Indian

Vida Doria: VD, venereal disease (the name of a Filipino beauty queen)

weather: to not care, to be unmindful (literal translation of the Tagalog word *panahon*)

Winnie Santos: to win (name of Tagalog female TV and singing personality)

Wilson-Phillips: in unison or harmony (name of an all-white female pop group)

Works Cited

Abelmann, Nancy, and John Lie. 1995. *Blue Dreams*. Cambridge, Mass.: Harvard University Press.

Adam, Barry. 1990. *The Rise of a Gay and Lesbian Movement*. Boston: Twayne Publications.

Adam, Barry, Jan Willem Duyvendak, and Andre Krouwel, eds. 1999. *The Global Emergence of Gay and Lesbian Politics: National Imprints of a Worldwide Movement*. Philadelphia: Temple University Press.

Aguilar-San Juan, Karin. 1998. "Going Home: Enacting Justice in Queer Asian America." In *Q and A: Queer in Asian America*, edited by D. Eng and A. Hom. Philadelphia: Temple University Press.

Alarcón, Norma. 1990. "The Theoretical Subjects of 'This Bridge Called My Back' and Anglo American Feminism." In *Making Face/Making Soul/Hacienda Caras: Creative and Critical Perspectives by Women of Color*, edited by G. Anzaldúa. San Francisco: Aunt Lute Books.

Alexander, Jacqui. 1997. "Erotic Autonomy as a Politics of Decolonization." In *Feminist Genealogies, Colonial Legacies, Democratic Futures*, edited by J. Alexander and C. Mohanty. New York: Routledge.

Almaguer, Tomas. 1991. "Chicano Men: A Cartography of Homosexual Identity and Behavior." *Differences* 3 (2): 75–100.

Altman, Dennis. 1996. "Rupture and Continuity?: The Internationalization of Gay Identities." *Social Text* 48: 77–94.

Amory, Deborah P. 1998. "Mashoga, Mabasha, and Magai: 'Homosexuality' on the East African Coast." In *Boy-Wives and Female Husbands: Studies in African Homosexualities,* edited by S. Murray and W. Roscoe. New York: Palgrave.

Anderson, Benedict. 1972. "The Idea of Power in Javanese Culture." In *Culture and Politics in Indonesia,* edited by Claire Holt, Benedict Anderson, and James T. Siegel. Ithaca, N.Y.: Cornell University Press.

Ang, Ien. 2001. *On Not Speaking Chinese: Living between Asia and the West.* London: Routledge.

Anzaldúa, Gloria. 1987. *Borderlands/La Frontera: The New Mestiza.* San Francisco: Aunt Lute Books.

Appadurai, Arjun. 1988. "Putting Hierarchy in Its Place." *Cultural Anthropology* 3 (1): 36–49.

———. 1990. "Disjuncture and Difference in the Global Cultural Economy." In *Global Culture: Nationalism, Globalization, and Modernity,* edited by Mike Featherstone. London: Sage.

———. 1991. "Global Ethnoscapes: Notes and Queries for a Transnational Anthropology." In *Recapturing Anthropology: Working in the Present,* edited by Richard Fox. Santa Fe, N.M.: School of American Research Press.

———. 1996. *Modernity at Large: Cultural Dimensions of Globalization.* Minneapolis: University of Minnesota Press.

———. 2000. "Grassroots Globalization and the Research Imagination." *Public Culture* 12 (1): 1–19.

Arteaga, Alfred, ed. 1994. *An Other Tongue: Nation and Ethnicity in the Linguistic Borderlands.* Durham, N.C.: Duke University Press.

Auge, Marc. 1995. *Non-places.* London: Verso.

Bailey, Robert W. 1999. *Gay Politics, Urban Politics: Identity and Economics in the Urban Setting.* New York: Columbia University Press.

Baudelaire, Charles. 1964. *The Painter of Modern Life and Other Essays.* New York: Da Capo.

Bech, Ulrich. 1997. *When Men Meet: Homosexuality and Modernity.* Cambridge: Polity Press.

Beeman, William. 1993. "The Anthropology of Theater and Spectacle." *Annual Review of Anthropology* 22: 369–93.

Behar, Ruth. 1996. *The Vulnerable Observer: Anthropology that Breaks Your Heart.* Boston: Beacon Press.

Bell, David, and Jon Binnie. 2000. *The Sexual Citizen: Queer Politics and Beyond.* Cambridge: Polity Press.

Bellah, Robert N., Richard Madsen, William M. Sullivan, Anne Swidler, and Steven Tipton. 1985. *Habits of the Heart: Individualism and Commitment in American Life.* Berkeley: University of California Press.

Benjamin, Walter. 1983. *Charles Baudelaire: A Lyric Poet in the Era of High Capitalism.* London: Verso.

Bergmann, Emilie, and Paul Julian Smith, eds. 1995. *Entiendes?* Durham, N.C.: Duke University Press.

Berlant, Lauren. 1998. "Introduction: Intimacy, A Special Issue." *Cultural Critique* 24 (2): 281–88.

Bernstein, Mary, and Renate Reimann, eds. 2001. *Queer Families, Queer Politics: Challenging Cultures and the State.* New York: Columbia University Press.

Berube, Allan. 1990. *Coming Out Under Fire.* New York: Free Press.

Bhabha, Homi. 1984. "Of Mimicry and Man: The Ambivalence of Colonial Discourse." *October* 28: 15–134.

——. 1992. "The Other Question: The Stereotype and Colonial Discourse." In *The Sexual Subject: Screen Reader,* edited by Mandy Merck. London: Routledge.

——.Blackwood, Evelyn, ed. 1986. *The Many Faces of Homosexuality: Anthropological Approaches to Homosexual Behavior.* New York: Harrington Press.

Blanc-Szanton, Cristina. 1990. "Collision of Cultures: Historical Reformulations of Gender in Lowland Visayas, Philippines." In *Power and Difference: Gender in Island Southeast Asia,* edited by Jane Monnig Atkinson and Shelly Errington. Palo Alto, Calif.: Stanford University Press.

Bleys, Rudi C. 1995. *The Geography of Perversion.* New York: New York University Press.

Bonus, Rick. 2000. *Locating Filipino Americans: Ethnicity and the Cultural Politics of Space.* Philadelphia: Temple University Press.

Bourdieu, Pierre. 1977. *Outline of a Theory of Practice.* New York: Cambridge University Press.

Boym, Svetlana. 1994. *Common Places: Mythologies of Everyday Life in Russia.* Cambridge, Mass.: Harvard University Press.

——. 1998. "On Diasporic Intimacy: Ilya Kabakov's Installations and Immigrant Homes." *Critical Inquiry* 24 (2): 498–524.

Brah, Avtar. 1996. *Cartographies of Diaspora: Contesting Identities.* London: Routledge.

Brown, Michael. 2000. *Closet Space: Geographies of Metaphor from the Body to the Globe.* New York: Routledge.

Browning, Frank. 1993. *The Culture of Desire.* New York: Crown Publishers.

Bruner, Edward M. 1986. "Experience and Its Expressions." In *The Anthropology of Experience,* edited by Victor W. Turner and Edward M. Bruner. Urbana: University of Illinois Press.

Bulosan, Carlos. 1973. *America Is in the Heart, a Personal History.* New York: Harcourt, Brace and Co., 1946. Reprint, Seattle: University of Washington Press.

Butler, Judith. 1990. *Gender Trouble: Feminism and the Subversion of Identity.* New York: Routledge.

——. 1991. "Imitation and Gender Insubordination." In *Inside/out: Lesbian Theories, Gay Theories,* edited by Diana Fuss. New York: Routledge.

——. 1993. *Bodies that Matter: On The Discursive Limits of Sex.* New York: Routledge.

Campomanes, Oscar V. 1992. "Filipinos in the United States and Their Literature of Exile." In *Reading the Literatures of Asian America*, edited by Shirley Geok-lin Lim and Amy Ling. Philadelphia: Temple University Press.

———. 1995. "Afterword: The New Empire's Forgetful and Forgotten Citizens: Unrepresentability and Unassimilability in Filipino American Postcolonialities." *Critical Mass: A Journal of Asian American Cultural Criticism* 2 (2): 145–200.

Cannell, Fenella. 1991. "Catholicism, Spirit Mediums, and the Ideal of Beauty in a Bicolano Community, Philippines." Ph.D. diss., London School of Economics.

———. 1995a. "The Imitation of Christ in Bicol, Philippines." *Journal of the Royal Anthropological Institute* 1: 377–94.

———. 1995b. "The Power of Appearances: Beauty, Mimicry, and Transformation in Bicol." In *Discrepant Histories: Translocal Essays in Philippine Cultures,* edited by Vicente Rafael. Philadelphia: Temple University Press.

———. 1999. *Power and Intimacy in the Christian Philippines.* Cambridge: Cambridge University Press.

Cariño, Benjamin. 1987. "The Philippines and Southeast Asia: Historical Roots and Contemporary Linkages." In *Pacific Bridges: The New Immigrants from Asia and the Pacific Islands,* edited by James W. Fawcet and Benjamin Cariño. New York: Center for Migration Studies.

Case, Sue Ellen, ed. 1990. *Performing Feminisms: Feminist Critical Theory and Theatre.* Baltimore, Md.: Johns Hopkins University Press

Case, Sue Ellen, Philip Brett, and Susan Leigh Foster, eds. 1995. *Cruising the Performative: Interventions into the Representation of Ethnicity, Nationality and Sexuality.* Bloomington: Indiana University Press.

Castles, Stephen, and Alastair Davidson. 2000. *Citizenship and Migration: Globalization and the Politics of Belonging.* New York: Routledge.

Chakrabarty, Dipesh. 2000. *Provincializing Europe: Postcolonial Thought and Historical Difference.* Princeton, N.J.: Princeton University Press.

Chambers, Iain. 1994. *Migrancy, Culture, Identity.* London: Routledge.

Chan, Sucheng. 1992. *Asian Americans: An Interpretive History.* Boston: Twayne.

Chauncey, George. 1994. *Gay New York: Gender, Urban Culture, and the Making of the Gay Male World, 1896–1940.* New York: Harper Collins.

Cheung, King Kok. 1993. *Articulate Silences.* Ithaca, N.Y.: Cornell University Press.

Chiang, Mark. 1998. "Coming Out into the Global System: Postmodern Patriarchies and Transnational Sexualities in the Wedding Banquet." In *Q and A: Queer in Asian America,* edited by D. Eng and A. Hom. Philadelphia: Temple University Press.

Circuit Boyz Productions. 1996. *Circuit Noize* 8 (summer).

Clifford, James. 1992. "Traveling Cultures." In *Cultural Studies,* edited by Lawrence Grossberg, Cary Nelson, and Paula Treichler. New York: Routledge.

———. 1994. "Diasporas." *Cultural Anthropology* 9 (3): 302–38.

Constable, Nicole 1997. *Maid to Order in Hong Kong: Stories of Filipina Workers.* Ithaca, N.Y.: Cornell University Press.

Cooper, Davina. 1994. *Sexing the City: Lesbian and Gay Politics within the Activist State.* London: Rivers Oram Press.

Cordova, Fred. 1974. *Filipinos: Forgotten Asian Americans.* Seattle: Demonstration Project for Asian Americans.

Cruz-Malave, Arnaldo, and Martin F. Manalansan, eds. 2002. "Introduction: Dissident Sexualities/Alternative Globalisms." In *Queer Globalizations: Citizenship and the Afterlife of Colonialism*. New York: New York University Press.

de Certeau, Michel. 1984. *The Practice of Everyday Life*. New York: Cambridge University Press.

Delaney, Samuel R. 1999. *Times Square Red, Times Square Blue*. New York: New York University Press.

Deleuze, Gilles, and Felix Guattari. 1987. *A Thousand Plateaus: Capitalism and Schizophrenia*. Minneapolis: University of Minnesota Press.

D'Emilio, John. 1983. *Sexual Politics, Sexual Communities: The Making of a Homosexual Minority in the U.S., 1940–1970*. Chicago: University of Chicago Press.

Desert, Jean-Ulrick. 1997. "Queer Space." In *Queers in Space: Communities, Public Places, Sites of Resistance*, edited by G. B. Ingram, A. Bouthillette, and Y. Ritter. Seattle: Bay Press.

Dollimore, Jonathan. 1991. *Sexual Dissidence: Augustine to Wilde, Freud to Foucault*. New York: Oxford University Press.

Douglas, Mary. 1966. *Purity and Danger: An Analysis of the Concepts of Pollution and Taboo*. London: Ark Books.

Duberman, Martin. 1994. *Stonewall*. New York: Plume.

Eng, David. 1997. "Out Here and Over There: Queerness and Diaspora in Asian American Studies." *Social Text* 52–53: 31–52.

Eng, David, and Alice Hom. 1998. "Q and A: Notes on a Queer Asian America." In *Q and A: Queer in Asian America*, edited by D. Eng and A. Hom. Philadelphia: Temple University Press.

Errington, Shelly. 1990. "Recasting Sex, Gender, and Power: A Theoretical and Regional Overview." In *Power and Difference: Gender in Island Southeast Asia,* edited by Jane Monnig Atkinson and Shelly Errington. Stanford, Calif.: Stanford University Press.

Espiritu, Yen Le. 1992. *Asian American Panethnicity: Bridging Institutions and Identities*. Philadelphia: Temple University Press.

Farmer, Paul. 1992. AIDS and Accusation: Haiti and the Geography of Blame. Berkeley: University of California Press.

Featherstone, Mike, ed. 1990. *Global Culture: Nationalism, Globalization, and Modernity.* London: Sage.

Ferguson, Roderick. 2003. *Specters of the Sexual: Race, Sociology, and the Conflict over American Culture*. Minneapolis: University of Minnesota Press.

Filipino Reporter. 1994. "2 OCWs Among AIDS Victims Found by DOH." August 4–11.

Fisk, John. 1992. "Cultural Studies and the Culture of Everyday Life." In *Cultural Studies*, edited by Lawrence Grossberg, Cary Nelson, and Paula Treichler. New York: Routledge.

Fitzgerald, Thomas. 1977. "A Critique of Anthropological Research in Homosexuality." *Journal of Homosexuality* 2 (4): 385–97.

Fleras, Jomar. 1993. "Reclaiming Our Historic Rights: Gays and Lesbians in the Philippines." In *The Third Pink Book: A Global View of Lesbian and Gay Liberation,* edited by A. Hendriks, R. Tielman, and E. van der Veer. Buffalo, N.Y.: Prometheus.

Fung, Richard. 1991a. "Center the Margins." In *Moving the Image: Independent Asian Pacific American Media Arts,* edited by Russell Leong. Los Angeles: UCLA Asian American Studies Center.

———. 1991b. "Looking for My Penis: The Eroticized Asian in Gay Video Porn." In *How Do I Look?: Queer Film and Video,* edited by Bad Object-Choices. Seattle: Bay Press.

Ganguly, Keya. 2001. *States of Exception: Everyday Life and Postcolonial Identity.* Minneapolis: University of Minnesota Press.

Gaonkar, Dilip Parameshwar. 1999. "On Alternative Modernities." *Public Culture* 11 (1): 1–18.

Garcia, J. Neil C. 1994. "Unfurling Lives: An Introduction." In *Ladlad: An Anthology of Philippine Gay Writings,* edited by J. Neal Garcia and D. Remoto. Manila: Anvil Press.

———. 1996. *Philippine Gay Culture: The Last Thirty Years.* Quezon City: University of the Philippines Press.

Geertz, Clifford. 1986. "Making Experience, Authoring Selves." In *The Anthropology of Experience,* edited by Victor W. Turner and Edward M. Bruner. Urbana: University of Illinois Press.

George, Rosemary Marangoly. 1992. "Traveling Light: Of Immigration, Invisible Suitcases, and Gunny Sacks." *Differences* 4 (2): 72–99.

Gibson-Graham, J. K. 1996. *The End of Capitalism (as We Knew It): A Feminist Critique of Political Economy.* Cambridge, Mass.: Blackwell Publishers.

Giddens, Anthony. 1992. *The Transformation of Intimacy.* Stanford, Calif.: Stanford University Press.

——— 2000. *Runaway World: How Globalization Is Reshaping Our Lives.* New York: Routledge.

Gilman, Sander. 1988. *Disease and Representation: Images of Illness from Madness to AIDS.* Ithaca, N.Y.: Cornell University Press.

Gilroy, Paul. 1993. *The Black Atlantic: Modernity and Double Consciousness.* Cambridge, Mass.: Harvard University Press.

Glick Schiller, Nina, Linda Basch, and Cristina Blanc-Szanton. 1992. "Transnationalism: A New Analytic Framework for Understanding Migration: Towards a Transnational Perspective on Migration." *Annals of the New York Academy of Science.* Vol. 645. New York: New York Academy of Science.

———. 1994. *Nations Unbound: Transnational Project, Postcolonial Predicaments, and Deterritorialized Nation-States.* New York: Gordon and Breach.

Goffman, Erving. 1959. *Presentation of Self in Everyday Life.* Woodstock, N.Y.: Overlook Press.

Gopinath, Gayatri. 1996. "Funny Boys and Girls: Notes on a Queer South Asian Planet." In *Asian American Sexualities: Dimensions of the Gay and Lesbian Experience,* edited by Russell Leong. New York: Routledge.

———. 1998. "Homo Economics: Queer Sexualities in a Transnational Frame." In *Burning Down the House,* edited by R. M. George. Boulder, Colo.: Westview Press.

———. n.d. *Contradictory Desires: Queer Diasporas and South Asian Public Cultures.* Unpublished manuscript.

Gupta, Akhil, and James Ferguson. 1992. "Beyond 'Culture': Space, Identity, and the Politics of Difference." *Cultural Anthropology* 7 (1): 6–23.

Gutierrez, Ramon. 1989. "Must We Deracinate Indians to Find Gay Roots?" *Out/Look* 1 (4): 61–67.

Guarnizo, Luis Eduardo, and Michael Peter Smith. 1998. "The Locations of Transnationalism." In *Transnationalism from Below,* edited by M. P. Smith and L. E. Guarnizo. New Brunswick, N.J.: Transaction Press.

Hagedorn, Jessica. 1991. "Homesick." In *Visions of America: Personal Narratives from the Promised Land,* edited by Wesley Brown and Amy Ling. New York: Persea Books.

Halberstam, Judith. 1998. "Transgender Butch: Butch/FTM Border Wars and the Masculine Continuum." *GLQ: A Journal of Lesbian and Gay Studies* 4 (2): 287–310.

Hall, Stuart. 1990. "Cultural Identity and Diaspora." In *Identity: Community, Culture, Difference,* edited by Jonathan Rutherford. London: Lawrence and Wishart.

Hannerz, Ulf. 1992. *Cultural Complexity: Studies in the Social Organization of Meaning.* New York: Columbia University Press.

——. 1996. *Transnational Connections: Culture, People, Places.* New York: Routledge.

Hardt, Michael, and Antonio Negri. 2000. *Empire.* Cambridge, Mass.: Harvard University Press.

Hart, Donn. 1968. "Male Homosexuality and Transvestism in the Philippines." *Behavior Science Notes* 2: 211–48.

Hart, Donn, and Harriet Hart. 1990. "Visayan Swardspeak: The Language of a Gay Community in the Philippines." *Crossroads: An Interdisciplinary Journal of Southeast Asian Studies* 5 (2): 27–49.

Hart, Linda, and Peggy Phelan. 1993. *Acting Out: Feminist Performances.* Ann Arbor: University of Michigan Press.

Harvey, David. 2000. *Spaces of Hope.* Berkeley: University of California Press.

Hawkeswood, William. 1996. *"One of the Children": Gay Black Men in Harlem.* Berkeley: University of California Press.

Hennessy, Rosemary. 2000. *Profit and Pleasure: Sexual Identities in Late Capitalism.* New York: Routledge.

Herdt, Gilbert. 1992. " 'Coming Out' as a Rite of Passage: A Chicago Study." In *Gay Culture in America: Essays from the Field,* edited by Gilbert Herdt. Boston: Beacon Press.

Herdt, Gilbert, and Andrew Boxer. 1992. "Introduction: Culture, History, and Life Course of Gay Men." In *Gay Culture in America: Essays from the Field,* edited by Gilbert Herdt. Boston: Beacon Press.

Herdt, Gilbert, and Shirley Lindenbaum. 1992. *The Time of* AIDS: Social Analysis, Theory, and Method. Newbury Park: Sage.

hooks, bell. 1992. *Black Looks: Race and Representation.* Boston: South End Press.

Hwang, David Henry. 1986. *M. Butterfly.* New York: New American Library-Plume Books.

Ileto, Reynaldo. 1979. *Pasyon and Revolution: Popular Movements in the Philippines, 1840–1910.* Quezon City: Ateneo de Manila University Press.

Itiel, Joseph. 1989. *Philippine Diary: A Gay Guide to the Philippines*. San Francisco: International Wavelength, Inc.

Iyer, Pico. 1988. *Video Nights in Kathmandu and Other Reports from the Not So Far East*. New York: Vintage.

Johnson, Mark. 1996. "Negotiating Style and Mediating Beauty: Transvestite (Gay/Bantut) Beauty Contests in the Southern Philippines." In *Beauty Contests in the Global Stage: Gender, Contests, and Power*, edited by Colleen Ballerino Cohen, Richard Wilk, and Beverly Stoeltje. New York: Routledge.

———. 1997. *Beauty and Power: Transgendering and Cultural Transformation in the Southern Philippines*. Oxford: Berg.

Joseph, May. 1995. "Diaspora, New Hybrid Identities, and the Performance of Citizenship." *Women and Performance: A Journal of Feminist Theory* 7 (2)–8 (1): 3–13

———. 1998. "Transatlantic Inscriptions: Desire, Diaspora, and Cultural Citizenship." In *Talking Visions: Multicultural Feminism in a Transnational Age*, edited by E. Shohat. Cambridge, Mass.: MIT Press.

Kaiser, Charles. 1997. *The Gay Metropolis*. New York: Harcourt Brace.

Kaplan, Caren. 1996. *Questions of Travel: Postmodern Discourses of Displacement*. Durham, N.C.: Duke University Press.

Kaplan, Caren, and Inderpal Grewal. 1994. "Introduction: Transnational Feminist Practices and Questions of Postmodernity." In *Scattered Hegemonies*, edited by Caren Kaplan and Inderpal Grewal. Minneapolis: University of Minnesota Press.

Kenney, Moira. 2001. *Mapping Gay L.A.: The Intersection of Place and Politics*. Philadelphia: Temple University Press.

Kleinman, Arthur. 1988. *The Illness Narratives*. New York: Basic Books.

Kleinman, Arthur, Veena Das, and Margaret Lock. 1997. *Social Suffering*. Berkeley: University of California Press.

Knopp, Lawrence. 1995. "Sexuality and Urban Space: A Framework for Analysis." In *Mapping Desire: Geographies of Sexuality*, edited by D. Bell and G. Valentine. London: Routledge.

———. 1998. "Sexuality and Urban Space: Gay Male Identity Politics in the United States, the United Kingdom, and Australia." In *Cities of Difference*, edited by R. Fincher and J. M. Jacobs. New York: Guilford Press.

Kondo, Dorinne. 1990. "*M. Butterfly*: Orientalism, Gender, and a Critique of Essentialist Identity." *Cultural Critique* 16: 5–29.

Kulick, Don. 1997. "A Man in the House: The Boyfriends of Brazilian Travestis Prostitutes." *Social Text* 52–53: 133–60.

———. 1998. *Travestis: Sex, Gender, and Culture among Brazilian Transgendered Prostitutes*. Chicago: University of Chicago Press.

———. 1999. "Transgender and Language: A Review of the Literature and Suggestions for the Future." *GLQ: A Journal of Lesbian and Gay Studies* 5 (4): 205–22.

Langness, L. L., and Gelya Frank. 1981. *Lives: An Anthropological Approach to Biography*. Novato, Calif.: Chandler and Sharp Publisher.

Larvie, Sean Patrick. 1999. "Queerness and the Specter of Brazilian National Ruin." *GLQ: A Journal of Lesbian and Gay Studies* 5 (4): 527–58.

Lavie, Smadar, and Ted Swedenburg, eds. 1996. *Displacements, Diasporas, and Geographies of Identity.* Durham, N.C.: Duke University Press.

Leach, Edmund. 1961. *Re-thinking Anthropology.* London: Athlone Press.

Leap, Bill. 1990. "Language and AIDS." In *Culture and AIDS,* edited by Douglas A. Feldman. New York: Praeger.

———. 1996. *Word's Out: Gay Men's English.* Minneapolis: University of Minnesota Press.

Lee, Robert G. 1999. *Orientals: Asian Americans in Popular Culture.* Philadelphia: Temple University Press.

Lefebvre, Henri. 1991. *Critique of Everyday Life.* Vol. 1. London: Verso.

Levine, Martin. 1990. "Gay Macho: Ethnography of the Homosexual Clone." Ph.D. diss., New York University.

———. 1992. "The Life and Death of Gay Clones." In *Gay Culture in America: Essays from the Field,* edited by Gilbert Herdt. Boston: Beacon Press.

———. 1998. *Gay Macho: The Life and Death of the Homosexual Clone.* New York: New York University Press.

Linmark, R. Zamora. 1995. *Rolling the R's.* New York: Kaya Production.

Livia, Anna, and Kira Hall. 1997. "It's a Girl! Bringing Performativity Back to Linguistics." In *Queerly Phrased: Language, Gender, and Sexuality.* New York: Oxford University Press.

Lloyd, David. 1996. "The Recovery of Kitsch." In *Distant Relations* edited by Trisha Ziff. New York: Smart Press.

Lorde, Audre. 1984. *Sister/Outsider: Essays and Speeches.* Trumansburg, N.Y.: The Crossing Press.

Lowe, Lisa. 1991. *Critical Terrains: British and French Orientalisms.* Ithaca, N.Y.: Cornell University Press.

———. 1996. *Immigrant Acts: On Asian American Cultural Politics.* Durham, N.C.: Duke University Press.

Luibheid, Eithne. 1996. "Obvious Homosexuals and Homosexuals Who Cover Up." *Radical America* 26 (2): 33–40.

———. 1998. "Looking Like a Lesbian: The Organization of Sexual Monitoring at the U.S.-Mexico Border." *Journal of the History of Sexuality* 8: 477–506.

———. 2002. *Entry Denied: Monitoring Sexuality at the Border.* Minneapolis: University of Minnesota Press.

Mahler, Sarah. 1998. "Theoretical and Empirical Contributions Towards a Research Agenda for Transnationalism." In *Transnationalism from Below,* edited by M. P. Smith and L. E. Guarnizo. New Brunswick, N.J.: Transaction Press.

Malkki, Lisa. 1992. "National Geographic: The Rooting of Peoples and the Territorialization of National Identity Among Scholars and Refugees." *Cultural Anthropology* 7 (1): 24–44.

Manalansan IV, Martin F. 1993. "(Re)locating the Gay Filipino: Resistance, Postcolonialism and Identity." *Journal of Homosexuality* 26 (2/3): 53–73.

———. 1995. "In the Shadows of Stonewall: Examining Gay Transnational Politics and the Diasporic Dilemma." *GLQ: A Journal of Lesbian and Gay Studies* 2–4: 425–38.

———. 2000. "Introduction: The Ethnography of Asian America: Notes Towards a

Thick Description." In *Cultural Compass: Ethnographic Explorations of Asian America,* edited by Martin F. Manalansan IV. Philadelphia: Temple University Press.

Mani, Lata, and Ruth Frankenberg. 1985. "The Challenge of Orientalism." *Economy and Society* 14 (2): 174–92.

Marcus, George. 1992. "Past, Present, and Emergent Identities: Requirements for Ethnographies of the Late Twentieth-Century Worldwide." In *Modernity and Identity,* edited by Scott Lash and Jonathan Friedman. Oxford: Blackwell.

———. 1998. *Ethnography through Thick and Thin.* Princeton, N.J.: Princeton University Press.

Margold, Jane. 1995. "Narratives of Masculinity and Transnational Migration: Filipino Workers in the Middle East." In *Bewitching Women, Pious Men: Gender and Body Politics in Southeast Asia,* edited by A. Ong and M. Peletz. Berkeley: University of California Press.

Mathews, Paul W. 1987. "Some Preliminary Observations of Male Prostitution in Manila." *Philippine Sociological Review* 35 (3–4): 55–74.

Mercer, Kobena. 1988. "Diaspora Culture and the Dialogic Imagination." In *Blackframes: Critical Perspectives on Black Independent Cinema,* edited by M. Cham and C. Watkins. London: MIT Press.

Mohanty, Chandra Talpade. 1990. "Feminist Encounters: Locating the Politics of Experience." In *Destabilizing Theory: Contemporary Feminist Debates,* edited by Michelle Barrett and Anne Phillips. Palo Alto, Calif.: Stanford University Press.

———. 1991a. "Cartographies of Struggle: Third World Women and the Politics of Feminism." In *Third World Women and the Politics of Feminism,* edited by Chandra Talpade Mohanty, Ann Russo, and Lourdes Torres. Bloomington: Indiana University Press.

———. 1991b. "Under Western Eyes: Feminist Scholarship and Colonial Discourses." In *Third World Women and the Politics of Feminism,* edited by Chandra Talpade Mohanty, Ann Russo, and Lourdes Torres. Bloomington: Indiana University Press.

Mollenkopf, John, and Manuel Castells, eds. 1991. *Dual City: Restructuring New York.* New York: Russell Sage Foundation.

Morris, Rosalind C. 1995. "All Made Up: Performance Theory and the New Anthropology of Sex and Gender." *Annual Review of Anthropology* 25: 567–92.

———. 1998. "Educating Desire: Thailand, Transnationalism, and Transgression." *Social Text* 52–53: 53–79.

Muñoz, Jose Esteban. 1999. *Disidentifications: Queers of Color and the Performance of Politics.* Minneapolis: University of Minnesota Press.

Munt, Sally. 1995. "The Lesbian Flaneur." In *Mapping Desire: Geographies of Sexuality,* edited by D. Bell and G. Valentine. London: Routledge.

Murray, David. 2000. "Between a Rock and a Hard Place: The Power and Powerlessness of Transnational Narratives among Gay Martinican Men." *American Anthropologist* 102 (2): 261–70.

Murray, Sarah. 1994. "Dragon Ladies, Draggin' Men: Some Reflections on Gender, Drag, and Homosexual Communities." *Public Culture* 8: 343–63.

Murray, Stephen O. 1979. "The Institutional Elaboration of a Quasi-ethnic Community." *International Review of Modern Sociology* 9 (21): 165–78.

———. 1987. *Male Homosexuality in Central and South America.* New York: Gay Academic Union.

———. 1992a. "Components of Gay Community in San Francisco." In *Gay Culture in America: Essays from the Field,* edited by Gilbert Herdt. Boston: Beacon Press.

———. 1992b. *Oceanic Homosexualities.* New York: Garland.

———. 1992c. "The Underdevelopment of Modern/Gay Homosexuality in Mesoamerica." In *Modern Homosexualities: Fragments of Lesbian and Gay Experience,* edited by Kenneth Plummer. London: Routledge.

———. 1996. *American Gay.* Chicago: University of Chicago Press.

Naficy, Hamid. 1991. "The Poetics and Practice of Iranian Nostalgia in Exile." *Diaspora* 1 (3): 285–302.

National Research Council. 1990. AIDS: The Second Decade. Washington, D.C.: National Academy Press.

Newton, Esther. 1972. *Mother Camp: Female Impersonators in America.* Chicago: University of Chicago Press.

———. 2000. *Margaret Mead Made Me Gay: Personal Essays, Public Ideas.* Durham, N.C.: Duke University Press.

New York City Lesbian and Gay Pride Guide. 1996. *The Official Guide to Lesbian and Gay Pride and History Month.* New York: Pride Access Corporation.

Ngai, Mai. 1998. "Illegal Aliens and Alien Citizens: United States Immigration Policy and Racial Formation, 1924–1945." Ph.D. diss., Columbia University.

Nierras, Ted. 1994. "This Risky Business of Desire: Theoretical Notes for and against Filipino Gay Male Identity." In *Ladlad: An Anthology of Philippine Gay Writings,* edited by J. Neal Garcia and D. Remoto. Manila: Anvil Press.

Nimmo, Arlo. 1978. *The Relativity of Sexual Deviance: A Sulu Example.* Papers in Anthropology. Norman, Okla.: Department of Anthropology, University of Oklahoma.

Niranjana, Tejaswini. 1994. "Colonialism and the Politics of Translation." In *An Other Tongue: Nation and Ethnicity in the Linguistic Borderlands,* edited by A. Arteaga. Durham, N.C.: Duke University Press.

Nubla, Gladys. 2002. "Hailing the Diasporic Nation: The Cultural History of Tagalog/Filipino in the United States." M.A. thesis, University of California, Los Angeles.

Oetomo, Dede. 1996. "Gender and Sexual Orientation in Indonesia." In *Fantasizing the Feminine in Indonesia,* edited by Lauri Sears. Durham, N.C.: Duke University Press.

Ogasawara, Dale. 1993. "Beyond the Rice Queen: Different Politics, Varying Identities." *Color Life: The Lesbian, Gay, Twospirit, and Bisexual People of Color Magazine* 1 (5): 1, 11, and 28.

Okamura, Jonathan. 1993. "The Filipino American Diaspora: Sites of Space, Time, and Ethnicity." In *Privileging Positions: The Sites of Asian American Studies,* edited by Gary Y. Okihiro, Marilyn Alquizola, Dorothy Fujita Rony, and J. Scott Wong. Pullman: Washington State University Press.

———. 1998. *Imagining the Filipino American Diaspora: Transnational Relations, Identities, and Communities.* New York: Garland.

Ong, Aihwa. 1999. *Flexible Citizenship: The Cultural Logics of Transnationality.* Durham, N.C.: Duke University Press.

Ong, Aihwa, and Donald Nonini. 1997. *The Cultural Politics of Modern Chinese Transnationalism*. New York: Routledge.

Ortner, Sherry. 1992. "Reading America: Preliminary Notes on Class and Culture." In *Recapturing Anthropology: Working in the Present,* edited by Richard Fox. Santa Fe, N.M.: School of American Research Press.

Paisano, Edna L. 1993. *We, the American - -: Asians*. Washington, D.C.: Government Printing Office.

Parker, Richard. 1999. *Beneath the Equator: Cultures of Desire, Male Homosexuality, and Emerging Gay Communities in Brazil*. New York: Routledge.

Parmar, Pratibha. 1993. "That Moment of Emergence." In *Queer Looks,* edited by M. Gever, J. Greyson, and P. Parmar. New York: Routledge.

Parreñas, Rhacel Salazar. 2001. *Servants of Globalization: Women, Migration, and Domestic Work*. Stanford, Calif.: Stanford University Press.

Patton, Cindy. 2002. *Globalizing* AIDS. Minneapolis: University of Minnesota Press.

Patton, Cindy, and Benigno Sanchez-Eppler, eds. 2000. "Introduction: Passport out of Eden." In *Queer Diasporas*. Durham, N.C.: Duke University Press.

Peacock, James. 1968. *Rites of Modernization: Symbolic and Social Aspects of Indonesian Proletarian Drama*. Chicago: University of Chicago Press.

Peña, Ralph. n.d. *Cinema Verite*. Unpublished manuscript.

Perez, Tony. 1992. *Cubao 1980 at iba pang katha: Unang Sigaw ng Gay liberation movement sa Pilipinas* [Cubao 1980 and other works: The first cry of the gay liberation movement in the Philippines]. Manila: Cacho Publishing House.

Personal Narratives Group. 1989. *Interpreting Women's Lives: Feminist Theory and Personal Narratives*. Bloomington, Ind.: Indiana University Press.

Povinelli, Elizabeth A., and George Chauncey. 1999. "Thinking Sex Transnationally: An Introduction." *GLQ: A Journal of Lesbian and Gay Studies* 5 (4): 439–50.

Pratt, Geraldine. 1998. "Grids of Difference: Place and Identity Formation." In *Cities of Difference,* edited by R. Fincher and J. M. Jacobs. New York: Guilford Press.

Quiroga, Jose. 2000. *Tropics of Desire: Interventions from Queer Latino America*. New York: New York University Press.

Rafael, Vicente. 1988. *Contracting Colonialism: Translation and Conversion in Tagalog Society Under Early Spanish Rule*. Quezon City: Ateneo de Manila University Press.

———. 1995. "Taglish or the Phantom Power of the Lingua Franca." *Public Culture* 8: 101–26.

Raquiza, Marie Antonette. 1983. "Bakla, Do They Have a Chance?" *Diliman Review* 31 (5): 35–37.

Read, Kenneth. 1980. *Other Voices: The Style of a Male Homosexual Tavern*. Novato, Calif.: Chandler and Sharp.

Realuyo, Bino A. 1999. *The Umbrella Country*. New York: Ballantine.

Reddy, Chandan. 1998. "Home, Houses, Nonidentity: Paris Is Burning." In *Burning Down the House,* edited by R. M. George. Boulder, Colo.: Westview Press

Reid-Pharr, Robert. 2001. *Black Gay Man: Essays*. New York: New York University Press.

Reyes, Eric Estuar. 1993. *Queer Spaces: The Spaces of Lesbians and Gay Men of Color in Los Angeles*. Master's thesis, University of California-Los Angeles.

Rich, Adrienne. 1986. *Blood, Bread, Poetry: Selected Prose, 1979–1985*. New York: Norton.

Rofel, Lisa. 1999. "Qualities of Desire: Imagining Gay Identities in China." *GLQ: A Journal of Lesbian and Gay Studies* 5 (4): 451–74.

Rosaldo, Renato. 1989. *Culture and Truth: The Remaking of Social Analysis*. Boston: Beacon Press.

———. 1994. "Cultural Citizenship and Education Democracy." *Cultural Anthropology* 9 (3): 402–11.

Rushdie, Salman. 1988. *Imaginary Homelands*. London: Penguin.

Said, Edward W. 1978. *Orientalism*. New York: Vintage Books.

Sanchez-Eppler, Benigno, and Cindy Patton. 2000. "Introduction: With a Passport out of Eden." In *Queer Diasporas*, edited by Cindy Patton and Benigno Sanchez-Eppler. Durham, N.C.: Duke University Press.

Sandoval, Chela. 1991. "U.S. Third World Feminism: The Theory and the Method of Oppositional Consciousness in the Postmodern World." *Genders* 10: 1–24.

San Juan, Epifanio. 1994. "Configuring the Filipino Diaspora in the United States." *Diaspora* 3 (2): 117–34.

———. 1998. *From Exile to Diaspora: Versions of Filipino Experiences in the United States*. Boulder, Colo.: Westview Press.

Sassen, Saskia. 1994. *Cities in a World Economy*. Thousand Oaks, Calif.: Pine Forge Press.

———. 1996. "Identity in the Global City: Economic and Cultural Encasements." In *Geography of Identity*, edited by Patricia Yaeger. Ann Arbor: University of Michigan Press.

———. 1998. *Globalization and Its Discontents*. New York: New Press.

———. 2001. *Global City: New York, London, Tokyo*. Princeton, N.J.: Princeton University Press.

Schein, Louisa. 1998. "Forged Transnationality and Oppositional Cosmopolitanism." In *Transnationalism from Below*, edited by M. P. Smith and L. E. Guarnizo. New Brunswick, N.J.: Transaction Press.

Scott, James. 1985. *Weapons of the Weak: Everyday Forms of Peasant Resistance*. New Haven, Conn.: Yale University Press.

Shah, Nayan. 1993. "Sexuality, Identity, and the Uses of History." In *Lotus of Another Color*, edited by Rahesh Ratti. Boston: Alyson.

Shohat, Ella, and Robert Stam. 1994. *Unthinking Eurocentrism: Multiculturalism and the Media*. London: Routledge.

Sinfield, Alan. 2000. "Diaspora and Hybridity: Queer Identities and the Ethnicity Model." In *Diaspora and Visual Culture: Representing Africans and Jews*, edited by N. Mirzoeff. New York: Routledge.

Slotkin, Richard. 1992. *Gunfighter Nation: The Myth of the Frontier in Twentieth-Century America*. New York: HarperCollins.

Smith, Dorothy. 1987. *The Everyday World as a Problematic: A Feminist Sociology*. Boston: Northeastern University Press.

Somerville, Siobhan. 2000. *Queering the Color Line: Race and the Invention of Homosexuality in American Culture*. Durham, N.C.: Duke University Press.

Stewart, Kathleen. 1992. "Nostalgia: A Polemic." In *Rereading Cultural*

Anthropology, edited by George E. Marcus. Durham, N.C.: Duke University Press.

Takaki, Ronald. 1989. *Strangers from a Different Shore: A History of Asian-Americans.* Boston: Little Brown and Company.

Tan, Michael. 1995. "From Bakla to Gay: Shifting Gender Identities and Sexual Behaviors in the Philippines." In *Conceiving Sexuality: Approaches to Sex Research in a Postmodern World,* edited by John G. Parker and John H. Gagnon. New York: Routledge.

Taussig, Michael. 1993. *Mimesis and Alterity: A Particular History of the Senses.* New York: Routledge.

Turner, Victor. 1987. *The Anthropology of Performance.* New York: PAJ Publications.

Tyner, James A. 1994. "The Social Construction of Gendered Migration from the Philippines." *Asian and Pacific Migration Journal* 3 (4): 589–617.

———. 2000. "Migrant Labour and the Politics of Scale: Gendering the Philippine State. *Asia Pacific Viewpoint* 41 (2): 131–54.

Valentine, David. 2000. "I Know What I Am: The Category 'Transgender' in the Construction of Contemporary U.S. American Conceptions of Gender and Sexuality." Ph.D. diss., New York University.

Wat, Eric. 2002. *The Making of a Gay Asian Community: An Oral History of Pre-AIDS Los Angeles.* Lanham, Colo.: Rowman and Littlefield.

Watney, Simon. 1995. "AIDS and the Politics of Queer Diaspora." In *Negotiating Lesbian and Gay Subjects,* edited by M. Dorenkamp and R. Henke. New York: Routledge.

Watson, Lawrence C., and Maria Barbara Watson-Franke. 1985. *Interpreting Life Histories: An Anthropological Inquiry.* New Brunswick, N.J.: Rutgers University Press.

Weston, Kath. 1991. *Families We Choose: Lesbians, Gays, and Kinship.* New York: Columbia University Press.

———. 1995. "Get Thee to a Big City: Sexual Imaginary and the Great Gay Migration." *GLQ: A Journal of Lesbian and Gay Studies* 2 (3): 253–77.

Whitam, Frederick, and Robin Mathy. 1986. *Male Homosexuality in Four Societies.* New York: Praeger.

White, Edmund. 1980. *States of Desire: Travels in Gay America.* New York: E. P. Dutton.

———. 2001. *The Flaneur: A Stroll through the Paradoxes of Paris.* London: Bloomsbury.

Wikan, Unni. 1990. *Managing Turbulent Hearts: A Balinese Formula for Living.* Chicago: University of Chicago Press.

Wong, Andrew, and Qing Zhang. 2001. "The Linguistic Construction of the Tongzhi Community." *Journal of Linguistic Anthropology* 10 (2): 248–78.

Woo, Jean M., George W. Rutherford, Susan F. Payne, J. Lowell Barnhardt, and George Lemp. 1988. "The Epidemiology of AIDS in Asian and Pacific Islander Populations in San Francisco." *AIDS* (2): 473–75.

Index

Adam, Barry, 22
African American gay men, 67–68, 78–80
AIDS, 152–83 passim; language and, 57–58. *See also* Language; Swardspeak; Tita Aida
Alexander, Jaqui, 5
Ang, Ien, 46, 59
Anzaldúa, Gloria, 8
Appadurai, Arjun, 6
Arteaga, Alfred, 60
Asian and Friends, 45

Bakla: definition, x–xi; the female heart, 25; the masculine bakla, 25–36; modernity and, 35–44
Bech, Ulrich, 65

Berlant, Lauren, 91
Bhabha, Homi, 60
Biyuti: and AIDS, 58; definition, ix, 15–16, 24–26; and everyday life, 92
Bourdieu, Pierre, 92
Boym, Svetlana, 91, 121, 123–24
Bruner, Edward, 133
Butler, Judith, 15. *See also* Performance

Cannell, Fennella, ix, 12–13, 35, 43–44, 139
Chauncey, George, 5, 9, 23, 64
Citizenship: crisis of, 13; and globalization, 13–14; performance of, 15. *See also* Cultural citizenship
Class: AIDS and, 157; Asian gay men and, 86–87, the bakla and, 25–26,

Class (*Continued*)
38–39; clones and, 69–70, 76–77;
coming out and, 34; language and,
55
Clifford, James, 18, 133
Clones, 66, 69
Coming out, 23, 27–35; the closet, 29–
35; silence and, 29–31
Cross-dressing, 127, 139–40; language
and, 54–55
Cultural citizenship, 14

de Certeau, Michel, 90, 92
Delaney, Samuel, 69–70
D'Emilio, John, 65
Drama: in everyday life, 92; as an
idiom, ix, 15–16

Eng, David, 91
Everyday life, 125–89; AIDS in, 162–66

Family, 94–114; and AIDS, 166–69
Farmer, Paul, 155
Filipino immigration, 10–12
Flaneur, 64–65, 87–88
Fleras, Jomar, 36–38
Fung, Richard, 16

Gaonkar, Dilip, 124
Garcia, J. Neil, 39–41
Gay Asian and Pacific Islander Men of
New York (GAPIMNY), 84, 128
Gay bars: as quintessential space of gay
identity, 2; rice bars, 81–83; as
spaces for queers of color, 71–72
Gay identity, 23–24
Geertz, Clifford, 132
Gender: and the bakla, 24–26; and lan-
guage (swardspeak), 53–55
George, Rosemary, 149, 151
Giddens, Anthony, 5
Gilroy, Paul, 91
Globalization, 5
Gopinath, Gayatri, 6, 91
Grewal, Inderpal, 8

Habits of the Heart, 22
Hall, Stuart, 150

Hart, Donn, 25
Hawkeswood, William, 66–68
Herdt, Gilbert, 23

Ileto, Reynaldo, 41
Immigration, 17; and mobility, 8–9;
narratives of, 21
Intimacy, 91; diasporic intimacy, 91
Itiel, Joseph, 85–86
Iyer, Pico, 12–13

Johnson, Mark, ix, 42–43
Joseph, May, 14

Kambal sa Lusog, 127
Kaplan, Caren, 9

Language, 46; and modernity, 50; and
silence, 29–31. *See also* Modernity;
Swardspeak
Levine, Martin, 66–67
Lloyd, David, 139

Mathews, Paul, 25–26
Mercer, Kobena, 156
Miss Saigon, 128
Modernity, 21, 124
Mohanty, Chandra Talpade, 8
Morris, Rosalind, 15
Munt, Sally, 65

"New Queer Studies," 6–7
New York City, 69–71, 88; as global
city, 64
Nierras, Ted, 190
Niranjana, Tejaswini, 60
Nostalgia, 136–40

Ogasawara, Dale, 16
Okamura, Jonathan, 11–12
Ong, Aihwa, 14
Orientalism, 140–47. *See also* Race

Parker, Richard, 64
Patton, Cindy, 155
Peña, Ralph, 141
Perez, Tony, 35–36
Performance, 15; and everyday life,

122; and language, 51–53. *See also* Citizenship; Language

Povinelli, Elizabeth, 4, 9

Race, 66; and language (swardspeak), 56–57

Rafael, Vicente, 41

Raquiza, Marie Antionette, 25

Realuyo, Bino, 12

Religion: and everyday life, 118–21; and the Santacruzan pageant, 114–21. *See also* AIDS; Santacruzan

Rice queen, 84–86

Rich, Adrienne, 8

Rofel, Lisa, 14

Rosaldo, Renato, 14

Sandoval, Chela, 8

Santacruzan, 127–36. *See also* Religion

Sassen, Saskia, 64

Schein, Louisa, 60

Scott, James, 43

Shohat, Ella, 14

Smith, Dorothy, 90

Stam, Robert, 14

Stewart, Kathleen, 136

Stonewall, 30–34

Swardspeak, 46–61. *See also* Language

Taglish, ix, 48

Tan, Michael, 38–39

Tita Aida, 169–82. *See also* AIDS

Translation, 45–47, 59–61

Tyner, James, 11

Umbrella Country, The, 12

Vogueing balls, 78–79. *See also* African American gay men

Watney, Simon, 3

White, Edmund, 65

Martin F. Manalansan IV is Assistant Professor of Anthropology at the University of Illinois, Urbana-Champaign. His previous books include the edited collections *Queer Globalizations: Citizenship and the Afterlife of Colonialism* (2002) and *Cultural Compass: Ethnographic Explorations of Asian America* (2000).

Library of Congress Cataloging-in-Publication Data

Manalansan IV, Martin F.

Global divas : Filipino gay men in the diaspora / Martin F. Manalansan IV.

p. cm. — (Perverse modernities) "A John Hope Franklin Center book."

Includes bibliographical references and index.

ISBN 0-8223-3204-3 (cloth : alk. paper)

ISBN 0-8223-3217-5 (pbk. : alk. paper)

1. Gay men — Philippines — Identity. 2. Homosexuality, Male — Philippines. 3. Filipinos — Ethnic identity. 4. Gay men — New York (State) — New York — Identity. 5. Homosexuality, Male — New York (State) — New York. I. Title. II. Series.

HQ76.2.P6M36 2003   305.38'9664'09599 — dc21   2003009459